FRANCE IN THE AGE OF HENRI IV

STUDIES IN MODERN HISTORY
General editors: *John Morrill and David Cannadine*
Titles already published

Titles already published

FRANCE IN THE AGE OF HENRI IV
  Mark Greengrass
VICTORIAN RADICALISM
  Paul Adelman

FRANCE IN THE AGE OF HENRI IV

the struggle for stability

Mark Greengrass

LONGMAN
London and New York

LONGMAN GROUP LIMITED
Longman House, Burnt Mill, Harlow
Essex CM20 2JE, England
Associated companies throughout the world

*Published in the United States of America
by Longman Inc., New York*

© *Longman Group Limited 1984*

First published 1984

BRITISH LIBRARY CATALOGUING IN PUBLICATION DATA
Greengrass, Mark
  France in the age of Henri IV.–(Studies in modern history)
  1. France–History–Henry IV, 1589–1610
  I. Title   II. Series
  944'.031   DC122
  ISBN 0–582–49251–3

LIBRARY OF CONGRESS CATALOGING IN PUBLICATION DATA
Greengrass, Mark
  France in the age of Henri IV.

  (Studies in modern history)
  Bibliography: p.
  Includes index.
  1. France–Politics and government–1589–1610.
I. Title.   II. Series: Studies in modern history
(Longman (Firm))
DC122.G73   1984   944'.031   83–18733
ISBN 0–582–49251–3

Set in 10/11 pt Linotron 202 Times
Printed in Hong Kong by
Commonwealth Printing Press Ltd

CONTENTS

v

LIST OF FIGURES AND MAPS

ABBREVIATIONS

Arch. cur. de l'hist. de France	*Archives curieuses de l'histoire de France depuis Louis XI jusqu'à Louis XVIII* (1st Series), (15 vols, Paris–Beauvais, 1834–7).
AD	*Archives Départementales*.
AN	*Archives Nationales*, Paris.
ANG	*Acta Nuntiaturae Gallicae* (*Correspondance du nonce en France*, Vols i–xiii appeared, Rome, Université pontificale grégorienne).
d'Aubigné	d'Aubigné Agrippa, *l'Histoire Universelle* (ed. A. de Ruble, 9 vols, Paris, 1886–97).
Bèze	*Histoire Ecclésiastique des églises réformées au royaume de France* (3 vols, 1883–89 – reprinted Niewkoop, B. de Graaf, 1974).
Bib. Mazarine	*Bibliothèque Mazarine*, Paris.
BN	*Bibliothèque Nationale*, Paris.
BL	*British Library*, London.
Cal SP For	*Calendar of State Papers Foreign*
Cayet	Cayet Palma, *Chronologie novenaire* (ed. Michaud and Poujoulat, *Nouvelle Collection des Mémoires*, Vol xii, 1881).
DBF	*Dictionnaire de biographie française* (Paris, 1954–)
Fontanon	Fontanon, A., *Les Edits et ordonnances des rois de France* (4 vols, Paris, 1611).
Haag/Bordier	Haag, E. and Bordier, H., *La France Protestante*, Geneva.
Isambert	Isambert, François, *Recueil général des anciennes lois françaises* (29 vols, Paris, 1829–33 – reprinted Burt Franklin, New York, 1964).
LN	Lindsay, Robert and Neu, John, *French Political Pamphlets 1547–1648* (Univ. of Wisconsin, Madison, 1969). This is an inventory of pam-

phlets including those held in the Newberry Library, most of which have been microfilmed and are available from Bell and Howell Ltd (Ref; Fr.3041). Individual titles have not been cited in the text but reference has been made to the inventory number of the pamphlet.

MC   *Mémoires de Louis I, prince de Condé* (6 vols, London, 1743).

ML   *Mémoires de la Ligue, contenans les événements les plus remarquables depuis 1576 . . .* (6 vols, Amsterdam, 1758–63).

de Thou, HU   de Thou, Jacques-Auguste, *Histoire universelle depuis 1543 jusqu'en 1607* (16 vols, London, 1734).

Valois   Valois, Noël, *Inventaire des arrêts du conseil d'Etat* (*règne de Henri IV*) (2 vols, Paris, 1886–93). Reference is made to *arrêts* by the inventory number.

PREFACE

'It is a thing to be wondered at', reflected Edmund Burke in 1790, 'to see how very soon France, when she had a moment to respire, recovered and emerged from the longest and most dreadful civil war that ever was known in any nation.' With the drama of the French Revolution evolving before his eyes, he had a good vantage point to look back to the remarkable recovery of France from the wars of religion 200 years previously. Less partisan presenters of modern history textbooks approach the period of France's wars of religion with sinking hearts. How can they readily make sense of the sordid, squalid successions of ambitious aristocrats, abetted by foreign powers, who, under the pretext of religion, organised endless coups and nearly destroyed the monarchy? Perceptibly relieved by the accession of the Bourbons, they explain the swift return to order in France, which had so impressed Burke, by referring to the anarchy of the civil wars which so wearied the country that it naturally turned to a strong and absolute monarchy.

Historians are now better informed about the nature of the propaganda, of sectarian conflict, of the operations of aristocratic patronage and the nature of provincial and municipal politics during the civil wars. Thanks to the published works of the last decade from a group of American scholars and the notable research of French historians such as Emmanuel Le Roy Ladurie, Denis Richet and Janine Garrisson-Estèbe and their pupils, it is now possible to be much more precise about the instabilities which afflicted France. The old-fashioned 'anarchy' is gradually being rendered intelligible. One of the purposes of this book is to present some of the interim conclusions of this recent research into the French civil wars.

A further purpose is to suggest a revision of historical perspective. It is possible to see that Henri IV had consciously to create the stability of his rule after the wars. There was nothing natural or automatic about it. It was a deliberate, in some senses artificial creation, which could have been easily overturned and which was constantly being tested, but which became stronger the longer it lasted. This is the perspective hinted at in Roland Mousnier's *Assassination of Henri IV*, an investigation of the background to the king's assassination in 1610, first published in French in 1964 at the time of the attempted assassinations of the first president of the fifth republic, Charles de Gaulle. As Mousnier suggested, the assassination crystallised a myth about the personality and achievement of the king which turned Henri IV into the man for all seasons, 'blessed of all ages' as Voltaire put it in his epic poem, the *Henriade*. To pious Catholics in the seventeenth century, he was a truly Catholic statesman; to Louis XIV, he was presented as a model of kingship, of the *métier du roi*. For the peasants of the Normandy rising in 1639, his epoch represented a golden age. In the Fronde, Parisians met under the shadow of the great equestrian statue of the king, the *Roy en bronze*, placed at one end of the Ile de la Cité, and in Fronde pamphlets, dialogues between this statue and *la Samaritaine*, a statue on the other side of the river, reminded Parisians of the first Bourbon's concern for their welfare. The legend reached its height in the next century when Voltaire praised the king as the champion of enlightened toleration while the Physiocrats saw in his reign, the beginnings of both a true respect for agriculture and free trade. Louis XVI presented himself as 'another Henri' while Marie Antoinette was pleased to regard herself as a romantic version of Gabrielle d'Estrées. If the legend of Henri IV became a focal point of uniting people in the *ancien régime*, this was because the whole emphasis of his rule was placed on the struggle for stability.

It is important, therefore, to penetrate beyond this myth, and arrive at an assessment of the political stability of France which does not depend on the legend and its inevitable stress on the undoubtedly considerable magnetism and personal charms of the monarch. The term 'political stability' has been chosen with some care. Stability does not exclude the possibility of continuing tensions of different sorts; the simple example comes to mind of a bridge which requires structural stress to keep it upright. It would be wrong to imagine that France, was, at any stage in the lifetime of Henri IV, politically apathetic or lacking a vigorous political debate about sectarianism, government weakness, the dangers of civil war and the possible social upheavals that followed periods of prolonged civil wars. The precise historical problem is to assess the reality of these tensions and the potential damage that they could do to the polity of France. To those tempted to suggest that 'political stability' is an anachronism or variety of historical impressionism, the reply would be that contemporaries were both precise and articulate in presenting stability, harmony and order as one of their clearest and most deep-rooted political aspirations.

This is a small book on a large subject. It can do no more than open up further lines of enquiry and indicate areas of agreement and disagreement and recent revisions of historical perspective. For this reason, I have kept manuscript references to a minimum, preferring to concentrate on referring to the rich amount of material which has appeared in print since 1945. When a primary source is used, the reference utilises the date of the printed edition and this is indicated in bold type.

I owe many debts of gratitude to those who have assisted me to express myself clearly and precisely and to avoid errors – especially to George Bernard, Joan Davies, Professor K. H. D. Haley, Roger Lockyer and Mrs. R. Potter. Many perspectives have their origins in conversations with Mrs Menna Prestwich. John Morrill and David Cannadine kindly welcomed the book to their series. I acknowledge the assistance of the Research Fund of the University of Sheffield and the British Academy towards a short period of research in Paris which proved invaluable in the completing of this manuscript.

MARK GREENGRASS
Sheffield

For Joyce and Philip

Chapter 1

THE FRENCH CIVIL WARS

SECTARIAN MEMORIES

During one of the French civil wars, Louis Le Roy (*c.* 1510–77), professor of Greek at the Collège Royale in Paris, published his world history. Among the notable changes in his own civilisation he was impressed by the invention of printing, gunpowder and the compass and alarmed by the lamentable spread of venereal disease. But the real disease of his own time, he wrote, was the 'sects [which have] sprung up in all nations, greatly disturbed the public order and withered the well-being of humans one to another. . . . Everywhere, states have been attacked, disturbed or overturned: everywhere, religions have been plagued with heresies. Everything is out of place and in confusion and nothing is as it should be.'[1] To him, there was no doubt that the decisive event of his century had been the Protestant Reformation. It had split Europe into two ideological camps, dividing families, cities and states, not just in terms of private convictions or theological beliefs but eventually into rival attitudes, values, political ideas, assumptions and shared experiences.

France could not have expected to escape from evangelism of persuasive Protestant preachers but, in comparison with Martin Luther's first decade of explosive and liberating influence in Germany, its impact in French-speaking Europe appears initially to have been muted. More went on than was apparent, for tolerably effective royal instruments for the repression of heresy, and a certain Catholic lay and clerical energy ensured discretion. Eventually there emerged a Protestant ideology at once less tolerant, more convinced of its righteousness and ultimately more violent than in German-speaking lands. This 'second-generation' Reformation – Calvinism – spread among exiles from France in the French-speaking parts of Europe – especially in the Imperial Free City of Strasbourg and the newly independent Geneva. Relatively free from constraint,

1

reformers like Jean Calvin (1509–64) were able to develop a strong sense of community within a new model church and to preach the pure kingdom of Christ. The pastors and elders of the Calvinist Church organised consistories to enforce a hard, clear moral code on believers. Refugees from Catholic persecution in France joined them in increasing numbers after 1545. Some of them became permanent exiles, but others were sent out again as an élite – the Saints – to conquer and destroy the 'great worldly Babylon' in their native country. Nicodemites, temporisers, those who refused to subscribe to the new faith, were to be cast aside. In 1557, the Huguenots (as the Calvinists became known in France) held their first National Synod in Paris and established their Confession of Faith and Ecclesiastical Discipline. Three years later, the king issued an amnesty for heretics which implicitly recognised that repression had failed. He admitted that 'great numbers of people of all sexes, ages, qualities and conditions' had become heretics. The licence of the times, the preachers and pamphlets from Geneva were to blame for leading astray the 'people of our realm who, lacking in judgement and knowledge, have no discernment in matters of doctrine'.[2]

How many Huguenots were there in France on the eve of the religious wars, and how were they socially and geographically distributed? These questions confused contemporaries as much as they have perplexed historians. Answers depend on whom you ask and where you look. Marshal of France and royal councillor, Gaspard de Saulx-Tavannes (1509–73) knew without a doubt that it was the townsmen, the lesser people (*paisans bourgeois, menu peuple*), women, children and vagabonds who were most infected in his native Burgundy.[3] Well-informed spy and smooth Venetian diplomat, Jean Michieli, reported that the nobility was the most contaminated and especially those 'under forty years old'.[4] His successor, Suriano, estimated that nine-tenths of the 16 million inhabitants of the kingdom were infected, early in 1562.[5] Elderly brutish Catholic lieutenant of Gascony, Blaise de Monluc (*c.* 1501–77), blamed heresy on his enemies among the royal officers and financiers of Bordeaux.[6] One of those judges, Florimond de Raemond (1540–1601), reflected from the comparative quiescence of his old age on how the schoolmasters had rendered pupils in his youth vulnerable to heresy by teaching them to read, think and, eventually, to act for themselves.[7] In the small Catholic *bastide* town of Gaillac, a hostile witness thought the rich merchants carried heresy with them. In Toulouse, another judge held the richer young men and the more beautiful young women among those most responsible. . . .[8]

For the Huguenots, a sense of imminent victory is the hallmark of those pages of the great Huguenot compilation, the *Ecclesiastical History of the Reformed Churches in France*, which relate to the period 1561–62.[9] Calvin could not believe what was happening and lamented that there were not enough well-trained ministers to supply the demand.[10] A report from the church in Paris to the Protestants in Zurich said that 'the harvest for Christ' had been excellent. Providence had protected them. 'We have confidence ... there is an extraordinary desire to see the Kingdom of God increase.' They talked of their congregation changing from being *petits gens* to becoming 'the élite of France' with 'many nobles and magistrates . . . women and honourable young ladies and from the best families' attending the sermons.[11] With an edict of toleration granting them a basic civil liberty (as in January 1562), they flaunted their respectability. A Paris merchant tailor spoke out in public against the Cardinal of Lorraine; leading members of the Paris congregation dressed up in their best clothes so that they could be seen by the queen mother on their way to a Huguenot church service.[12] To those who had been so recently persecuted, this sudden degree of recognition was, in itself, a sign of the Lord at work. In provincial cities, public meetings were held in markets, main streets and even town halls, demonstrating that Huguenotism had become part of the social fabric of French city life. Communal singing, marriages between the faithful, public burials, organised rallies of the new sect were not just moments when the Huguenots called on the Lord, but ways of demonstrating to those who took part that He really was on their side.[13]

Attempts to quantify this consciousness within a statistic are doomed to failure. It is frequently said, for instance, that there were 2,150 Calvinist churches established by May 1562.[14] It is clear that some kind of review was carried out then to establish how many troops the Huguenots could muster in the event of a war. But this figure is also a highly inflated one, designed to impress the queen mother and her advisors of the overwhelming strength of Huguenot numbers. Attempts to reconstitute a list of those churches which had a minister or a deacon around this date arrive at nowhere near this figure and the best estimate is of about 1,400 communities running right across France with 800 of them concentrated in a broad crescent sweeping across western France and down through the Midi to the Alps.[15] The size of congregations varied enormously, so that any estimate of the numbers of believers is nothing more than an educated guess. Suriano, the Venetian ambassador, was clearly exaggerating their strength when he spoke of nine-tenths of the kingdom; it may have been only as many as 2 million. From these churches came many of the 20,000 who assembled at Orléans under the Prince of Condé for the beginning of the civil wars.[16]

The impressions of contemporaries were all, in their way, correct; and modern, highly sophisticated analysis directed towards discovering the social status and religious experience of Huguenots in various cities, provinces and individual social groups has confirmed

3

in one way or another the diverse and profound effect of Huguenotism within the French polity.[17] But the Huguenots paid a high price
for their success. Far from the approaching victory of the New Jeru-
salem of their dreams, they faced bitter Catholic hostilities. This
swiftly erased their naive optimism which, while it returned to parts
of the Huguenot world again in 1566 and 1572 and at the time of the
peace of Monsieur in 1576, was to be once more crushed by Catholic
reaction and civil war. France was, in fact, officially at war for most
of the time during 1562–63, 1567–70 and 1572–77. Sectarian tension
in these years has a distinctive rhythm and ritual which provides a
kind of seismograph to these religious tremors.[18] Massacres occurred
at the beginning of formal periods of warfare, when passions were
at their height. They were over long before the military campaigns
reached their stalemates. Cities where the two religions existed in
close proximity were most at risk. Moments when official Catholic
leaders tried to control or proscribe Huguenots were the most
dangerous ones. Advent and Lent were the seasons of greatest fear,
partly because they were traditionally times of great Catholic
preaching. Long sermons by Catholic preachers openly criticised
royal policy and invited their congregations to take the law into their
own hands. Royal and municipal authorities were almost powerless
to restrain them for the arrest of a Catholic preacher could produce
the rising which the authorities were trying to avoid.[19]

The resulting massacres were frequently extremely bloody: one
Protestant pamphleteer with a happy knack of endowing his work
with a spurious certainty estimated that 765,000 people had been
killed in the wars to 1581 of whom 36,300 had been massacred, 4,500
of whose bodies had floated down the Seine.[20] His figures were
inventions, but it is clear that the massacres of this period were on
a scale and intensity which was unmatched anywhere else in Europe.
In one sectarian battle in the streets of Toulouse in May 1562, the
battle raged for days and between 3,000 and 4,000 people died inside
and outside the city walls.[21] The Huguenot defeat was remembered
in an annual procession in the city which Voltaire later described as
a commemoration 'to thank God for four thousand murders'. The
massacre of Saint Bartholomew was the most notorious; beginning
in Paris on 24 August 1572, it lasted for six days there before
spreading to several provincial towns like Lyons, Bordeaux, Orléans
and Toulouse to create a 'season' of massacres.[22] The death-toll was
enormous; the Huguenot pamphlet *Le Reveille-Matin* (*The Morning
Call*) of 1573 – the first in French to create the Protestant legend of
a premeditated attempt by the authorities to annihilate every
Huguenot in the kingdom – spoke of 100,000 murdered at that time.[23]
This was an evident exaggeration but other estimates are of little
value and incapable of verification. Perhaps 3,000 died in Paris and
a further 8,000 in the provinces.[24] It was frequently the case that the

authorities could not control the killing, once it had started, and sometimes they did not try. The *parlement* of Toulouse legalised the pillage and slaughter of any heretic by any individual in May 1562.[25] 'Kill them all, the king commanded it', the Duke of Guise was reported to have told the Catholics in Paris in August 1572.[26] Priests and ministers of the reformed religion legitimised or sanctioned violence and bloodshed. Massacres involved both rich and poor and could, unless checked, manifest a sense of class hostility with the indiscriminate pillaging of rich people's property on the assumption that it belonged to Huguenots or sheltered suspects.[27] Private scores were settled as well. The hangman of the city of Carcassonne took the opportunity of the religious riot of 1562 to kill five of his personal enemies, 'eating the liver of one of them' and then 'knifing another . . .'.[28] Women played their part and children helped to foment disturbances and were prominent among the participants on both sides.[29] The Huguenots aimed particularly at the destruction of images, crosses, stained glass and relics.[30] To the cry of 'the Gospel', they went about their work with a sense that they were undertaking God's purpose and created in the minds of many contemporaries the impression that, by destroying such symbols of authority and removing a priesthood, they were, in fact, creating a new and dangerous equality. This was particularly the case in rural areas and among the nobility, although the expressions of equality were also heard in those towns where Huguenotism had taken root at the lower level of the social scale.[31]

Ritual elements in the massacres have been stressed and it is not surprising that they should have been present. Calvin repeatedly described the Catholic ritual as being polluted with idolatry and Calvinists believed this to be truly the case.[32] When Catholics found the Sacred Host thrown to the dogs, the statue of the Virgin Mary covered in mud, the crucifix roasted on a spit, holy oil used to smarten up the soldiers' boots and human excrement filling the fonts and holy water basins, their hostility naturally took the form of demanding the ritual cleansing of a city or locality from the taint of Huguenot impurities.[33] They first ridiculed Huguenotism by burning its Bibles or stuffing them into victims' mouths. Catholic pamphlets had already taught them to believe that Protestants held their services at night as sexual or drunken orgies, and that Protestant clergy married women as the first step on the road to polygamy.[34] Huguenot victims were thrown in the river Garonne in Toulouse in May 1562 and part of the city was burnt to the ground as ritual cleansings of an impure city. It must also be admitted that they were 'necessary' steps in an urban war when the prisons were full and part of the city proved recalcitrant to Catholic attack. Children were used in 1572 to castrate and disembowel the body of the Huguenot leader, Admiral Coligny (1519–72) and then drag the remnants through the sewers. Why else was this so, if not to ensure that their innocence should transcend his heretical filth?[35] After sectarian troubles, Catholics held processions and undertook pilgrimages to ensure that the Saints were not offended. They built commemorative crosses to purify particular quarters – the most famous of which was the Gâtines cross in the rue Saint-Denis of Paris, constructed in August 1571 on the site of a house inhabited by a Huguenot family which had been host to secret meetings of the Paris congregation there. The house was pulled down by order of the *parlement* of Paris and the cross itself was later removed on 20 December 1571 by the king after Protestant protests. The operation provoked Parisian riots and popular discontent. Inevitably there were miracles. A hawthorn bush in the cemetery of the Holy Innocents in Paris, for example, spontaneously burst into flower at the beginning of the massacre of Saint Bartholomew.[36] In Troyes, eleven years previously, a copper cross, the healing powers of which had apparently lapsed at the turn of the century, changed its colour and began to cure people again after the first public sectarian disturbances in the city.[37] Even the 'happy day' of the massacre of Saint Bartholomew was treated as a kind of miracle in some Catholic circles.[38] Ritual thus became one of the first steps by which Catholics created for themselves a common memory of the sectarian tensions of the civil wars.

Acting together in a common cause also left its imprint on the collective Catholic consciousness. Confraternities, traditional institutions for Catholic laymen, became the most common instrument; with municipal (or other) support, they acted like vigilante groups in some localities.[39] In May 1568, for example, over 400 people gathered in the ruined cathedral at Mâcon to swear an oath to the newly re-formed confraternity of the Holy Ghost in which the city's Catholics agreed to protect each other by force of arms if necessary, to expiate the invasion of the city by the Protestants in 1562 and 1567, and to rebuild the churches (every one of which had been destroyed). Two months later a Calvinist nobleman from Coligny's brother's cavalry company was killed by six masked men outside his house in Mâcon. The first fruits of the confraternity's malevolence, asserted the admiral.[40] Other confraternities along the Saône valley acted in concert with one another and the pattern was repeated elsewhere.[41] In towns with sovereign courts in the south of France, confraternities united with *syndicats* of judges to maintain order and city loyalties in the face of Huguenot attack.[42] Distinctive clothing and badges identified the participants – red bonnets in the *Bande cardinale* in Bordeaux of 1562, the crucifix in Toulouse at the same time, rosaries and special feathered hats with white crosses on them in Aix-en-Provence.[43] The band in Aix, led by the first consul and a Franciscan, was particularly violent; 'Huguenot-hunting' became a legitimate pastime after 1572 in towns like Troyes.[44] Royal efforts to disband these confraternities were only partially successful; the group in Bordeaux, for instance, reappeared and, in 1578, the queen mother had to order its removal.[45]

By 1577, in fact, the massacres were past history. In some provinces such as Champagne and Burgundy, Huguenotism was effectively wiped out in 1572.[46] In some northern cities like Amiens, it became a minority faith, restricted to the textile workers and deprived of support from city notábles.[47] In others, such as Rouen, it began a period of numerical decline, assisted by emigration.[48] South of the Loire, the Huguenots concentrated their forces in fortified towns like La Rochelle, Sancerre, Montauban, Nîmes and Gap where they were numerically and politically predominant and began a period of stubborn military resistance. Only towns like Montpellier with large populations of mixed religious persuasion found themselves a prey to religious tensions of the old style as late as 1577.[49] The two religious communities were, to some extent, apart; but the memories of sectarian tension were kept alive, particularly for the Protestants, by the poetry, paintings, drama and pamphlets which it had generated.[50]

Calvin had, of course, taught that the seed of the true church lay in the blood of martyrs and the respect accorded to martyrdom became a vital part of the Huguenot tradition. Jean Crespin (1520–72), a lawyer who had trained in Paris and fled from persecution to become a printer in Geneva, produced his famous *History of the Persecuted Martyrs* in 1554 and it was revised during the civil wars to keep it up to date.[51] Immensely important to French Huguenotism, it stressed the continuity between earlier heresies in the life of the church and Calvinism and attempted to demonstrate that God had inspired martyrs to be constant so that their deaths proved the Huguenot Church to be the true one.[52] But Crespin's book was only one in a world of propaganda through which the memories of sectarian tensions were relived and fought over again. The growth of the printing press in regional centres in France had been prodigious in the early sixteenth century and many of the printers and workers were Protestants. Their efforts were supplemented by the imports of book-pedlars (*colporteurs*) bringing editions from the Protestant printing centres of Geneva, Strasbourg and, later, Amsterdam. The language and tone of these works was of scarcely controlled abuse. Sometimes they were collected together and issued as one volume – as, for instance, the misleadingly entitled *Memoirs of Condé*.[53] Many pamphlets engaged in calculated slander which could do great damage. One Venetian ambassador remarked: 'It is necessary to beware of these little books that are being spread about ... People are by nature curious and, although without intending any evil, they open these books, they read them as though they had the authority of Scripture and cannot imagine that passages may be falsified, altered and they are therefore confused.'[54] They were widely read and the king had to rebuke the Duke of Guise for reading broadsheets while at Mass.[55]

Pamphleteering wars were waged as fiercely as the real ones. They began in earnest after the conspiracy of Amboise in March 1560. This was an attempt by some Protestants to capture the king and rescue him from what they regarded as the illegal domination of his court by the Catholic family and noble House of Guise. The plot failed ignominiously and Catholics launched a diatribe against the 'detestable conspiracy and fiendish enterprise' of the Protestants. Protestants replied with pamphlets which slandered the Cardinal of Lorraine (of the House of Guise), accusing him of atheism, corruption and cruelty.[56] The most savage attack came from François Hotman's *Letter Addressed to the Tiger of France*. Hotman even hinted that it would be necessary to remove the cardinal from public life by force.[57]

Personal vilification led to public vendetta. François, first Duke of Guise was assassinated towards the end of the first civil war on 18 February 1563. The assassination became the subject of many pamphlets (twenty-five different titles of which have survived) and created a vendetta between the House of Guise and a group of wanted and hated Protestant leaders.[58] Among these was Gaspard de Coligny, Admiral of France, who had been incriminated in the duke's assassination. Coligny's assassination in August 1572 (following numerous abortive attempts) was the prelude to the massacre of Saint Bartholomew, itself the subject of a long and fruitful pamphleteering campaign in France and Europe.[59] Although there was a certain pacifist literature during the civil wars (which has yet to be properly studied), it was the 'discourses, replies, advertisements, alarums and apologies' which 'started the braziers of rebellions', as Estoile (who systematically collected them) remarked in April 1587.[60]

We have only scratched the surface of the sectarian tensions which went through French society in the civil wars. It was clearly immensely difficult for political leaders to stand aside from them. When they tried, they were accused by one side or the other (and sometimes by both) of being *politiques*. The historian de Thou recorded of the Guise clan in 1568:[61]

For those who opposed their ambitions, there was no end of calumnies which they invented to disgrace their enemies; they called them *politiques*, a name which they invented to designate their enemies. Those *politiques*, if they were to be believed, were more dangerous than even the heretics. They included Catholics who were against factions and disturbances and, thus, unfavourable to their side, such as the cardinal of Bourbon, the chancellor l'Hôpital and the marshals Montmorency.

Cardinal Granvelle wrote from Brussels in 1564 that Coligny was 'more *politique* (as they say in France) than *dévot*'.[62] The term became used by the Catholic preachers to attack 'all statesmen who worked for peace' and, in their political careers, every major figure in the civil wars with the exception of the Guise family was accused of *politique* sympathies at some point or other. It is now a received wisdom among historians that there was a 'politique' political group around in the civil wars and that it congregated around the Montmorency family and its allies.[63] The historian de Thou (with one eye, perhaps, on the old Constable of Montmorency who was in high favour at the time he was writing) wrote his great work of history in which the *politiques* appear as heroes of the hour. Nineteenth-century historians were very sympathetic towards these kindred spirits to whom the state was more important than religion, and who had apparently saved France from the worst excesses of the civil wars.[64]

It must be said, however, that the Montmorency family did not regularly espouse the *politique* cause. The elderly Constable Anne de Montmorency, who died in the second civil war in 1567, made common cause with the Guise against the heretics. After his death, his family split in several directions so that, by 1577, the eldest of his sons was in retirement on his estates, having been imprisoned by the king for his part in a coup d'état in 1574. Meanwhile, his second son, Henri de Montmorency-Damville (1534–1614), was fighting the Huguenots around Montpellier for the king and against his younger brother, Thoré (1546–75), who was a committed Huguenot: Montmorency-Damville's allies were malcontents who were as interested in dismembering royal authority as they were concerned to appeal to religious sympathies when it seemed politically advantageous to them to do so. In a general sense, everyone in royal service was a *politique* and they acted as such, even when faced with orders (as in the aftermath of the massacre of Saint Bartholomew) to eliminate the Huguenots. With the exception of the Guise family and their clients, provincial governors and military lieutenants in provinces with substantial Huguenot minorities refused to carry out royal instructions in August 1572 to eliminate Protestants. Instead they prevaricated in the face of a clearly erratic decision which appeared to damage royal authority in the localities.[65]

The most notorious *politique* was undoubtedly Catherine de Médicis, queen mother to the three kings who ruled France from 1559 to 1589.[66] The propaganda branded her as a malevolent influence on her sons, corrupt, cruel, treacherous, Machiavellian, immoral and *politique*.[67] She avidly read and annotated it, apparently unperturbed by the 'hate and imputations which are piled on her'.[68] Her attempts to woo the Protestants to support her were endless and ingenious. She organised the colloquy of Poissy in 1561, drafted the edict of toleration of January 1562, was the architect of the first pacification in 1563 and ensured its enforcement in a lavish progress round the kingdom, visiting many of the sensitive localities most disturbed by heresy.[69] She played a leading part in the pacification of St Germain-en-Laye in 1570 and the edict of peace at Bergerac in 1577 was enforced through her tremendous efforts of diplomacy in 1578–79, again involving extensive journeys through the southern provinces. She energetically recruited historians, painters, lawyers and astrologers to the task, engaging them to search history, mythology, legal precedent and every agreed wisdom to show that female rule was beneficent, that two religions could be tolerated within one society and that repression of one by the other was rarely successful. Even Louis Le Roy was persuaded to turn his pen to the task.[70] But few people in public life had the queen mother's staying power or determination. Michel de l'Hôpital (1507–73), her chancellor, was forced to surrender the seals and retire. Clerical servants in her entourage found their positions particularly vulnerable.

The case for toleration as a matter of principle was never heard anywhere in France during this period. Those who did support a pacification with the Protestants did so on purely prudential grounds.[71] Etienne Pasquier (1529–1615) for instance, wrote a poem in defence of the pacification of St Germain-en-Laye in 1570.[72] His views were those of an *habitué* to a refined salon world of Paris lawyers, and he reflected their opinions that peace in the kingdom ensured law and order whereas civil war did not ensure religious triumph because the Huguenots were too large a minority to dispose of by force. The force of this argument (to the author as well as to others) depended on how well or how badly the wars were going.[73] For nobles in the provinces, fidelity was frequently more important than faith in a religious cause. Many changed their sides with their clan leader unquestioningly. La Popelinière cited the example of the sieur de Passac, client of the Count of Lude, who followed Lude to fight for the Protestants in the first religious wars, and then lost his life fighting for Lude on the Catholic side in September 1569 having spent 'the greatest part of his wealth and, in the end his own life . . . .'.[74] Lude's change of sides was notorious, but he was not alone in being unclear where his loyalties lay. And, in the wider French polity, conformity and confusion played a much larger part in people's individual choices. La Popelinière, a soldier and historian for the Huguenot cause, thought that more than two-thirds of France had remained neutral in the first decade of the civil wars – 'the friends of fortune and of the good life' as he calls them.[75] He also recalled that the wars were fought substantially with foreign troops (the Protestant army in 1569 spoke six languages; the royal forces included Italians, Germans, Swiss and Albanians as well as French).[76] He also said that, for 'un million de bandoliers fleurdelize', the religious focus of the wars was less important than the opportunities that political disorder provided to form a *bandonil* – or irregular armed band – and live off the countryside.[77] Increasingly the problem of disorder in the countryside came to the fore in the course of the hostilities.

HUGUENOTS AT WAR

The year 1572 was a watershed for the Huguenots for it largely eliminated their noble leadership. It also led to the most remarkable hostilities undertaken by the Huguenots during the civil wars. As de Thou recalled in his history[78]:

> After the murder of so many generals and the dispersal of what remained of the Protestant nobility, the fright of the people in every town, there was no one who did not regard this cause as absolutely defeated. However, against the opinion of those who took up arms and without premeditated design, a war which began feebly, restored the affairs of the Protestants in the space of a year without the help of a foreign prince and despite the lack of resources. . .

The classic works of Huguenot political thought all appeared during this period and the institutions which one historian has christened the 'United Provinces of the Midi' became as mature as they ever would in the civil wars.[79] But it is wrong to draw too clear a divide at this date. Although the works of political theory appeared after 1572, many of the ideas were formulated in the years before that date. François Hotman's *Francogallia* (1573) was composed in the period 1567–69 and the three volumes published by the Genevan Simon Goulart and entitled *Memoirs of the State of France* . . . (1576–77) – another compendium of pamphlets produced in the civil wars – included many writings from the first decade of civil war as well as the famous reactions of the Huguenots to the massacre, the *Politique, Political Discourses* and Beza's *Right of Magistrates*.[80] Elective Huguenot political assemblies, attended by lay and ecclesiastical representatives from across a province, can also be traced back to the beginning of the civil wars, exercising all the powers with which they were formally endowed after 1572.[81]

In a society which equated obedience with good order and stability, the development of a view that in certain circumstances it was right to resist lawful authority, comes as an enormous shock. It is one of the most perceptible signs of the instability of the civil wars. Huguenot theorists only espoused it circumspectly. In April 1562, the Prince of Condé had claimed that the young king had been captured and the lawful government usurped by an aristocratic faction.[82] The Huguenot rebellion was thus a loyal uprising to free the king and this view received very cautious support from Geneva for princes of the blood had a limited authority (its origins were unclear) to resist manifest tyranny and maintain the monarchy in a minority. In 1567, Condé's manifesto reflected a more uncomfortable reality since it was the Protestants who, at that moment, were attempting to capture the king. This time, the manifesto spoke of the fundamental 'ancient constitution' of the realm which was being perverted by a king who needed guidance by, among others, a prince of the blood and an estates general. [83]

The appeal to a fundamental constitution was taken to theoretical conclusions in François Hotman's *Francogallia*.[84] This long, highly persuasive book had a powerful effect on contemporaries. Hotman was, in many ways, the perfect ideologue; scholar and lawyer by training, he was a natural propagandist, a fast worker and capable of writing with the right mixture of evidence, argument, anger and wit to suit the occasion. Exiled early in his career (in Geneva and Strasbourg from 1548), he learned to make friends among many different groups. He had a knack of anticipating events and was used by Protestant princes as a negotiator and diplomat. He relished his reputation as a 'seditious and tumultuous person' even though it twice cost him his belongings in escaping the sudden tensions of civil war.[85] The *Francogallia* was intended by its author to be 'the work of history, the history of a fact'.[86] That the fact – or rather, ideal – was that France had once been a free country – Free Gaul – whose fundamental liberty had been gradually enslaved, first by the Roman empire and latterly, by the 'great beast of Rome' the Papacy. France's lawyer-historians had uncovered the complex laws and precedents of France's feudal past and, with the aid of the Renaissance tools of philology and the study of Roman law, were in the process of codifying and classifying them.[87] Hotman subordinated this legal antiquarianism within a wider picture which appealed to a certain French patriotism, a mythical view of the past.[88] At the same time, he revealed the richness, complexity and variety of French institutions beyond the French monarchy.

His conclusions were unambiguous. Kings were, he said, elected by the people.[89] They were magistrates, responsible to the people for the exercise of power. 'The supreme power of deposing kings was also', he wrote, 'that of the people.'[90] Valois monarchs had become Roman in their attitudes – imperial, Catholic and absolutist – 'bloody tyrants', as he does not hesitate to call them at one point. It was essential that France recover the institutions of its 'mixed constitution' which enshrined their former freedom.[91] These were not the *parlements*, lawcourts which could be relied on to ratify the king's worst 'Roman' pretensions.[92] (They had even usurped the term 'parlementum' which had originally and properly applied only to the elected estates of the realm.) The principal institution for Hotman was the estates general, which had once had extensive powers to deliberate on the general welfare and which had been 'held as something sacrosanct' in France's feudal past.[93] Provincial estates, town councils, elected clergy, provincial and municipal privileges were all cited as evidence of former Gallic freedoms which it was essential to recover in order to return to a properly constituted order.

For Hotman, like other Huguenot theorists, was concerned at the damage the civil wars were doing to France and the massacre of Saint Bartholomew had genuinely shocked him.[94] He regarded the work as 'throwing a bucket of water' on the flames of civil war, hoping that it would contribute to 'the recuperation, and even the restoration, of our French state'.[95] His book had a widespread readership, as Hotman was the first to acknowledge. Even in Paris it was 'well-received by all men of good sense and all good Frenchmen'.[96] It wore its Calvinism lightly and it did not sneer at *politiques* like more intemperate Huguenot writings of the period. The appeal to a national identity, threatened by foreigners, was widely supported by those of every religious persuasion who believed that in the Italianate atheism and Machiavellianism attributed to the queen mother, her entourage and the Italians of the royal service lay the true source of the instability in France.[97] Hotman presented the reality of complex, non-royal institutions operating in a mixed government within a royal context and this was precisely what the deputies to the various political assemblies in the Midi wanted to hear. He gave them legal, historical and political reasons for a limited right of revolt which, in a more inchoate way, those assemblies were struggling for in 1572–73.[98]

The king, Henri III, and the queen mother read *Francogallia* and it horrified them. They tried to have it banned and commissioned various refutations of its arguments from the Italian lawyer, Matteo Zampini, and Louis Le Roy among others.[99] The criticisms which were eventually levelled at Hotman's work cast serious doubts on its historical veracity.[100] This is why the last great work of Huguenot resistance theory, written towards the end of the 1570s, rested its case less on specifically legal, historical or French grounds and more on a thoroughly scholastic argument.[101] It stipulated that there were two essential bonds of society. These were the pact, or treaty, between king and people and the more sacred covenant or bond linking God, king and people. This work, the *Vindicae Contra Tyrannos* or *Vindication against Tyrants*, became the starting point for discussion of the question of the nature of political obedience in Huguenot circles at the end of the civil wars.[102] This was an indication of the way in which the internal hostilities had destroyed the common assumptions of automatic obedience to the powers that be, which had been taken as the theoretical basis for the French polity.

Meanwhile, the Huguenots' political assemblies and councils of what de Thou called 'a raw kind of republic' demonstrated their own more practical independence. They negotiated with French kings as with a distant respected foreign power in 1573–76 and displayed a boldness and canny persistence that exasperated royal councillors.[103] 'Gens de la boutique', 'inexperienced in affairs', scorned the governor of Languedoc, Henri de Montmorency-Damville, but they were a match for his mercurial politics.[104] They put together finance on a considerable scale to support the foreign mercenary leader John Casimir, Palatine Count of the Rhine and duke in Bavaria (1543–92) in 1576.[105] They ran their affairs with a minimum degree of deference to noble authority and a pronounced leaning towards the commons. Montmorency-Damville is supposed to have said that he had learnt 'that they were enemies to all the nobility and wanted popular and communal domination'.[106] La Popelinière, gentleman, historian, Protestant and moderate, had personal experience of the Protestant assemblies for he was deputed to the assembly of Millau in 1574. He remarked that the *esprit des marchands* and that of soldiers rarely was reconcilable and he noticed that the liberties of nobles 'were not compatible with the equality of the Third Estate'.[107] The Protestants provided councils to advise and control the actions of their protector and his lieutenants. They tried to reconcile differences of opinion between their military lieutenants, and imposed oaths of allegiance on them all. This passion for order and upright government under a civil constitution reflected the strict puritan morality they enforced on their cities (even during the civil wars) through the consistories and colloquies operating under the ecclesiastical constitution. Both the civil and ecclesiastical constitution provided new opportunities for power, status, wealth and achievement for those with the necessary tenacity and luck to make use of them.

REFORM OF THE REALM AND ITS FAILURE

Civil war created a demand for a reform of the French polity from those of both religious persuasions. Catherine de Médicis recognised it during her tour through the provinces in 1564–65 (following the first civil war) and she organised an assembly of notables at Moulins in January 1566. The results included the great reforming statute of eighty-six articles promising, among other things, major changes in the *parlements*, the establishment of *grands jours* (or assizes) to deal with endemic crime and disorder and the appointment of better judges and royal officials (where venality was believed to have rendered them corrupt and partial).[108] It promised to limit the authority of provincial governors (to prevent their appropriating royal revenues as they had done in the civil wars) and to stamp out the pillage and abuse of civilians by the royal cavalry companies. Hospitals, confraternities, sumptuary and blasphemy laws, the regulation of printing, all appeared within it. Finance was also involved and Catherine was acutely aware of the considerable royal debts (600,000 *livres* was necessary at that moment to keep the royal creditors prepared to enter future loans).[109] Financial pressure and royal attempts at reform were never separable during the civil wars.

Renewed hostilities prevented the Moulins *ordonnances* from taking effect and rendered the royal financial postion much worse. Further loans were entered into from Italian bankers on the customs at Lyons, advances were made by the *bonne ville* of Paris, and a further 2 million *livres* of clerical wealth were alienated, beginning in November 1568. There were the first signs of a serious collapse in the coinage.[110] The same expedients were used when war began again in 1572–74, but this period coincided with poor harvests, shortages of salt and a more serious collapse of the currency. Preparations for another assembly of notables in 1573 were shelved with the king's death in 1574; but a rich crop of printed polemics in 1574 from Catholic and Protestant sources displayed the extent of the malaise.[111] The new king was reminded that 'the ruin of his people is the ruination of his state'. He was told that offices, sold to the low-born, damaged the social structure of the country. He was reminded that treasurers were suspected of pocketing public revenues; that the church was being made to pay for royal extravagance. 'People are being fleeced, the gendarmerie go unpaid, all piety, religion and discipline have been despised and let slip. . . .'[112] The remedy lay in a 'free meeting' of the estates general in which Protestants and Catholics could remonstrate to the king on the defects in administration of the state, church and in justice. From the remonstrances laid before the king by the people of Champagne in 1575 and the independent report of the Venetian ambassador who passed through the province that year, it was clear that conditions were desperate. Villagers sheltered in churches, once-prosperous towns were half tumbled down and the bourgeois were forced to ransom themselves from ravaging troops if they left the comparative security of town walls. In November 1575, it was reported in Paris that 'the nobles and people of Brittany, Normandy, Burgundy and the Auvergne are in league, one with another and have decided to pay no more imports, aids, subsidies, loans, *tailles*, increases and charges above those levied in the reign of Louis XII'. In December 1575, the *prévôt des marchands* in Paris, Charron, laid before the king a remonstrance which left little unsaid. The 'wrath of God' (a phrase the king was fond of using himself to explain the civil wars) was the result of the 'universal corruption in all the estates and orders of the realm' and it required royal action.[113] The Duke of Anjou (the king's brother) also pressed for the holding of an estates general and a promise to do so was contained in the peace of Monsieur (edict of Beaulieu) in 1576.[114]

The promise was fulfilled by the summoning of the estates general to Blois towards the end of the year. The previous history of estates general as agents of reform of the kingdom was not encouraging; the elective procedures, the method by which the *cahiers* of grievances were gathered and the debating arrangements of such assemblies all stood in the way of constructive solutions. Clearly, royal finances were parlous in the wake of the pressures of war and the enormous burdens of paying for the removal of the German mercenary troops that the Protestants had hired and the king had undertaken to pay off.[115] Figures presented to the estates (and doubtless exaggerated for impact) suggested that the overall royal debt was of the order of 101 million *livres* and the annual deficit stood at about 4 million *livres*.[116] A serious attempt at government reform would have been worth the granting of substantial taxation. But the estates general began, instead, to question the royal accounts and to propose the dismantling of royal authority in justice and finance. The estates were then dissolved.

The initiative lay next with the provincial estates to whom the king turned for assistance in dealing with the enormous burdens of royal debts. Some piecemeal reforms were successfully accomplished in the meantime, particularly for stabilising the currency.[117] From the estates of Burgundy came the demand in October 1578 that 'the reformation of the kingdom be attended to' before they grant further assistance to the king. Normandy's estates threw the royal treasures out of their assembly in the following month and a clerical representative there, after insulting the *premier président* (senior judge in the *parlement* of Normandy and a royal appointment) turned to the provincial governor and asked: 'When, Monseigneur, when will our afflictions cease? When will we see an end to the violent seizure of our goods and belongings by the tax sergeants?' They proceeded, like their colleagues in Burgundy, to refuse the taxation that the king demanded of them. Instead, at a specially convened meeting in March 1579, they demanded that their grievances be met before they granted any further taxation. These included a reform in the church, schools, hospitals and the council of state; the removal of extraordinary royal commissions in the province and the establishment of a temporary commission of impartial judges to replace the venal *parlement* at Rouen; the establishment of a chamber to investigate and punish corrupt financial officials; the suppression of the provincial treasurers and the *élections* (local royal tax officials) as the first step towards the return of the provincial estates to their former importance.[118] The king gave his consent to their demands verbally in reply to their deputies in April 1579. When they asked him to put this assent into writing, he replied icily (Henri III had a studied ability to deliver a wounding rejoinder) 'that they ought to content themselves that the king had given them his word concerning that assembly, which is more to be valued than any written guarantee which might be given to them'. When their deputies were later arrested and imprisoned, the estates of Normandy were given good cause to doubt the king's good faith.

The clergy also spent most of the year haggling with the king over his proposals for substantial new taxes on the clergy.[119] They compared the church to the 'good Joseph who, being forced to obey the squalid wish of his mistress, would rather emerge naked, leaving his coat behind him, rather than soil his soul by such a grave adultery'. They also demanded reform – the publication of the decrees of the Council of Trent in France by the king and royal cooperation in removing corruption and heresy from the episcopate. Their demands were either ignored or rejected. When, in December 1579, they felt on the point of agreement, the king abruptly increased his demands. The clergy also began to doubt his good faith. In order to dispel the mounting suspicions, the king signed the ordinance of Blois.[120] This substantially reflected the demands of the estates of Blois in their final *cahiers* to the king. Like the reforms edicted from Moulins in 1566, those from Blois were a promise of better things to come. But few of the promises were put into practice.

The conditions of a half-made peace made it difficult to do so. There was renewed Huguenot disaffection in some provinces, peasant insurrections, disruptive seigneurs and town riots which made any enforcement of law difficult.[121] Pressure for reform, however, led to the final attempt by the last Valois to produce a coherent and successful recovery. A string of reforming measures appeared in royal ordinances in the early summer of 1582. The English ambassador reported that Henri III was closeted with his secretaries for several days, dictating to them his plans for reform, the copies of which he then locked away in a desk to which he alone kept the key. Then, in early August 1582, he announced that he would hold an assembly of notables which was to be properly informed of all the problems in the localities.[122] To this end, commissioners toured the provinces in the autumn and winter of 1582 with detailed instructions to visit all the main towns and listen to complaints, and also to stop every seven leagues and hear villagers' laments.[123] Many examples of local corruption were thus unearthed.[124] After several delays, the assembly of notables met in December 1583 and sat for two months. It was attended by the king's closest advisors and by the masters of requests who possessed specialist knowledge about trade, currency and law. Senior prelates were also present and they established a special commission on ecclesiastical reform. Some former ambassadors and provincial governors and lieutenants also took part.[125] The debates, proposals, schemes and resolutions of the assembly were well informed, extremely wide-ranging and imaginative. Some of the most accurate information on the state of royal debts in the course of the civil war was prepared by this assembly.[126] The breadth and seriousness of their discussions are a sign of the deep-rooted instabilities which they discovered within the French polity.

They were not entirely pessimistic. If the series of measures which they proposed were adopted in full, then, with the assistance of a period of at least ten years of peace, the kingdom could expect to see real recovery. There was to be no mass repurchase of offices; but some *bureaux* of offices were to be disbanded among the *trésoriers* and *élus*.[127] Royal offices were gradually to fall vacant on death so that this part of the royal debt would gradually amortise itself without immediate and painful political repercussions. Reform of the domain had already begun in 1578.[128] It was to be pushed forward and inquiries would root out fraud while other parts of the domain which had been mortgaged would be repurchased over a number of years. Forest inquiries were also to be undertaken. A chamber of justice would investigate corrupt financiers and tax farmers.[129] Commissioners would also be sent to provinces to investigate *taille* registers, render the tax equitable and eradicate the corruption and fraud that *trésoriers* and *élus* had introduced. Investigations of falsely claimed nobility were to be continued.[130] Farms on salt and customs duties would be promptly renegotiated and consolidated to ensure that the king was gaining an economic return.[131] Customs were to be so rated as to protect native manufacture without damaging (by total prohibition the import of certain goods, notably cloth from England) France's reciprocal trade abroad.[132] Reform of hospitals would, among other measures, strengthen the hand of the royal almoner over their financial affairs. The muster, review and payment of cavalry companies was considered and a series of reforms produced.[133] The policing of towns was dealt with, and roving assizes despatched to deal with provincial brigandage.[134] Reforms already set in hand at court in the numbers, provisioning, discipline and routine of those attending the king were strengthened with controls designed to limit pensions, the soliciting of favours and the recording of the decisions of the councils of state. The reforms put together at the assembly of notables at St Germain-en-Laye constitute the most thoroughly conceived measure of reforming endeavour undertaken during the period of the civil wars.

Why was it that so many attempts had achieved so little? Was it not the case that the failure to reform the state was the cause of provincial dissension and the frustrations which led to the Catholic League? To many knowledgeable contemporaries like Estoile, Cobham (English ambassador), Moro (Venetian ambassador), Busbecq and de Thou, the assembly of notables of 1583 was a kind of propaganda exercise, a way of gaining more time in the struggle against disorder in the state.[135] There was plenty of evidence for their view that reform was so intimately connected with the imperious demands of the appalling royal debts, and that the need for more revenue and the desire for reform were so incompatible, that reform was never going to succeed. Their pessimism was shared by some reactions in the provinces to the appearance of the commissioners in 1582. Lyons was uncooperative and the commissioners spent two months in the city trying to elucidate their information. The estates of Picardy greeted them by saying that they were delighted that the king wanted to remedy abuses 'although very late'. For, during the years of civil wars, they had seen: 'So many fine assemblies, so many fine ordinances, the estates (general) so solemnly convoked and held at Orléans and then at Blois, the colloquies and assemblies at Poissy, Moulins, Paris and elsewhere, all of them full of great hopes for the relief of the people: we see, however, that all this has achieved nothing.'[136] There was a widespread doubt as to whether the means, will and confidence existed to achieve any measure of reform, a real pessimism that France was ungovernable on the terms that pre-war France would have understood and that political stability was not an achievable goal but an unrealisable ideal belonging to the golden age of Henri II.

Who was to blame for this? The Italians; the financiers; the favourites; the quarrels in the royal family; the rival clans of nobles; the size, luxury and morality of the court in general; the king himself – were all cited and received some share of the resulting acrimony. Every explanation contained a degree of truth among a great deal of misinformation and prejudice. For the court and its members were not completely apart, cut off from the rest of France, but a reflection of the strains and tensions in its society. The Italians, for instance, were not as malevolent an influence as a growing xenophobic French attitude wanted to believe. It is true that, politically speaking, they were prominent in the councils of state.[137] It is also the case that they occupied a proportion of French benefices and even gained admittance into French noble orders.[138] But their political advice was independent of the noble factions among the French nobility and they were good soldiers whose companies attracted ambitious Frenchmen and Italians alike. The painters, architects, musicians, dancing masters and fencing teachers who became part of royal and princely retinues were merely a reflection of Italian pre-eminence in these spheres. More worrying was the influence of Italian merchants and banking houses at court.[139] But their presence was necessary to provide the king and other courtiers with essential short-term liquidity.[140] Their participation in army-funding, tax-contracts and the mortgaging of the royal jewels was not a sign of their malevolent influence in court but an indication of the extensiveness of the royal debts which they funded. Inevitably, they used their credit to secure influence at court and positions as gentlemen of the chamber, *maîtres d'hôtel du roi* and *écuyers* to the queen and queen mother. Naturally this ensured both adverse comment and also some favourable deals for them in their financial affairs. Sebastian Zametti (the queen mother called him by his diminutive, 'Zamet') was reputedly pompous, arrogant and difficult to deal with, even by the king.[141] Louis d'Adjiaceto was found to have secured favourable contracts on tax-farming by the *chambre des comptes*.[142] Scipio Sardini even published an edict in 1587 on his own authority increasing a tax on certain products, for which he was imprisoned by the *cour des aides* but the king secured his release.[143] Some of the Italian financiers became extremely wealthy from their time at the royal court and attracted resentment for the overt, liberal display that they made of it. When Orazio Rucellai left the French court to return to Italy in 1586 (having found the attacks and resentments unbearable) he took with him 1.6 million *livres*.[144] But one tends to forget those Italian financiers who, like Mario Bandini, were bankrupted and broken by their activities at the French court.[145] In any case, the native *intendants de finance* were easily as corrupt. Only Claude Marcel, a former *prévôt des marchands* in Paris, enjoyed a reputation for honesty among those who served the last Valois in this capacity. Benoît Milon, sieur de Videville, the son of a locksmith from Blois, who rose (as Estoile said) 'like the mushrooms, in one night' was chased from the royal chamber by an irate king for his corruption and took flight in the Netherlands.[146] The only difference was that the Italians had no ignoble stigma attached to them and, therefore, could insinuate themselves the more easily into high court positions.

The *mignons* (as the royal favourites were called from about 1574) were as easy a target to blame for the failure of reform as the Italians. They were believed to be the epitome of luxury at court, a force for evil around the king.[147] In fact, the king did not (except for a brief period after 1586) restrict his favours to one favourite for any length of time. The ease with which disgrace befell the favourites of Henri III was one of the reasons for their intense jealousies. Henri III wrote inside the leaf of the prayer book of Epernon (the most subtle and able of the *mignons* and the one who did dominate the king after 1586)[148]:

> I beg you, my friend, to remember me when you pray as I love no one else in the world more than you.

But, five years later, in 1588, Epernon was banished from the court by royal demand. It is clear that the existence of the *mignons* performed a useful political function. As Catherine de Médicis acknowledged, able young men were being trained for future service to the king.[149] Also, the court contained many gentlemen of modest fortune and the rise of a favourite from their ranks gave them hopes of social ascension. Henri III needed men on whose loyalty he could depend. The problem was that, after 1586, Epernon did gain control of the privy purse, the *comptants à la main du roi*.[150] He also dominated access to the king. But in this respect he was unusual and attracted the particular vilification of other courtiers. More generally, the *mignons* were attacked for their extravagance which was occasionally tactless and excessive. But in some ways they were no different from the court in which they had been educated. There is little sign that they were the homosexual companions of the king, as hostile pamphlets insinuated (particularly at the beginning and end of the reign). Davila, Estoile, Gassot and Brantôme, all knowledgeable contemporaries, gave the rumours no credence.[151] Among foreign diplomats, only the Savoyard ambassador was disposed to accept the malicious gossip.[152] They were *camarades*, military companions, to whom Henri's liberality *was* excessive. But Henri II, his father, had behaved in the same fashion towards his favourites, without attracting any homosexual criticism. That the slander existed, that it could have been given credence, is a sign of the gap between the court and the rest of France in this period.

The contrast between the lavishness at court and the conditions in the provinces struck deputies to the king forcibly and did little to strengthen confidence in royal ability to undertake a reform and spend cash frugally. A further paradox was that poets and writers owing their livelihood to the liberality of the Valois court developed hostile attitudes to the institution of the court. Inspired by Virgil and Horace, they made nature a virtue and dwelt on the servility, ambition, flattery and false attitudes that made a good courtier.[153] The Italianate forms of the Valois court – its studied artificiality (mirrors, emblems, *trompe-l'oeil*, masques, costume, exaggerated respect for the points of honour, and a delight in the macabre) – helped them present the court as a flamboyant and unreal world which Protestants like François de La Noue had already denounced as vicious.[154]

More unfortunate were the legacies of family quarrels and noble hostilities which Henri III inherited and which he could periodically control but never eradicate. There was a sad contrast between the loyalty and fidelity he enjoyed from the illegitimate members of the Valois and the resentments and hatreds manifested by his brother and sister. His stepbrother and namesake Henri d'Angoulême was a companion from youth, enjoyed the same tastes, and served the king loyally in Provence until his assassination by local factions in 1586. His stepsister, Madame Diane, ten years older than himself, became his trusted councillor. Even the illegitimate son of his brother, Charles d'Angoulême, received favour from Henri III after 1586. To Epernon's scarcely concealed dismay, the king toyed with the possibility of making him legitimate and an heir to the throne.[155]

No such confidence and trust existed between the king and his sister Marguerite, married in an evidently ill-suited match to Henri of Navarre; or between the king and his brother, François Hercules, Duke of Alençon (later, Duke of Anjou), who was the heir to the throne from 1574 until his death in 1584. Morally, emotionally and sexually, François and Marguerite behaved alike. They were violent, uncontrollable and unstable. Together, they plotted, planned, intrigued and conspired both in and outside the kingdom. Henri III's gauche attempts to restrain them merely increased their animosities towards him. There was little the king could do except divert and distract their destructive energies. The comedies of feigned reconciliations, put together by the queen mother or members of the royal and ducal entourage, or by the mediation of Henri of Navarre with his wife, could not disguise the lasting and sustained hatreds. There is no doubt that many hostile pamphlets, writings and accusations against Henri III originated from these two members of his family.[156] They were either indifferent towards reform, or actively hostile. Anjou refused to attend the assembly of notables in 1583 and the queen mother had to be despatched to try to persuade him to come.

The destructive tensions and animus between noble clans were also beyond the ability of the king and his court to dissipate. Henri III had inherited the kingdom with the King of Navarre in close confinement and the Duke of Montmorency in prison. Navarre escaped from court in 1576 and never returned to it. François, Duke of Montmorency, was released and lived largely on his estates until his death in 1579. His brother, Henri of Montmorency-Damville, narrowly escaped from an assassination attempt on his life in Turin in 1574 which he blamed on the king. He swore a solemn oath that he would never see the king again, except in effigy, and so it was.[157] Removed from the exercise of his powers as governor of Languedoc in the same year, he joined the Huguenots and only signed a formal reconciliation with Henri III in 1577. He did nothing to help the reform initiatives and, still suspicious, he refused to leave his province for fear that he would jeopardise his authority there. In 1582 he began to resent the growing authority of one of the royal *mignons*, Anne de Joyeuse, whose father was his lieutenant in Languedoc. His response was to begin negotiations with the king of Spain for a permanent alliance and subsidy, negotiations about which the king learnt as the assembly of notables of 1583 began its debates. In 1585 Montmorency-Damville was declared deposed from his government of Languedoc and his family's property in northern France was confiscated by the king in 1586. He responded with an open revolt and renewed alliance with the Protestants and the King of Navarre. Henri III's influence in the Midi was lost.

Things went little better with the powerful family of Guise. They began the reign in high favour. At the royal coronation in 1575 (where the king married into their house) the Cardinal of Guise took the service; his brothers, nephews and cousins, the Duke of Guise, Mayenne, Aumale and Elboeuf, were the principal lay peers and chamberlain to officiate at the ceremony. The council of state even met from time to time in the *hôtel* of Guise in Paris in 1575 and the queen mother feared their predominance.[158] In the following year, the king signed the edict of Beaulieu, a peace agreement with the Protestants which gave them large concessions as well as huge privileges to the Duke of Alençon. By way of reprisal, the Guise clan ostentatiously left the court. By the end of 1577 the Guise found that peace with the Protestants had strengthened royal authority and rendered the king more independent of them. So they returned to court, fanned the quarrels between royal favourites and supporters of the Duke of Alençon (pitched battles at court reduced the king to tears), and then staged a new, menacing departure. Perhaps the refusal of the estates of Normandy and Burgundy to grant taxation before redress of grievances owed something to stimulus from Guise and Alençon.[159] In May 1579 another feigned reconciliation between Henri III and the Guise family was followed by four tiresome years in which the king tried, through *mignons*, to exclude them from the powerful offices of the kingdom while winning over some members of the family (Elboeuf, Mayenne) with pensions, promises and lavish entertainments.[160] Even so, the Guise barely cooperated at the assembly of notables in 1583 and actively resisted reform in the church at the assembly. The king's tactics were astute, desperately clever – a tribute to his political skills – but the Guise were not fooled. In 1584, 'they say privately to their friends that they well understand the mortal hatred in which the king holds them'.[161] As champions of Catholicism *à outrance* in France, they would not pass over the opportunity created for them by the death of the heir to the throne and the threat of a Huguenot accession. They also signed an alliance for subsidy from Spain, gathered support from their kinsman the Duke of Lorraine, and accompanied a declaration from Péronne on 28 March 1585 with a premature insurrection in several parts of the kingdom. They received the active cooperation of former members of Alençon's disruptive entourage, while Marguerite of Valois established a small sovereignty in Agen to support them. The king was forced to bend before their menacing threats and to cancel Protestant privileges. Then began another superficial reconciliation with the Guise clan; more tense encounters at court where mutual suspicions and antagonisms were only just beneath the surface, to be followed by yet another threatened departure from court in 1587. The stage was set for the Day of Barricades in May 1588.

The failures of a generation were blamed on its king. No other sixteenth-century monarch was quite so vilified by his subjects; none has received such opprobrium from historians.[162] It was symptomatic of the collapse of political stability that its traditional bulwark was so excoriated in public. The attacks on the court and Henri III can be followed in the pamphlets and engravings collected by the contemporary Estoile, or in the large pamphlet collection in the *Bibliothèque Nationale*.[163] Their volume and abrasiveness varied in direct relation to the confidence or pessimism attached to the king's reforming endeavours. The themes of the criticism of the king are well known and need little rehearsal here. They would be summarised and repeated by pamphleteers and preachers in the League. Contemporaries like Estoile did not take all they read at face value.[164] Their views altered and changed in the face of political circumstances. Many were aware of the king's abilities; his oratory, his learning, his historical awareness, his knowledge of politics. They knew of his periodic, assiduous attention to the business of state, punctuated by moments of profound paralysing depression. He sometimes attended to all his own correspondence; he even arranged for a glass window to be cut into the cabinet rooms of the council of state in his châteaux so that he could watch over their deliberations.[165] Even as late as 1589 he sat in council all afternoon examining the *cahiers* from the estates of Blois – 'a miracle' as one contemporary recorded 'amidst such tumult and perturbation.[166] Those who served him and knew him well were impressed with his abilities; his superintendent of financers, Bellièvre, when asked by Henri IV to tell him frankly about his predecessor, refused to say anything against the memory of his previous master.

The king's strengths and weaknesses, and the extent to which he was misunderstood, appear readily from an examination of his personal religious attitudes and public attitudes towards them. Nothing struck more deeply than the charge that Henri III was a *politique* and, worse, an 'atheist'. It reached to the heart of the divinity of the French monarchy in which Henri III believed and to which he had been educated. Ominously, Catholics recalled that the crown had slipped twice from Henri III's head during his coronation at Reims in 1575 and that the liturgy of the service had been improper – sure signs of God's disapproval.[167] In fact, the king was intensely religious in both a public and a private way. He healed for scrofula with genuine zeal and regarded this as one of the ways in which he could contribute to curing the commonweal's afflictions. At Blois in 1576 and again in the following year at Poitiers, the centre of one of the most devastated regions, he applied his thaumaturgical powers. Catholic preachers scurrilously intimated later that Henri III had rendered his healing powers inofficacious by his compromise peace with the Protestants.[168] The king kept a Catholic court, employing few, if any Protestants. Services in his chapels were immaculately presented in accordance with Tridentine liturgical forms. He avidly collected relics and religious pictures, cutting the latter from medieval manuscripts.[169] The most important relics of the royal collection were those of the Passion in the Sainte Chapelle in Paris. When a fragment of the Holy Cross disappeared in 1575 (its theft was blamed on the queen mother and Italian financiers) the king ensured that the remaining fragment was given a special reliquary and attended in person the processions to venerate it.[170] Other processions were regularly organised by the king to sustain the realm in times of greatest danger. He required them to be impeccably organised, with no women taking part; 'for there is no devotion to be found when they are around'.

He conceived of reform in religious terms, expending enormous personal effort to create a new noble Order, the Order of the Holy Spirit. That of St Michael had become debased in the civil wars (entitlement had been given to those serving in the cavalry companies instead of arrears of pay).[171] The new Order was to surround the sovereign with a group of nobles of high birth, sworn by a special bond of fidelity to sustain royal authority and the Catholic Church and restore the natural leadership of the nobility in the kingdom. The scheme provoked years of bitter controversy with the Papacy over the ecclesiastical revenues that the king required to sustain it. When it was finally established in December 1578, it was criticised by some as too lavish, by others because they had not been appointed to it and then by Alençon because he feared its success.[172] In fact, it probably did encourage some members of the upper nobility to convert from Calvinism back to Catholicism and those appointed to the order were carefully chosen to be political supporters of the Valois monarchy.[173]

Reform on a personal plane he also perceived in religious terms. He founded private chapels and retreats in the *bois* at Vincennes and the Faubourg St Honoré where he could go on retreat for penance, mortification and contemplation. These retreats were criticised by contemporaries as ill-becoming a king. But they only lasted for fifteen to twenty days each year and, to those close to the king, it was the severity of his devotions and the effect on the king's fragile health which alarmed them. Other monastic orders in France mistrusted the Jeronimites and (later) Minims of Vincennes for precisely this austerity.[174] But these periods of retreat were important; from his retreat in 1582 sprang the royal initiatives for reform in 1583, for instance. They were essential in maintaining a royal sense of purpose amid a hostile climate.

The popular counterpart to the Order of the Holy Spirit and the Jeronimites in Vincennes was the penitent movement. The king was introduced to the penitents at Avignon in 1574 by his confessor, the Jesuit Edmund Auger. Impressed by their ritual of processions, pilgrimages and confessions, he envisaged they might stimulate moral and religious revival in Catholic France without the political dangers of the local confraternities. He helped to establish the penitents in Lyons in 1582 and introduced them in the following year to Paris.[175] Cardinal Joyeuse and Bishop Gondi, prominent clerical courtiers, introduced other branches of the penitent movement to the capital city. The processions were ridiculed by the Parisian notables and called, contemptuously, the *battus* and the 'flagellants', despite the fact that the scourges hanging from their belts were purely symbolic.

Above all else, contemporaries could not understand the royal attitude to heresy. How was it that the young prince who had played a prominent part at the massacre of Saint Bartholomew in 1572 could sign and sustain the edict of pacification at Bergerac (1577) which had granted the Protestants substantial rights in his kingdom? They ignored the massacre's profound effect on him (he was taciturn for days after the slaughter). His later political experience taught him that force against an ideological opposition was useless. As he said to his ambassador in Venice, a most prudent Catholic, Arnaud du Ferrier (*c.* 1508–85): 'I have learnt by experience that the evils so long afflicting this realm cannot be healed by force of arms. Softer and more gentle means are needed and these I am resolved to use....'[176] Some Catholics understood the realism of this position. Arnaud Sorbin, chaplain to Charles IX and Henri III, believed that force would not win back the heretics and Edmund Auger preached the same message. But there were many Catholic clergy to whom the message of the reintroduction of the Inquisition and renewed fighting made more sense. They would have agreed with Father Panigarola (who was removed from Henri III's court for such sentiments) that, with heretics, 'it was pious to be cruel'.[177]

THE DISPUTED SUCCESSION

On 10 June 1584, the direct heir to the throne, François, Duke of Anjou, died. François had been a political menace to his brother while alive. His death was a disaster, for the lack of a clear legal succession further eroded royal authority. As the Savoyard ambassador reported, 'Every day he [the king] has the sound of death in his ears, whether from the letters of his friends or the mouths of his servants and subjects. Everything in France comes down to this subject: 'If your majesty dies this could happen. . . .'[178] Succession problems had a habit of festering and poisoning sixteenth-century states unless they were quickly resolved. According to royal apologists, the custom in France was that 'la mort saisit le vif', whereby a king was declared by dynastic right and not by coronation and, to that extent, disputed successions could be avoided. The problems facing the country in 1584 could not be quickly or painlessly despatched. Not only was Henri III legally bound not to make a will or declare his successor but, as contemporaries well understood, he was under powerful pressures not to declare his own political demise by naming his successor.[179]

Claims of the most speculative kind about the legitimacy of Valois rule in France had been made since the beginning of the century. In 1510, Symphorien Champier, physician and historian to Antoine, Duke of Lorraine (d. 1544) had asserted on the basis of a charter in 1070 that the Dukes of Lorraine were directly descended from Charlemagne. The assertion received support in the reign of Henri II, partly from cleverly forged documents; in the wars of religion, its importance grew as other authors like François Hotman attempted to prove that the Capetians (and, therefore, the Valois) were usurpers to the throne of Charlemagne. The Duke of Lorraine was, in 1584, one of the candidates in a position to assert his right to the throne.[180]

The kingdom of France was not, of course, bereft of fundamental laws governing the succession. The problem was that they were difficult to apply in the particular case. The principal law was the Salic law – an invention of the French lawyers in the Hundred Years War to exclude Plantagenet claims to the French throne – which stated that the French crown was hereditary only through the male line. Were it to apply strictly, the claim of the Duke of Lorraine would fall away (since the succession from Charlemagne passed through two females). But the Salic law was not accepted entirely without question at the end of the sixteenth century. It did not conform to the general principles of Roman law and certainly conflicted with private customary law in some regions (for instance, Lorraine, where territories 'devolved' through the female line).[181]

But the Salic law was imprecise on the law of inheritance. If the inheritance passed into a collateral line, whose was the better case? By strict primogeniture, the first in line of succession was Henri of Navarre, followed by his uncle Charles, Cardinal of Bourbon. But by consanguinity (the principle used in Roman law to decide an intestate inheritance) the first in line was the Cardinal of Bourbon, since the cardinal was only twenty degrees removed from the Valois king.[182] The case of strict primogeniture was argued by François Hotman whom Henri of Navarre approached in a letter of August 1584 to sustain him in 'this huge and complex question, so vital for the future, and which needs to be enlightened'.[183] No one, Navarre told Hotman, could do it better – 'Work with diligence and attention . . . and I assure you I will reward your useful service.' By April 1585 Hotman's *Disputes on the Succession Controversy* had appeared. It was a theoretical work of great sophistication, arguing the case for the *suitas regiae* or the *ius filiationis vel sanguinis*, the royal birthright or succession, not governed by blood or degree but by declared, public law, solemnly enacted in the estates general of the kingdom. He used extensively a work of a fifteenth-century jurist, Jean de Terre Rouge, an edition of whose treatise he appended to his publication. At the same time, he hastened to amend the fourth edition of *Francogallia* by adding a chapter on the laws of succession in the French monarchy.[184]

The case for consanguinity was argued by Hotman's former enemy, the Italian Matteo Zampini. He produced a treatise *On the Law of Succession*, which circulated widely in manuscript before appearing in print in 1588.[185] Zampini criticised Hotman's case for primogeniture. The birthright of the succession always lay with the dauphin, the heir apparent. Antoine de Bourbon, King of Navarre and Henri's father (1518–62), had never been the first prince of the blood for he was in a collateral line and Valois princes had denied him the possibility of *ever* being the dauphin. Therefore, there was no *suitas regiae* to Navarre. When there was no direct birthright then, by historical precedent, the succession passed to the next proximate kin by consanguinity. The chief historical precedent was the succession of Louis the Pious as against Bernard, son of Pepin (*c.* 754). Zampini's case was a strong one, although later he was lampooned by those of a Navarrist persuasion as a 'senseless and scurrilous' foreign lawyer. There were, however, residual problems connected with the way in which precise consanguinity was to be calculated.

In any case, Catholics argued the case for another fundamental law in favour of the Cardinal of Bourbon, that of 'Catholicity'. The case was, again, an imposing one. The French king was 'the Most Christian King' in Europe, with powers to heal scrofula, to appoint bishops and take revenues from the Catholic Church. The mystique of monarchy, the symbolism of crown, coronation, and the ritual which gave the institution its social significance and political authority, relied on Catholicism. But the case for 'Catholicity' was made more complex by the famous papal bull read by Sixtus V to the consistory in Rome on 9 September 1585 excommunicating both Henri of Navarre and Henri Prince of Condé and declaring Navarre ineligible for the French throne.[186] This turned the issue of Catholicity into part of a much older question, that of papal rights and authority in France. Hotman, again, was responsible for the famous reply to the papal bull, the *Brutum Fulmen* (translated into English as the *Brutish Thunderbolt or Rather Feeble Fire Flash*). In his best cavalier style he accused Sixtus V, the 'stupid cuckoo', the 'purple whore', of the seven cardinal crimes (impiety, heresy, tyranny, sacrilege, treason, forgery and illegality) and pointed out the dangers of papal interference in the law of Catholicity. The pamphlet went through four editions in two years and the Curia placed a contract of 2,000 crowns for Hotman's assassination.[187] Nevertheless, the pressure on Henri of Navarre to convert to Catholicism was very great. It is doubtful, if he had, whether he would have had an undisputed succession, for his basic dynastic right was still in doubt. It is certain that he would not have carried the Protestants with him and it is possible that he would have become the prisoner of the Catholic League.[188] The Cardinal of Bourbon was, in his own way, a prisoner of circumstances too. The 'red ass' (as Hotman spitefully called him), the 'old dotard, drunk with ambition' (as de Thou dismissed him) was aware that his age and clerical condition told against him. Although Henri III eventually declared (and registered in *parlement*) that the cardinal was his dauphin (on 17 August 1588) the cardinal knew that this had been in response to pressure from the Guise. He eventually publicly acknowledged that 'the Guise, fatal enemies to his name and his house, had used him to advance themselves'.[189]

REFERENCES AND NOTES

1. L. Le Roy, *De la vicissitude ou variété des choses en l'univers* (Paris, 1576, *BL* C115, hl/2). Cf. W. Gundersheimer, 1966.

2. Still the best way to observe the growth of French Protestantism is through Calvin's correspondence (*Calvini Opera, corpus reformatorum* Vols X–XX, **1863–1900**). Cf. D. Kelley, 1981, N. M. Sutherland, 1980. *Edict du roy, contenant la grace et pardon pour ceux qui par cy devant ont mal senty de la foy* (Paris, 11 Mar. 1559, N.S. 1560).

3. G. de Saulx-Tavannes, **1881**, Vol. VIII, p. 368.

4. N.Tommaseo, **1838**, Vol. I, p. 413.

5. *Ibid.* p. 541. Cited in I. Cloulas, 1979, p. 137.

6. B. de Monluc, **1964**, p. 472.

7. F. de Raemond, *l'Histoire de la Naissance, Progrez et Décadence de l'Héresie de ce siècle . . .* (2 vols, Paris, 1605) p. 261.

8. M. Blouyn, **1976**, p. 74. G. Bosquet, *Recueil de pieces historiques . . .* (Toulouse, 1862) pp. 47–8. Bosquet's was a common Catholic belief – see Jean de La Vacquerie, *Catholique remonstrance aux roys et princes chrestiens . . .* (Paris, 1560), where Huguenotism was believed to have taken root in the 'banquets & assemblées de femmes . . .'.

9. Bèze, Vol. I, Bk IV and V.

10. R. Kingdon, 1956, ch. viii.

11. F. Aubert, 1947, p. 97.

12. D. Richet, 1977, pp. 766–9.

13. Bèze, Vol. II, pp. 432–5, 712–18; III, pp. 1–14, 249–55. N. H. Galpern, 1976, pp. 155–6. P. Benedict, 1981, ch. ii. D. Kelley, 1981, pp. 96–118. M. S. Lamet, 1979, ch. iv.

14. R. Kingdon, 1956, p. 79. L. Romier, 1925, Vol. II, p. 180.

15. J. Garrisson-Estèbe, 1980, pp. 63–4.

16. D. Kelley, 1981, p. 225.
17. E. Le Roy Ladurie, 1966, pp. 348–56 and tables for lower Languedoc and the growth of Protestantism among the Cévennes hill towns. J. M. Davies, 1979, analyses the proscription lists of Toulouse's Protestants. N. Z. Davis, 1975, ch. i (Lyons' printing workers); ch. iii (city women and religious change). D. L. Rosenberg, 1978, on textile-workers of Amiens. D. J. Nicholls, 1977, on the growth of Protestantism in Normandy generally. M. S. Lamet, 1979, chs iv and v on Protestantism in Dieppe and Caen. J. C. P. Meyer, 1978, on the lack of social conflict in La Rochelle's vigorous Protestantism. N. H. Galpern, 1976, pp. 125–80 stresses the different mental outlooks and assumptions of Protestants in Champagne.
18. D. Richet, 1977, pp. 770–2.
19. *Ibid.* G. W. Sypher, 1980, pp. 80–4. Inflammatory arrest of Lenten preachers in Toulouse 1561, in Bèze, Vol. I, pp. 904–5. Cf. references to Bordeaux, pp. 869–71, Béziers, pp. 965 and Beaune, pp. 864–5.
20. N. Froumenteau [pseud.] *Le Secret des Finances de France* (n.p. 1581, *BL* 283, c 14). He provides a survey, diocese by diocese, of deaths in the following categories: canons, monks (by religious orders), Catholic and protestant nobles, soldiers, foreigners, girls violated, villages damaged, houses destroyed. The precision of the figures renders the work fictitious, but their relative order of magnitude may constitute a valuable impression of the worst affected regions of France.
21. M. Greengrass, 'The anatomy of a religious riot in Toulouse in May 1562', *Journal of Ecclesiastical History,* Vol. XXXIV (1983), pp. 367–91
22. J. Garrisson-Estèbe. 1968. chs viii–ix.
23. *Le Reveille-matin des Français* (Edinburgh [Basel?], 1573). Q. Skinner, 1978, Vol. II, pp. 304–5.
24. Estimates in P. Joutard *et al.*, 1976, p. 68. I. Cloulas, 1979, p. 297, puts the figures substantially higher.
25. Bèze, Vol. III, p. 17.
26. D. Richet, 1977, p. 772. N. Z. Davis, 1975, pp. 152–87.
27. N. Z. Davis, 1975, pp. 175–6. J. Garrisson-Estèbe, 1968, p. 196. Bèze, Vol. III, p. 17 (Toulouse, 1562 – 'No shortage of houses to pillage or people to kill'.)
28. *Ibid.*, Vol. I, pp. 963–4.
29. *Mèmoires de Condè* (cited as *MC*) Vol. I, p. 82, for little children of Paris, taking the bodies of two Protestants executed at the Halles in May 1562 and burning them. Examples also in Toulouse, 1562, Brignolles, 1562, Pamiers, 1566 and Paris, 1572.
30. Objects of destruction discussed in N. Z. Davis, 1975, p. 174. Garrisson-Estèbe, 1980, pp. 163–5. Also Bèze, Vol. I, p. 887.
31. G. de Saulx-Tavannes, **1881**, Vol. VIII, p. 368. The murder of the prominent Baron Fumel in the Agenais on 22 Nov. 1561 provoked many fears in that locality. In Bordeaux, the first *président* of the *parlement* said: 'When the common people attack great men to whom obedience is due, that is a sign that the madness is extreme and the

hopes of cure slender' (*Secret registers, parlement* of Bordeaux, Vol. XI, p. 203). Cf. Bèze, Vol. I, pp. 885–7. De Thou, *Histoire Universelle* (cited as *HU*) Vol. IV, pp. 370–1. Antoine de Nouailles told his brother that the Protestants were planning to burn all titles to property and destroy the nobility (*BN MS Fr* 6910, fol. 138). On the refusal to pay tithes, J. Garrisson-Estèbe, 1980, pp. 162–3; E. Le Roy Ladurie, 1966, Vol. I, p. 382.

32. Calvin, *Institutes of the Christian Religion*, Bk IV, ch. 18, paras 18 (the Mass); 19 (Holy Oil); Bk I, chs 11–12 (Images); Bk III, ch. 20, para. 22 (Veneration of Saints). Cf. Coligny (Actes du Colloque, 1972), 1974, pp. 451–87.

33. N. Z. Davis, 1975, p. 180. N. H. Galpern, 1976, p. 160. G. Bosquet, *op. cit.*, p. 148 (cited n. 8).

34. G. W. Sypher, 1980, pp. 59–84. Also the work of Jean de la Vacquerie. cited above, n. 8.

35. E. de Barthélemy, *Journal d'un curé ligueur*, 1866, p. 165.

36. J. Garrisson-Estèbe, 1968, pp. 133–4.

37. N. H. Galpern, 1976, pp. 159–60.

38. P. Joutard *et al.*, 1976, pp. 55–6.

39. M. Orlea, 1980, pp. 33–4. R. Harding, 1980, pp. 85–107.

40. *Catherine de Médicis, Lettres*, **1880–1909**, Vol. III, p. 163.

41. Dijon, Chalon-sur-Saône, Beaune, Tournus and Couches.

42. Bèze, Vol. I, pp. 871–4. F. Hauchecorne, 1950, pp. 329–40.

43. M. Orlea, 1980, p. 34.

44. N. H. Galpern, 1976, p. 178. D. Kelley, 1973, p. 250.

45. I. Cloulas, 1979, p. 419.

46. H. Drouot, 1937b, pp. 31–9. N. H. Galpern, 1976, p. 178.

47. D. L. Rosenberg, 1978, p. 52.

48. P. Benedict, 1981, ch. v.

49. J. Philippi, **1918**, p. 183.

50. F. Charbonnier, 1919 and 1923. J. Pineaux, 1973. Coligny (Actes du Colloque, 1972), 1974, pp. 390–405. D. Kelley, 1981, pp. 276–87. Cf. the engravings of Tortorel and Périssin as well as *les Tragiques* of Agrippa d'Aubigné (composed *c.* 1577).

51. J-F. Gilmont, 1981.

52. D. Kelley, 1981, pp. 118–24. A. Soman, 1974, pp. 181–202.

53. *MC* (5 vols, ed. Secousse, London). A sixth volume was published from The Hague in the same year. See H. Hauser, 1912, Vol. III, pp. 103–4.

54. N. Tommaseo, **1838** Vol. II, p. 138. Cf. *Avertissement sur la faussété de plusieurs mensonges* . . . (n.p. 1562, *LN*, No. 258). 'We now see a stock of defammatory libels by which the most excellent persons – princes and seigneurs – are outrageously attacked . . . .'

55. Cayet, p. 103. Estoile says that pamphlets were produced 'as much by one party as by another so that nothing was talked of at Paris and at court except new libels containing reasons and defences and the accusations of each party'. Estoile, **1943**, pp. 189–90.

56. D. Kelley, 1981, pp. 266–7 and pamphlets cited from *MC*. G. Guilleminot, 1977, pp. 77–83.

57. J. Poujol, 1955, pp. 33–7.

58. H. Warren, 1967, pp. xlii–xliii. Coligny (Actes du colloque, 1972), 1974, pp. 323–39. N. M. Sutherland, 1973.
59. P. Joutard *et al.*, 1974. A. Soman, 1976.
60. Estoile, **1943**, p. 490 (April 1587).
61. De Thou, *HU*, Vol. v, p. 524. Cf. G. de Saulx-Tavannes, **1881**, Vol. VIII, p. 118.
62. Granvelle, **1841–52**, Vol. VIII, p. 118.
63. J. E. Neale, 1943, pp. 84–5. L. Romier, pp. 215–16. D. Buisseret, 1972, p. 64. Q. Skinner, 1978, Vol. II, p. 249 rightly talks of the 'so-called party of politiques'.
64. F. Decrue de Stoutz, 1890.
65. P. Benedict, 1978, pp. 205–25.
66. Among recent biographies, that of I. Cloulas, 1979, is undoubtedly the best, but there is no substitute for the magnificent edition of her correspondence to grasp the measure of her contribution in the civil wars.
67. The notorious *Discours merveilleux de la vie, actions et déportements de la reine Catherine de Médicis* (n.p. 1574) contains most of the criticisms levelled against her.
68. N. Tommaseo, **1838**, Vol. II, p. 245. Also Brantôme, **1864–82**, Vol. VII, p. 373.
69. V. W. Graham and W. M. Johnson, 1979. Also P. Champion, 1937.
70. W. L. Gundersheimer, 1966, ch. vi.
71. E. M. Beame, 1966, pp. 250–65.
72. *Congratulation au Roy Charles IX sur l'Edict de Pacification* . . . in E. Pasquier, **1723**, Vol. II, cols 913–20.
73. E. M. Beame, 1966, pp. 256–8. D. Thicket, 1979, pp. 95–115.
74. La Popelinière (L. de Voisin, sieur de) *La Vraye et entière Histoire des Troubles et choses memorables depuis l'an 1562* . . . (Basel, 2 vols, 1572, *BL* 284, a 31) Vol. II, fol. 478. The notoriety of Lude's indecision can be judged from the following message attached to the maypole in front of his lodgings in Niort in 1576: 'The nobles were the only protected ones in these civil wars . . . they know so well how to maintain and protect themselves that, neither in their wealth or their personnages, do they receive any inconvenience, but, rather, they profit from the troubles. By their behaviour, it is easy to judge that these wars were no longer about religion. 20,000 Catholics and Huguenots, no longer able to bear such behaviour, were willing to rise up and do away with them.' Quoted in Y-M. Bercé, 1974, Vol. I, p. 284. For nobles who married across the sectarian divide to protect their fortunes, see C. Pradel, **1894**, pp. 41–2.
75. La Popelinière, *op. cit.*, fol. 478 (cited n. 74),
76. *Ibid.*, fol. 304.
77. *Ibid.*, fols. 39 and 392–3.
78. De Thou, *HU*, Vol. VII, p. 61.
79. J. Delumeau, 1968, p. 181. J. Garrisson Estèbe, 1980, p. 185.
80. S. Goulart, *Mémoires de l'état de France sous Charles IX* (2nd edn, 3 vols, Middelburg [Geneva], 1576, copy in London Library).
81. J. Loutchizky, **1873–96**. A. Dussert, 1929, pp. 110–18.
82. Q. Skinner, 1978, Vol. ii, p. 302. Condé's *Declaration* as well as his *Traité d'Association* are in LN, Nos. 261 and 271.

83. Q. Skinner, 1978, Vol. II, pp. 303–4. Cf. *Discours véritable* (n.p. 1567, LN, No. 505) and *De la Necessité d'assembler les estats* (n.p. 1567, LN, No. 511).
84. F. Hotman, **1972**.
85. D. Kelley, 1973.
86. *Ibid.*, p. 254.
87. D. Kelley, 1970, parts II and III and 1973, pp. 240–1.
88. M. Yardeni, 1971. D. Kelley, 1970, part III. D. Kelley, 1973, pp. 241–2.
89. F. Hotman, **1972**, pp. 220–33. R. A. Jackson, 1972, pp. 155–71.
90. *Ibid.*, p. 235.
91. *Ibid.*, pp. 287–331.
92. *Ibid.*, pp. 496–505.
93. *Ibid.*, pp. 332–49.
94. D. Kelley, 1973, pp. 218–26.
95. *Ibid.*, p. 247.
96. *Ibid.*, p. 252.
97. M. Yardeni, 1971, pp. 163–81.
98. For example, the opening remarks of the *procès-verbal* of the assembly at Anduze, 7 Feb. 1573 in J. Garrisson-Estèbe, 1980, pp. 339–41. Cf. *Declaration des causes qui ont meu ceux de la religion à reprendre les armes pour leur conservation* (Montauban, 1574, LN, No. 789).
99. Kelley, 1973, pp. 253–60. Q. Skinner, 1978, p. 318. W. L. Gundersheimer, 1966, pp. 81–3. G. Bontems *et al.*, 1965, pp. 155–71.
100. Q. Skinner, 1978, pp. 318–9.
101. Etienne Junius Brutus [pseud], *Vindicae contra Tyrannos*, **1979**. Cf. Q. Skinner, 1978, Vol. II, pp. 319–38. The work is frequently ascribed to Philippe Du Plessis-Mornay, but the important distinction between 'writing' and 'publishing' is drawn by H. Weber in the 1979 edition, pp. i–v.
102. R. Schnur, *Die französischen Juristen im konfessionellen Bürgerkrieg* . . . Duncker and Humblot, Berlin, 1962.
103. J. Garrisson-Estèbe, 1980, pp. 184–5. Catherine de Médicis's famous angry reaction to their demands in the autumn of 1573 is contained in d'Aubigné, Vol. IV, p. 183. There is no satisfactory account of the negotiations in 1575–6.
104. J. Loutchizky, **1875**, p. 83.
105. Details of the complex agreement with Casimir in I. Cloulas, 1979, pp. 386–9. Cf. B. Vogler, 1965, pp. 51–85.
106. J. Gassot, **1934**, p. 142. Catholic propaganda of the period contained the same theme. Cf. *Advertissement à la noblesse de France tant du party du Roy que des rebelles, & conspirateurs contre luy & son estat* . . . (Paris, 1574, LN, No. 795).
107. La Popelinière (L. de Voisin, sieur de), *Histoire de France* (n.p. 1581, *BL* 183, d 7, 8), Bk XXXVII, fols 101, 225, etc.
108. Isambert, Vol. XIV, pp. 189–212 (Feb. 1566). Summarised in J. H. M. Salmon, 1975, pp. 154–56.
109. I. Cloulas, 1979, p. 221.
110. *Ibid.*, p. 257. Coligny (Actes du colloque, 1972), 1974, pp. 651–705. Cf. H. Hauser, 1932.

111. Memoirs for the assembly were compiled in some regions and reveal the scale of the problems in French society, e.g. C. Douais, **1890**, pp. 473–89; Devic and Vaissète, **1872–1904**, Vol. XII, cols 1065–71. For the agitation in Champagne, C. Haton, **1857**, Vol. II, p. 760. Pressure for holding estates came from the Protestants – *Articles contenans la requeste presentee au Roy par les deputez des Eglises Reformee* (Basel, 1574, *BL* 3900, a 1). See also the *Advis et tres humbles remonstrances a tous Princes, Seigneurs, Cours de Parlement & nombre de catholiques* . . . (n.p. 1574, LN, No. 760). For Poitou, La Popelinière, *Histoire de France* (1581), Vol. II, fol. 206v.

112. LN, no. 760.

113. *Registres de Paris*, **1866**, etc., Vol. VII, pp. 313–17. Also printed as *Remonstrances faictes au Roy en son château au Louvre, xix de Decembre 1575*.

114. Clause 58. A. Stegmann, **1979**, pp. 116–17.

115. There is no satisfactory study of the estates general of Blois. *Cahiers*, debates and organisation of the estates are touched on in E. Charleville, 1901; M. Orléa, 1980, pp. 87–96; G. de Taix, **1625**; J. Bodin, **1789**.

116. I. Cloulas, 1979 p. 401. M. Wolfe, 1972, pp. 158–68.

117. F. C. Spooner, 1972, pp. 90–2. Summary in J. H. M. Salmon, 1975, pp. 226–7.

118. J. R. L. Highfield and R. M. Jeffs, 1981, pp. 166–7; J. Russell Major, 1980, pp. 208–10, 213–16.

119. L. Serbat, 1906, pp. 89–108. Pamphlets in LN, Nos 958 and 1002.

120. Isambert, Vol. XIV, pp. 380–463 (May 1579).

121. S. H. Ehrman, 1936, Vol. II, pp. 600–41. M. Foisil, 1976, pp. 25–40. L. Scott Van Doren, 1974, pp. 71–100. A. Dussert, 1931, pp. 123–89. J. H. M. Salmon, 1979, pp. 1–28.

122. A. Karcher, 1956, pp. 115–62. The decision was in the wake of an Eastertide series of intense devotions.

123. Commission is published in G. Hanotaux, 1884, pp. 187–8. That for Brittany is dated 3 August 1582. Evidence for their activity is in E. Pallasse, 1943, pp. 364–9.

124. In Aix-en-Provence, Blois, Niort, Marseilles, etc. See *BN MS Fr* 16228 and *Cal SP For*, Vol. XVII, p. 239.

125. Karcher, *op. cit.* (cited n. 122).

126. Surviving evidence from the assembly includes the royal speech, BN Dupuy *MS* 87 fol. 151–2. Reports of its considerations in *BN MS Fr* 7248, 3961 and 15567 fol 80.

127. Evidence in Fontanon, Vol. II, p. 88, 591–601, 603–4 (suppressions of *bureaux des finances*, 20 *élections*, certain *greniers* and *trésoriers*).

128. January 1578; a scheme for the domain to be repurchased presented by the *prévôt des marchands*.

129. *BN MS Fr* 4352 (established May 1584 and suppressed May 1585).

130. See reports to the council in *BN MS Fr* 16231–2.

131. This was a slow process, but it led eventually to the engrossed tax farm, the *cinq grosses fermes*, in 1585.

132. *Bib Mazarine*, 2635 fols 67 *et seq*. General background in R. Gascon, 1971, Vol. II, pp. 698–727.

133. The assembly envisaged a small, well-equiped, well-paid standing army of 2,400 men serving and training in garrisons for four months each year. Attempts to reduce the size of the army in Fontanon, Vol. IV, pp. 129–39. The admiralty was also reorganised in March 1584.

134. The assizes established at Troyes were extended in November 1582. Others had already been held in Poitou (pamphlets in LN, Nos 963, 967–8; 1058–62) and Guyenne. The English ambassador recorded: 'Truly justice is done in them marvellously severely.' (*Cal SP For,* Vol. XVI, p. 252)

135. Estoile, **1943**, pp. 350–1. Busbecq, **1845**, p. 68. De Thou, *HU*, Vol. IX, pp. 81–2.

136. A. Karcher, 1956, p. 121.

137. Especially towards the beginning of the realm – René de Birague, the Dukes of Nevers and de Retz were members of a much smaller council than had existed under Charles IX – hence some of the dislike directed against them.

138. Of 115 bishoprics in the period from 1570–95 about 27 were held by bishops born in Italy. Among these who gained titles of French nobility were the Dukes of Nevers and de Retz, the Marquis de Villars, the Bishop Philippe de Gondi, Alphonse d'Ornano and Guillaume de Gadagne.

139. D. Richet, 1965, pp. 27–33.

140. Among innumerable references, I. Cloulas, 1979, pp. 373, 397 and 451. *Catherine de Médicis, Lettres*, **1880–1909** Vol. V, pp. 303–4 and 375. A. Desjardins, **1859–65**, Vol. IV, pp. 327–31. The debts to the Italians outstanding for the period 1585–89 appear in Henri IV's council of state papers (Valois, Vol. I, Nos 3120–22, 3039, etc.).

141. R. de Lucinge, **1964**, pp. 107–8 (June 1585).

142. A. M. de Boilisle, **1873**, No. 166 (Aug. 1576).

143. Estoile, **1943**, p. 483 (20 Jan. 1587).

144. E. Picot, 1901, p. 133.

145. Diz. biog. degli Italiani (Rome, *Institute della Enciclopedia*, XXV vols in prog., 1960), Vol. V (Bandini). J. Delumeau, 1959, Vol. II, pp. 899–900.

146. Milon rose through army contracting and salt-tax farming. He eventually became a secretary to the royal chamber. His ignoble origins and peculation were widely known. When he went to Spa to be cured of the stone (*calcul*) there were jokes about his 'art des calculs' (Estoile, **1943**, pp. 150–1). He returned from the Netherlands to favour before 1588.

147. Estoile, **1943**, pp. 72–3, 134, 154–5, 235, etc. In 1588, the 'Gaverston' literature, comparing Epernon with Edward II's favourite – F. Baumgartner, 1975, pp. 86–8.

148. *Cal SP For,* Vol. XVII, pp. 256–8.

149. I. Cloulas, 1979, p. 427 – 'Les vieux s'en vont et il faut dresser les jeunes.' But Epernon, for instance, was only four years younger than the Duke of Guise.

150. See below, p. 90. The court expenses were not excessive and probably compare favourably with those of Henri IV's court. See also H. Michaud, 1972, pp. 87–150.

151. H. C. Davila, **1647**, pp. 477–80. Estoile, **1943**, p. 201. Gassot, **1934**, pp. 159–60.

152. R. de Lucinge, **1954–55**, pp. 104–5; **1964**, p. 92. Lucinge was irritated at the king's obstruction of the proposed marriage of the Duke of Nemours and Christine Duchess of Lorraine.

153. Impressions created by the literary works of Ronsard, Philippe Desportes, A. Janyn, N. Rapin, Pibrac *et al*.

154. F. de La Noue, **1967**, 1st and 5th discourse.

155. Henri d'Angoulême, son of Henri II and Lady Fleming. Mlle Diane, daughter of Henri II and a Piedmontese noble. The king visited her frequently at Chantilly (Brantôme, **1864–82**, pp. 141–5). Charles d'Angoulême's favour after 1586 is recalled in *Catherine de Médicis*, *Lettres*, **1880–1909**, Vol. IX, pp. 77-a–8. A. Desjardins, **1859–86**, Vol. IV, pp. 704–9.

156. J. H. Mariéjol, 1928. No satisfactory study of the Duke of Anjou. For the hostile pamphlets see *Catherine de Médicis*, *Lettres*, **1880–1909**, Vol. VI, pp. 235–6; VIII, pp. 116–17. The queen was also supposed to have been responsible for the 'Sonnet of the young La Bourdaisière' in May 1575 (Estoile, **1943**, pp. 72–3). In 1588 she wrote a vicious memorandum against her brother (K. de Lettenhove, 1891, pp. 161–95).

157. J. Gaches, **1879**, p. 199. M. Greengrass, 1979.

158. *Cal SP For*, Vol. XI, pp. 20–1, 44, 67.

159. *Ibid*., Vol. XII, pp. 655–60; XIII, pp. 264–5, 300–3.

160. With the exception of the Duke of Mayenne, they were all heavily indebted and in no position to refuse the king's gifts (see below, p. 175). For example, 100,000 *écus* to d'Aumale for his wedding; 100,000 *livres* to Mayenne for his; 500,000 *écus* to the Duke of Guise on salt receipts in 1582.

161. *Mémoires de la Ligue* (cited as *ML*), Vol. I, p. 567.

162. Among the more ignorant: A. J. Grant, 1951, 'The historian wishing to understand this strange creature [Henri III] should probably have to seek the help of an expert in brain disease' (p. 427). V. H. H. Green, 1969, 'Clearly a psychological case' (p. 247).

163. There are over 800 pamphlets in their collection for this period.

164. It is sometimes implied that Estoile's views were those of the pamphlets he collected. But he was evidently outraged by some of them and said that only foolish people believed what they read in them. His support for the king after 1584 was less equivocal.

165. *Cal SP For*, Vol. XVI, 112. J. Gassot, **1934**, pp. 23, 159. Hurault de Cheverny, **1881**, Vol. X, pp. 496–7; even R. de Lucinge, **1954–55**, p. 106. His intellectual pursuits brought him to employ Giordano Bruno, the famous natural philosopher (F. Yates, 1947, p. 101). His study of politics included Aristotle (Louis Le Roy dedicated his edition to him in 1576). He read Tacitus, Polybius, Machiavelli's works. His historian, du Haillan, told Henri IV that his predecessor studied history closely 'which might serve as an inspiration to reform many of

the corrupt and altered things in his state which had need of remedies, reformation and correction' (du Haillan, *Estat et succez des affaires de France* (Paris, 1609, *BL* 1059, b 3), preface.

166. E. Halphen, **1880**, pp. 69–75.
167. Estoile, **1943**, p. 67. K. Cameron, 1974, pp. 152–63.
168. M. Bloch, 1973, pp. 177, 193.
169. This was unlike the Cardinal of Guise who scandalised the nuncio by not holding Tridentine services at Reims (*ANG*, Vol. VII, pp. 574–6).
170. Estoile, **1943**, pp. 71, 112.
171. R. Harding, 1978, pp. 81–2.
172. J. Boucher, 'L'ordre du Saint Esprit dans la pensée politique et religieuse d'Henri III', *Cahiers d'Histoire* (1972) pp. 129–42. *ANG*, Vol. VIII, pp. 258–60; 176–7.
173. Sully's two brothers were attracted to Catholicism in this way, to his disgust (Sully, **1970**, p. 122).
174. The oratory in Vincennes was ready in 1584 (A. Desjardins, **1859–65**, Vol. IV, pp. 485–7) and that of St Honoré in *C*. 1585 (*ibid.*, pp. 600, 631). François Hotman thought the king had gone mad with superstition and remorse for his tyranny (R. Dareste, 1850, p. 88). Estoile reported Parisian views of 'le roi se faisant moine' in **1943**, p. 417, 498.
175. A. Lynn Martin, 1973, *Cal SP For*, Vol. XVII, p. 184–6. Statutes of the congregation in *Arch. cur. de l'hist. de France*, Vol. X (1st series), pp. 437–9.
176. *Henri III, Lettres*, **1965–**, Vol. III, p. 409. For Arnaud du Ferrier, *DBF*, Vol. XI, col. 1393. He died of 'chagrin' at the renewed civil wars and was Henri of Navarre's chancellor for a period.
177. Fr. Panigarola, *Leçons catholiques* ... (Trans. G. Chappuys, Lyons, 1586, *BN* D 46834), pp. 591–2.
178. R. de Lucinge, **1954–55**, p. 106; **1964**, pp. 171–3.
179. F. Hotman, **1972**, pp. 463–4. Cf. *Discours sur les calomnies* (Paris, 1588, LN No. 1245) – 'To declare a successor is almost . . . to condemn a prince.'
180. L. Davillé, 1909, pp. 2–22. The case was publicly refuted by Philippe Du Plessis-Mornay in 1583 – *Discours sur le droit pretendu par ceux de Guise sur la Couronne de France* (n.p. 1583, LN, No. 1054).
181. L. Davillé, 1909. The queen mother did not accept it (Brantôme, **1864–82**, Vol. VIII, p. 45).
182. F. J. Baumgartner, 1973, pp. 87–98. The position can be presented as follows:

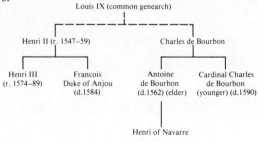

183. D. Kelley, 1973, p. 292.
184. F. Hotman, **1972**, pp. 452–72.
185. C. Bontems *et al.*, 1965, pp. 171–86. Published in Latin and French in 1588 – *De la Succession du Droict et Prérogative de premier Prince du sang de France* (Paris, 1588, *BL* 1059, a 15).
186. *Sanctiss. d.n. Sixti papas V declaratio . . .* (Rome, 1585, LN 1094).
187. D. Kelley, 1973, pp. 300–6.
188. Huguenots left his service in the summer of 1589 because of the fear of his conversion (*Henri IV, Lettres*, Vol. III, p. 72).
189. De Thou, *HU*, Vol. VIII, p. 255; *MC*, Vol. IV, p. 3.

Chapter 2

THE CATHOLIC LEAGUE

The Catholic League was the culmination of the ideological struggle of the wars of religion. It had its roots in the failure of reform in the French state and seized the opportunity created by the succession problem after the Duke of Anjou's death. Formally speaking, the League took shape in complicated negotiations which arose in northeast France between September 1584 and March 1585.[1] The venues were Nancy, capital of the duchy of Lorraine; Joinville, principal château of the House of Guise in Catholic Champagne; and Reims, the great cathedral city, symbol of Catholic France where its kings were traditionally crowned. Those present at various times included Charles III, Duke of Lorraine (1543–1606) and every member of the House of Guise who could attend. François de Roncherolles, sieur de Maineville, acted as an agent for the Cardinal of Bourbon. Philip II, King of Spain, was represented by Jean-Baptiste de Tassis (*c.* 1530–1610) who had just been replaced as Spain's ambassador in Paris; also by Philip's chief agent in France, Juan Moreo. Claude Matthieu, a Jesuit from the Duke of Lorraine's new Jesuit university, attended in order to carry news of the discussions to Rome. Each party had its own interests to pursue, but the issue of the succession to the French crown and the possibility of exploiting the lively hatred of the Valois court united them splendidly. The results were an agreement at Joinville on 31 December 1584 to support the Cardinal of Bourbon's claim to the throne, by war if necessary, supported by substantial sums of money from Spain and guaranteed by the Duke of Lorraine. Three months later, in the so-called declaration of Péronne, the League for the reform of the state and the defence of the Catholic faith was publicly proclaimed.[2]

As with the Huguenots, the most lively and committed part of the League lay in major cities where, following the example of Paris, groups of men, dedicated to the preservation of the Catholic faith, seized power in 1589. In Paris, they were known as the *Sixteen* (*Seize*) after the number of quarters (*quartiers*) of the capital from which the members of its organising committees were elected. Many features of the League in the cities – its apparent spontaneity, the oath, secrecy and vigilante attitudes – reflected the Catholic confraternities of earlier civil wars. They certainly inspired genuine fears and social conflict among Catholic city notables: 'This is true anarchy' reported Etienne Pasquier in Paris.[3] The *Sixteen* plotted against the king and expelled him from his capital in 1588. They remained a powerful force for over three years in the capital and their popularity and organisation were such that, in 1589, they seemed to be invincible. Yet, by 1594, the League had collapsed in many traditionally Catholic localities. How did the *Sixteen* acquire such influence and how was it so quickly lost? To what extent did its defeat assist France's struggle for political stability? The confused history of the Catholic League is that of its own internal quarrels, but from them, something can be learned of the instabilities in France towards the end of the sixteenth century.

THE SIXTEEN AND THE DAY OF BARRICADES IN PARIS (12 May 1588)

Two documents, written in very different circumstances, supply all our information about the 'prehistory' of the *Sixteen*. One was a passionate dialectic called the *Dialogue between the Noble and the Townsman* (1593) probably written by the ardent League supporter, François Cromé, sieur de Morin.[4] The other was a dossier, compiled by Nicolas Poulain, lieutenant of police in Paris and a double agent in the *Sixteen* for the king almost from its instigation until the Day of Barricades.[5] Both accept that the *Sixteen* began to meet late in 1584. Charles Hotman de la Rocheblond, younger brother to the Huguenot author and a treasurer to the Bishop of Paris, was to be its 'Moses'. He consulted three clerical colleagues about 'the misery of the times, the ambition of the nobles, the insolence of the people, and, above all, the loss of the Roman Catholic religion'.[6] They all agreed on the necessity for action and Hotman and his three friends, Jean Prévost (*curé* of the prestigious Paris church of St Séverin), Jean Boucher (*curé* of St Benoît and a former rector of the University of Paris) and Mathieu de Launoy (canon in Soissons cathedral and a former Huguenot) nominated further Catholic zealots and figures of respect within the city to join the group. Nearly all the notables who were later to play a leading part in the history of the *Sixteen* joined at this early stage. They included Etienne de Neuilly (d. 1598), Michel Marteau, sieur de la Chapelle (d. 1605), Louis Dorléans (1540–1627) the prominent League controversialist, Jean Guincestre their theologian and Jean ('le Bussy') Clerc, later the *Sixteen*'s governor of the Bastille.[7] In many ways, therefore, the movement was originally clerical, respectable and thoroughly well integrated into the professional cadres of Paris urban life. Several of these notables had already been involved in past associations to defend the Catholic faith so that, to some extent, the spontaneity of the *Sixteen* was more apparent than real.[8]

Its growth was, nonetheless, remarkable. It recruited with care and required a strict oath of secrecy and loyalty to other members.[9] The council of the *Sixteen* – initially a large, informal meeting – was transformed into a small inner council, probably in 1587, more suited to its larger membership.[10] Members reported daily on the activities of their *quartier*, just as they would have done if they had been serving on the watch committees. Cash was plentiful, collected, it was said, by voluntary donations.[11] They managed to penetrate all the important groups in Parisian public life so that, by 1587, the *Sixteen* had adherents among the printers, the royal mint, the treasury, the *parlement*, the royal messenger service, the clerks and attorneys as well as the horse traders, the Seine lightermen and the retail butchers. For Hotman's funeral in 1587 (he was the 'chief and leader of its affairs') the *Sixteen* provided an impressive cortège.[12] It is not difficult to explain why the League should have been popular in Paris. It was a large city with a substantial population. It had a well-established urban political consciousness with corporate institutions which looked to orthodox Catholicism to provide them with their rituals and respectability. They were capable of representing their own grievances effectively and speaking also for those of a wider French polity. When threatened by an apparently common enemy, even if it was the king, it was only natural that some of them should have thought to create a 'syndicate' to react in unison.

Paris was a city which knew that suppression of heresy by violent means worked and the lessons of the Saint Bartholomew Day massacre were reiterated from the press, pulpit and university. Paris was a major printing centre in Europe and its printers (about 120 of them joined the League) exploited the profitable markets in works of Catholic casuistry and piety.[13] For them the League was an immense business opportunity. As Estoile noted: 'There is not a single, small, poor printer who does not have the means to roll off his press some new stupidity or scandalous libel against His Majesty. . . . I have collected more than 300 examples, all printed in Paris and sold publicly in the streets.[14]

Initially, the *Sixteen* exploited their clandestinity, publishing the papal bull excommunicating Henri of Navarre and the Prince of Condé (it was banned by the king) and distributing copies only to their supporters.[15] Other sonnets and pasquinades developed hidden anagrams and *double entendre*s. One fine example was the verse which could be read in a Royalist/Bourbon or Lorraine/Guise direction[16]:

Plus ne fault endurer
La Ligue de Lorraine

Ils tiennent en leurs mains
Le fer pour nous tuer.
(Royalist)

La race de Bourbon
Est la paix de la France
(Guisard)

De l'estat la defense
C'est la Religion.

They then began a remarkable series of propaganda exercises which presented the League as the only logical political option for French Catholics. In 1585, the issue was the declaration of Péronne; the following year it was the necessity for war against the Huguenots. This was when Louis Dorléans produced his famous *Advertisement of the English Catholics to the French Catholics*, which the historian de Thou later described as the 'general call to arms' of the League.[17] The moderate Huguenot, Palma Cayet, was shocked by its crudity.[18] It painted the heretics as ravaging wolves with whom there could be no peace or security. They should all be burned, beginning with the author of *Francogallia*. The courage and bravery of the Duke of Guise was praised, the pirates of La Rochelle would be defeated. Heresy was a contagion and the lesson of the English Catholics and their miseries under the wicked 'Jezebel' queen, Elizabeth I, should be learned before it was too late.[19] The attacks on the king multiplied and 'corroded the hearts of the people' so that, by the end of 1587, he was spoken of as a puppet prince.[20] Royalist printers were liable to find their copies seized and burnt by preachers.[21] The Sorbonne refused to censor works with which, at heart, it agreed. On 16 December 1587, the doctors of the Sorbonne accepted the proposition that 'if a prince did not do as he should, then he could be dismissed in the same way as dismissing a child's guardian for improper behaviour . . .'.[22] The growth of League propaganda in Paris and in major provincial cities during this period is crudely demonstrated in Fig. 1 (p. 226).

The press appealed to the literate. Engravings, billboards and paintings reached the illiterate. In July 1587, for instance, Henri III ordered the removal of a painted poster erected in the cemetery of St Séverin (the church of the Latin quarter) which depicted the cruelties and tortures suffered by the English Catholics while men stood by with pointers to emphasise that this was what Parisian Catholics could expect from a heretic king.[23] Organised processions also were employed, leaving the historian de Thou with a powerful impression of their popular appeal[24]:

Processions were ordered in all the churches of the city; altars full of gold, silver and jewels were set up to attract the people . . . peasants also took part, and the duke of Guise sent a party of men and women

dressed in white robes ornamented with crosses from Champagne. . . .
These devout ones forming long lines and crossing Paris while
mumbling prayers that could scarcely be heard attracted everyone's
attention.

The king could scarcely forbid an activity which he himself had
encouraged.

From the pulpit, League preachers delivered the same message at
Advent and Lent. Contemporaries were impressed with their liberty
and the extent to which they were believed by their congregations.[25]
In September 1587, Estoile complained (with some exaggeration)
that it was difficult to find a preacher who was not a League
supporter.[26] His contemporary, Etienne Pasquier, recognised the
power of the pulpit in one of his letters from the capital in 1587[27]:

[Preachers] are dangerous tools in a civil war, whether they lend their
tongues to one side or the other. . . . They say that, when they preach,
the Holy Ghost is directing their lips and that, from the pulpit of truth,
they are allowed to speak as it moves them . . . their enemies,
however, say that they are only men and that, in a civil war, they sell
their tongues to the highest bidder.

The king tried to curb their enthusiasms by inviting them to private
audiences to admonish them, but with little effect. Jean Boucher
(1548–1644) (called 'the butcher' and, about whom Estoile cruelly
remarked that 'in the kingdom of the blind, the one-eyed are kings'
– Boucher was blind in one eye) apparently harangued the king on
the evils of his court and royal weaknesses when he was invited to
the Louvre.[28] Attempts to arrest three League clergy at St Séverin
on 2 September 1587 produced a riot in the Latin quarter.[29] Others
were accused of preaching 'democracy, or popular government', of
refusing to have the 'peace of God' in the Mass lest it tempered
people's ardour against 'closet' heretics in their neighbourhood, and
of even refusing the sacraments to prominent judges of the *parlement*
because they were reputed to be hypocrites and dissembling heretics.[30] Popularism – the underlying theme of the civil wars – was again
in the ascendant.

While Paris became a crucible for Catholic aspirations and ideals,
the 'good town' of Paris was called on to make particular sacrifices
by its Valois monarch. The demands for forced loans and 'gracious
gifts' (*dons gratuits*) came with a monotonous regularity, and
although the king could rely on the city provost and councillors
(whom he either appointed or nominated) to agree to such additional
taxation, he could be less confident of the urban militia, with its colonels and watch committees appointed in each *quartier*. He attempted
to appoint his own militia captains in 1585, but this only increased
the suspicion of the monarch's interference in Parisian liberties and
many came to view the *Sixteen* as a kind of alternative or provisional

municipal defence corps.[31] Traditionally, too, war meant the creation of new royal offices and these affected Paris more than any other city in France because of the number of tribunals in the capital and the size of its legal and professional groups. Creations came in accumulations and their prices were very high.[32] For those on the foothills of the world of the office holders – attorneys, *procureurs* and, to a certain extent, clerks – this kind of excessive office creation was badly received. The sovereign courts in Paris issued strong remonstrances in 1586 and refused to register these new edicts.[33] When the king resorted to a formal *lit de justice*, the legal staff of the royal courts went on strike.[34] It is not surprising that many of the *Sixteen*'s most active supporters would come from the legal world of France, and particularly in Paris.

A *fronde* of royal servants was engendered by other forms of fiscality which affected the *officiers*. These included periodic failures to pay their salaries and the seizure of the revenue assigned to pay the interest on the government bonds, issued through the *hôtel de ville* in Paris (*rentes*), in which they had invested heavily.[35] The *parlement* told the king bluntly in May 1587 that, by failing to honour his commitments to the *rentiers* he was attacking 'poor widows and orphans' and that he had received more in revenue in 10 years than his predecessors had in the previous 200 years.[36] Senior judges were particularly incensed by an interview which the king held in the Louvre earlier in 1587. The king had begun the meeting with a heartfelt declaration of his intention to fight heresy until he won. Pausing to allow the judges to express their enthusiastic support, the king then turned to the city provost to demand 600,000 *écus* from Paris by means of a levy on the wealthiest of its citizens. The judges came away murmuring that the king was like a nasty insect whose sting lay in its tail. . . .[37]

Beyond the official world of law and government lay the Paris of the Halles, the merchants who, through their guilds, corporations, confraternities and parochial activities, played a vigorous part in civic life. A devalued currency, new indirect taxes on imports to the city, adverse trading conditions in wartime affected them, but it was the sermons and the pamphlets which influenced them most. They were apparently afraid of losing *their* religion, the traditional Catholicism which guaranteed their status, rendered their notability honourable, blessed the substantial dowries they endowed to their daughters and made sense of the corporate life in which they played such an important part.[38] They were more aware than most of the desperate conditions in the French countryside created by the poor harvests of 1586–87. Louis Dorléans' *Advertisement* went out of its way to prove that heresy was the cause of these natural disasters.[39] Merchants probably experienced at close hand the conditions that deputies came to Paris to describe to the king in May 1586[40]:

One from Zaintonge and the other from Périgord, who, on their knees have humbly desired the King to make a peace and to have pity upon his poor people, whose want was such as they were forced to eat bread made of *ardoise* [tiles] and of nut-shells which they brought and showed to the King. They told him also that the famine was so great as a woman in Périgord had already eaten two of her children and the like had been done in Zaintonge. The King, at the hearing of this, changed countenance. . . .

Two weeks later, the English ambassador reported that the news in Paris was that there were 'many thousand' in the Auvergne 'already dead for hunger, and that, in that extremity . . . they feed upon grass . . . like horses and die with grass in their mouths'.[41]

Paris was unique among French cities in that it saw the king and court more often than any other city. When the preachers and printers retailed scurrilous gossip, it was frequently from courtiers themselves that it had been learned. Estoile often remarked on the inappropriateness of royal lavishness at a time of municipal stringency and he was reacting to the sharp contrast, more easily seen in Paris than elsewhere, between city and court. It was unfortunate, too, that the less secure the king felt in Parisian loyalty, the longer he felt obliged to spend there, and the more vulnerable he became to rumour and sedition. It was reported in 1585 that he no longer trusted its citizens and, the following year, he hastily returned to his capital when it was feared that a rising in Troyes might spread to Paris.[42] He only left the city on occasions of absolute necessity from then until he was forced from it in May 1588.[43] The proximity of the court led the *Sixteen* towards planning a *coup d'état* at a relatively early stage.[44] Details of their plots remain vague and, while it would seem that they were well timed it is also true that they were too complicated and ambitious. Most is known about that of March 1587 when, it seems, the *Sixteen* planned to capture the Bastille, assassinate the governor, murder many prominent judges, overwhelm royal institutions of the capital and starve the palace guards from the Louvre. The king was to become a puppet ruler while a massacre took care of the *politiques*. Barricades were envisaged, partly to keep the populace under control and partly to divide the city into sections for guerilla warfare.[45] The Duke of Mayenne, for whom the plan was prepared, was notably uncommittal, doubtless aware of the overwhelming difficulties of an operation on this scale; the preparations were leaked to the king by Nicolas Poulain and an arrest of a member of the *Sixteen* was made.[46] By this, and other, failures in the eighteen months before May 1588, the *Sixteen* became more nervous that their position was vulnerable and that they were in danger of arrest and trial for treason.[47]

On Saturday 7 May 1588, the king ordered house-to-house searches to be made throughout the capital city and replaced suspect members of the civic militia with individuals of proven loyalty, an indication that the *Sixteen* had little time left. Two days later, at 1 p.m., the Duke of Guise, ignoring repeated orders from the king not to, entered Paris with a small retinue. The king became terrified by the explosion of popular support for the duke among Parisians and took some necessary precautions. On Thursday 12 May, at about 4 o'clock in the morning, eleven Swiss and four French detachments of troops entered Paris and took up positions on the bridges, at the Louvre and in the Latin quarter. The city woke to find itself a garrisoned stronghold. In response to the military presence, and with a degree of coordination which is surprising, barricades of barrels and chains began to be erected at 50-yard intervals in streets in the Latin quarter, on the Iles and around the Louvre. The royal troops were thus enveloped in a city revolt; balconies bristled with muskets and arquebuses pointed at them and awnings were removed to clear the range of fire. Every street in Paris was like a town to be besieged, commented the king's military advisor. The Duke of Guise offered to mediate but the king, preferring to withdraw rather than admit to a military defeat in his capital, hastily left the Louvre by the Tuileries (the only exit left to him) at about 6 p.m. on Friday 13 May.

It is ironical that the Day of Barricades itself was not, therefore, the result of a plot by the *Sixteen*, but the result of a series of panic measures by the king. It was not the arrival of the Duke of Guise in Paris, nor the activities of his troops to the east of the capital, nor yet the advanced military preparations of the *Sixteen* which determined the timing of the erection of the barricades, although they undoubtedly contributed to the city's tensions. Rather, it resulted from the house-to-house searches and the introduction of the Swiss guards to take possession of key points of the capital so that, as one League commentator said, it gave the League 50,000 volunteers.[48] The threat to city liberties produced a popular and spontaneous uprising which resulted in Henri III's prudent and hasty retreat from the capital.

The precise part of the Duke of Guise and his brothers in the events leading to the Day of Barricades remains a matter for conjecture. The Guise were certainly the heroes of the Catholic cause in Paris and some historians have seen the *Sixteen* as a Guisard conspiracy, the product of Guise ambitions to overthrow the Valois. But the evidence points to a more delicate and tenuous involvement than that. The Duke of Guise and his brothers and cousins clearly had a substantial clientele of purveyors, debtors and servants in the city.[49] He had his agent, Maineville, keeping him informed of their activities.[50] His assistance was sought for supplying arms and he could be relied on to offer some protection.[51] But the duke was compromised in one of the plots in 1587 and the *Sixteen* had to placate him with a suitably generous gold chain for the embarrassment they had caused him.[52] When he finally arrived in Paris in May 1588, it was not to raise a popular revolt against the king but, as he himself said, to justify himself against his critics and impose his will on the king's council.[53] There is a reliable report that the duke was taken unawares by the sounds of the tocsin in the city on 12 May. Realising that he was unarmed, he hastily rummaged through the armoury of the *hôtel* de Guise to find his father's old pike, convinced that the commotion was the signal for his own assassination.[54] If the Day of Barricades had been intended to impose the duke's will on the king by popular revolt, then it failed. For it had driven the king into the hands of Henri of Navarre and committed him to a popular movement which might not be successful and which would certainly leave him open to a charge of inciting sedition and treason.

For the Spanish ambassador in Paris, Bernadino de Mendoza, the Day of Barricades was immensely satisfactory news, for it prevented the French king from interfering with the Spanish Armada which was due to sail up the English Channel shortly. This has led some historians to suggest that the *Sixteen* were in concert with Philip II.[55] The Spanish king certainly knew of their existence and it would have been untypical of the high quality of Spanish intelligence if they had not made some contact. But there is no incontrovertible proof of it and there is an impression that Mendoza was more concerned about activities round the French channel ports than with what was going on in Paris.[56] Mendoza and Philip II counselled the Duke of Guise to keep away from Paris in the crucial weeks before the Day of Barricades. Mendoza appeared surprised when the rising took place, although it is difficult to read very much into his dry diplomatic despatches.[57] Even if one admits that the ambitions of the Duke of Guise and the strategems of Spain did play a part in what happened before May 1588 (they clearly did so afterwards), it is still evident that the explosion in Paris owed more to the popular resentments of the capital and the autonomous activities of the *Sixteen*.

A 'HOLY UNION'

Between the Day of Barricades and the assassination of Henri III on 1 August of the following year, the *Sixteen* became a national movement with distinctive and radical solutions to the nation's problems. At an early stage, they had sought support in the provinces. Nicolas Ameline, an attorney in the Châtelet (the Parisian lawcourt) was despatched to tour (in disguise) the cities of northern and central France.[58] His message was that Paris had collected large sums of money to rid France of heresy in three years and required the support of every Catholic. In some cities, he clearly enjoyed an encouraging response.[59] In 1587, Paris suggested an elaborate federal structure for these provincial contacts. Each town was to be responsible for raising its own money and troops within an overall defensive union – 'a Holy Union' – with Paris at its head. This was to be the Catholic answer to the 'United Provinces of the South' – the 'Catholic Cities of the Holy Union'.[60] Whether they developed governing councils like that in Paris is not clear.[61] So much documentation was destroyed afterwards in the rush to conform to Henri IV (he ordered the destruction of all the documentation of the League in order to erase the memories of past sedition) that only fragments survive now.[62] By the Day of Barricades, there were perhaps 300 towns supporting Paris – most of them towns of secondary importance in the provinces. St Malo, for instance, became the League counterpart to Huguenot La Rochelle. Abbeville, centre of the collapsed Picardy cloth industry, became an enthusiastic League stronghold in the north.

The months between May and October 1588 were especially favourable to the growth of the 'Holy Union'. The atmosphere was not revolutionary. The revolt against the king would be healed with a truce in July 1588, the edict of Union. The *Sixteen* did not overturn the Paris municipal constitution but worked with it to organise elections of suitably minded delegates to the estates general which the king had agreed to summon to Blois in October 1588. In many towns, the *Sixteen*'s agents secured the election of their delegates, despite royal efforts to influence the elections against them.[63] Even before the official opening of the estates, the Paris delegates (La Chapelle Marteau and Neuilly were among them) held meetings among the newly arriving 191 representatives of the third estate to coordinate their demands and strategy. The Duke of Guise did the same thing among members of the other two orders.[64]

The estates of Blois enabled the Holy Union to articulate its political ideas and to gain support for them. These appear in the magnificent *cahier des doléances* of the city of Paris, drawn up under League auspices, to present to the estates in October.[65] Underlying its highly specific and wide-ranging clauses runs the general theme of the purification of the state. An excessive liberality had smashed religion into a hundred fragments and the state into a hundred fragments. The king had listened to the demands for reform but little had been achieved. It was 'difficult, even impossible' to expect any more from either his, or his council's efforts. Only the estates general could succeed. Heresy was a 'cancer . . . filled with filth and infectious putrefaction'. It must be removed by force. 'All heretics, whatever their quality, condition or estate, must be imprisoned and punished by being burned alive.' The same fate was to await sorcerers and magicians whose activities had, they claimed, become so prolific during the civil disorders. The lawcourts should swear to keep, and to publish, the act of Holy Union with the king in July 1588. This was to be treated as a kind of 'fundamental law', guarded by the estates general, the 'corps' of France, which would be reconvened every three years to undertake the necessary purification of the state. Epernon and his brother should present themselves before the estates to answer the charges laid by the delegates and 'purge' themselves. Tax farmers – *sangsues* – and other foreigners were to be investigated by a powerful commission from the estates general which would reconvene automatically every five years and be responsible to the delegates alone. Superfluous noble titles acquired by cash were to be abolished. All taxation, apart from revenues of the royal domain, was to be approved by the estates. The royal domain was also to be the subject of the estates' investigations. The royal court was to be cleansed, the pensions cut, even the courtesans were to be sent home. Nobles who were apprehended in the act of duelling were to be hanged 'les vivants et les morts ensemble'. Taverns, banquets and festivities were to be curtailed. No games of dice, darts, cards or chequers were permissible for 'they rendered youth useless to the Republic'. Senior clergymen were to be elected and royal influence in the appointments to the church curtailed. Looking back from this *cahier* to the clandestine pamphlets produced in Paris in the years before 1588, the source for many of these notions becomes clear. Looking further back, they bear a striking resemblance to Huguenot ideas in the 1570s. A recourse to the estates general and the sovereignty of the people; a renewed insistence on a fundamental law that the estates general guarded; a belief in the restorative power of elections in both church and state; an underlying puritanism and suspicion of the old nobility – these notions would soon be joined by another shared notion, that of the right to revolt against a tyrant.

Henri III knew how to deal with estates general. He would make promises and concessions as he had done in 1576. 'Je le ferai', he replied to their demands, while reminding delegates that some of his advisors told him that he would become, like the Doge of Venice, little more than a figurehead.[66] The critical change came on 23 December 1588 when the king organised the assassination of the Duke of Guise by members of his bodyguard at the entry to the royal chamber. The assassination was followed the next day by that of his brother, the Cardinal of Guise. The Cardinal of Bourbon was also imprisoned. These massacres provoked an explosion of popular outrage in the major cities of France, turning them into League centres almost overnight. Henri III (who had carefully ensured that the bodies had been burned in quicklime so that there would be no relics to venerate) produced his justification for his actions – the Guise had planned 'pernicious enterprises against the state and the king's person' – but this had little effect and, in the weeks following 23 December, Rouen, Blois, Amiens, Reims, Dijon, Orléans,

Toulouse and Marseilles all joined the League in Paris.[67] The Catholic Union had eventually been achieved not round a common purpose but against a common enemy.

It is difficult to recapture the language and mood of violence in Catholic circles in the early months of 1589. In Paris, the preachers went on to the streets crying 'Au meutre! Au feu! Au sang! A la vengeance!' against the king.[68] An extraordinary account of the emotion raised in Rouen has been preserved for us by a refugee English nun. She attended a sermon by the Jesuit, Jacques Commolet, on December 29[69]:

> When he came into the pulpytt, all eyis and mowthes gapying upon hym, the good man was in such a passyon that he seemyed lyke to burst and could scars brying out hys words for weepying, the passyon of that tyme had so alteryd hys voyce. Hys matter was of blessed St Thomas (of Canterbury), declarying to the people the cause of hys martirdome in the behalfe of Chrystes churche, and of the quarrel betwyxt hym and the kyng, and how hys braynes were stroke out uppon the pavement before ye altar. Thys thyng was so apt for hys purpose that the people could by and by apply ytt that the preacher had no soner named the slaughter of theyr 2 prynces but thatt all fell out into weepying, and the preacher ther sobyng allowde could saye no more. Butt after a preatty space, stryving with himself to speake, he, clappying of hys hands cryed aloude, o pover eglese galicane. . . .

This passion – calculated or sincere – was accompanied by the formalities of funeral processions and masses for the royal victims. The number of extant titles of pamphlets produced reaches its peak in this year in Toulouse and Lyons (see Fig. 1) and the engravings in them illustrate their intensity.[70] Many people were also influenced by the decision of the Sorbonne on 7 January 1589 to release France from the obedience it owed its king and to justify the taking up of arms against a nefarious tyrant. Thereafter, tyrannicide became a principal motif for League propaganda. In one procession on 10 January 1589, little children in Paris were assembled from the various parishes to march from the cemetery of the Innocents to the church of the abbey of Ste Geneviève. Each child carried a lighted candle and, at the entrance to the church, trampled it underfoot 'as a sign that the cursed tyrant [Henri III] was excommunicated'.[71] Wall posters emphasised the same message.[72] Its attractions were to be demonstrated by a twenty-four-year-old monk from the convent of the Jacobins in Paris, formerly noted only for his stupidity who, having been absolved by his confessor, gained martyrdom in the eyes of the League by accomplishing the assassination of Henri III. Jean Boucher hastily revised his pedantic treatise on *The Just Abdication of Henri III* and hailed Clément as a 'new David' who had killed Goliath, a new 'Judith' who had exterminated Holofernes.[73]

The massacres at Blois created a powerful sense of unity without directing political mechanisms. The League had lost its king (excommunicated), their aristocratic leaders (massacred), their municipal leaders (imprisoned with several other delegates to the third estate at Blois). Necessity drove them, as it had driven the Protestants after 1572, to form an alternative government. They did so by drawing on their political experience and developed elective councils to fill their needs. In Paris, special ward committees in each quarter elected representatives to a council of the Union which then, in February 1589, constituted another council, the General Council of the Union.[74] This general council of about forty members had as wide and as representative a membership as possible and it appointed the Duke of Mayenne (the Duke of Guise's surviving brother) as its military commander. He took his oath before it on 13 March 1589.[75] In its first few months, the General Council was enormously active. It corresponded with cities elsewhere in France. It organised purges of known royalists from the great institutions of the capital and forty judges were led away from the Palais de Justice to the Bastille on 15 January 1589. Many were replaced in their posts by nominees of the General Council such as Barnabé Brisson, the Union's first president, and Molé, the royal *procureur* for the Union. As Palma Cayet remarked, 'the leaders of the *Sixteen* all have some post now'.[76] The Council also raised revenues by voluntary contributions, fined those who wanted to leave the city and selected pillaging of the property and wealth of those who had left. Pierre Molan, the treasurer of the king, left 36,000 *écus* in his house and this was appropriated to Union coffers.[77] The Council became responsible for the security of Paris and the reimposition of order. This was a period of great exhilaration for them. Enjoying widespread support, the Union appeared to be a reality and the death of the king was a fitting climax, their first real success. Madame de Montpensier, the Duke of Guise's sister, distributed green – the colour of fools – scarves to the public in celebration of it. Only one thing, she said, disappointed her and that was that the tyrant had not known that she had organised his assassination. She rode round the streets crying 'Bonnes nouvelles! Bonnes nouvelles!'[78]

In the longer term, the king's assassination was not such good news, for it opened up the contradictions within the Union which their unity against the tyrant had masked. Some of the behaviour of those nominated to their posts by the Union gave offence. The social tensions in the capital and other provincial cities grew more marked. Another rift occurred between the *Sixteen* and its military commander, the Duke of Mayenne, who was suspicious of the independence of the General Council. He appointed his own clients to it and then ignored its decisions. Finally, he disbanded it altogether. Already on the horizon was the difficult relationship between capital and provinces in an ill-defined federation at a time of war when communications were disrupted. Everywhere, suspicions of 'royalists' and *politiques* divided Catholics from each other and were at the root of the waning of the Holy Union.

FROM UNION TO PARTY

In the Catholic cities of the Union, the coming to power of a new political group brought with it the threats of social revolution. Royalist propaganda stressed that the one led ineluctably to the other. 'Consider', exhorted the *Manifesto of France to the Parisians*,[79]

> the state of your town . . . into whose hands has it now fallen? . . .
> You will find that it is in the hands of those who went from door to door collecting refuse, butchers' and slaughterhouse boys, the filth and excrement of your town. . . . Are you not ashamed, solid bourgeois and good merchants whose wealth has been acquired by just means . . .?

Those judges who escaped to the royalist *parlement* of Tours reported their fears of indiscriminate arrests, and of arbitrary pillage. They explained how they had escaped and spoke of their fears of popular violence and *la racquaille du peuple*.[80] Some had seen the bodies of *politiques* floating down the Seine; others had been threatened with elimination unless they conformed.[81]

To some extent, it was the behaviour of the members of the Union as much as their social inferiority which alarmed contemporaries. The pages of the diarist Estoile and the *Dialogue* give many instances of their arrogance and enjoyment of their new-found status and power. Bussy le Clerc, governor of the Bastille and a former solicitor, was the most notorious. He was a masterly demagogue and one of his first acts was to celebrate with a procession the discovery of a piece of the true cross in the Bastille. Solicitor turned gaoler and judge, he presided over the imprisonment of judges in January 1589.[82] Later, he dined with the Archbishop of Lyons and had meetings with the Duke of Nemours. But he had a violent streak as well. When an aunt of one of the *politiques* in the Bastille came to visit her relation, she was told that he had died in custody and that his body had been thrown to the dogs 'because he was a dog'.[83] Another important figure in the Union was the council's secretary Pierre Senault. Estoile provided a vivid description of his behaviour at its meetings[84]:

> For a clerk, i.e. a 'valet' of the council (for such he calls himself), he has an extraordinary degree of authority. . . . He calls them 'his masters' but when he finds something proposed in council meetings which is not to his liking . . . he rises to his feet and loudly says: 'I

forbid and oppose it in the name of 40,000 men.' At the sound of his voice, they lower their heads like dogs and not another word is heard about it.

The *Dialogue*'s ironic epithets for the leaders of the *Sixteen* reveal something of the same resentments – Jean Louchard 'the swaggerer', M. de La Rue 'formerly draper on the pont St Michel and now one of the 100 gentlemen and councillors of the Union . . . '. La Bruyère is described as the 'saffron seigneur', a common expression for the socially ambitious.[85]

The bullying swagger and aggression of the Unionists was partly their response to the real fears of a royalist conspiracy in the capital. The *Sixteen* recognised that it was weak in certain quarters and its fears were given considerable encouragement by a series of royalist plots. In fact, the failure of the Potier de Blancmesnil conspiracy in August 1589, the 'Bread or Peace' rising of 8 August 1590, and the 'Day of Flour' in January 1591 demonstrated that, in the business of conspiracy, the *politiques* were even less competent than the *Sixteen* had proved to be before 1588. The problem was that the fears about royalist sedition were self-justifying. It was impossible to be sure of everyone's loyalties. Oaths were sworn, of course, but this meant little. As one pamphleteer said, it was easy to pretend to be a supporter of the *Sixteen*[86].

> As soon as two or three of us are together, I take up the subject of the death of M. de Guise. I praise the list of his good deeds to the skies and then I begin to insult the king . . . thus I am respected as the best man in the world and a good Catholic. Of course, I do not believe what I say. I only do it to avoid going to prison, and consequently of having my goods seized and my house ransacked.

Suspects who were detained, fined or imprisoned, came from among the wealthy Parisians in the royal administration. The League, almost in spite of itself, came to attack those with status and authority in the community whose natural clannishness and desire to protect each other merely heightened the suspicions of the *Sixteen*. Friends, relatives, those who were strangers in the capital, all became vulnerable to the charge of being a *politique*. The local watch committees ceased to include office holders in several quarters and removed their influence towards moderation from within the Union.

In some respect, the *Sixteen* was the victim of its own propaganda. The violence of the preachers' language encouraged members of the League's committees to violent action. In March 1591, Boucher preached 'nothing but killing', according to Estoile. He excited his congregation 'in words and gestures' to do away with the *politiques*, and Estoile feared that he would descend from his pulpit and dismember one before their eyes.[87] The incumbent of the parish of St André wanted to be the first one to 'cut the throats of these "politiques" and he knew who they were . . .'.[88] The suspects had only the weapons of the impotent against such hostility – the anonymous wall-poster, hand-written flysheet pushed under doors and the satirical drawing. Estoile used the privacy of his diary to express his moral revulsion at, for instance, a preacher saying that it was better to kill your own children than to accept a heretic king. Thinking men of the *Sixteen*, like Louis Dorléans, eventually reacted against Unionist thuggery. In 1590, he wrote a brave pamphlet called the *Second Advertisement from an English Catholic* in which he warned his confederates that[89]:

> Paris is no longer Paris but Babylon. . . . Several have been thrown into your Union who have brought it neither clean hands nor clear consciences. They have taken gold and silver, clothes and other precious things to their own homes. . . . They have grown very rich and the city very poor. . . . Who wishes to be associated with the crimes of such robbers and brigands?

The siege of Paris from May to August 1590 contributed to the waning of the Union in an indirect way. The economic life of the city became seriously damaged by the most crippling siege in the history of any major European city since that of Constantinople in the fifteenth century. Bread disappeared from the diet. The numbers estimated by contemporaries to have died from malnutrition and associated diseases varies from 5,000 to 12,000.[90] Estoile reported one man to be eating candlewax. Madame de Montpensier encouraged experiments in the milling of cemetery bones for flour. There were reports of cannibalism and some extraordinary fantasies gripped the minds of those whose stomachs had been empty for too long.[91] The siege was only partially lifted on 27 August 1590 by the arrival of the Duke of Parma and an army from Flanders. Paris remained completely surrounded with all its major routeways blocked by royalist garrisons. Grain was allowed through only after the payment of extortionate levies. Royalist pamphlets argued that conditions were better in every royalist city compared to those in Paris and the *Sixteen* began to criticise its military leader, the Duke of Mayenne, whose defeat at Ivry (14 March 1590) had led to the blockage of the capital. By the spring of 1591, Mayenne chose to reside in the city's suburbs rather than endure the preachers' hostility. 'In private', Estoile noted, 'when they retired with the *Sixteen* they said that he was only a big pig who slept with his whore . . . and that he could only fight a war with [wine] flagons. . . . '[92]

Anxious to reinforce its waning authority in the autumn of 1591, the *Sixteen* formed a secret committee of ten. Three members of it persuaded the others to sign a blank piece of paper which was eventually to become the death warrant for three members of the *parlement* who were accused of treating a suspected *politique* leniently. In a demonstration of authority, they murdered the first *président*, Barnabé Brisson, the royal attorney Molé and another judge on 15 November 1591. The events surrounding this turning point in the fortunes of the League are well known. These deaths were intended to be the first in a series of show trials of *politiques* whose names were already inscribed on a register (known as the PDC register because, after each name, there was an initial indicating the victim's fate – *pendu, dagué, chassé*).[93] The council of ten proposed to create a special legal tribunal to deal with these cases, staffed with young graduates, not by established judges at law. It was to be a calculated extension of the authority of the *Sixteen*.[94] In fact, the three murders proved how far the Catholic Union had become a faction. There was no great Parisian uprising at these deaths. The bodies were unmutilated, not even touched. The small crowd that gathered round them outside the Palais de justice on the morning of their execution was sullen and quiet. Within a month, the Duke of Mayenne had arrived in Paris, determined to amputate the political power of the *Sixteen*. He came with 1,000 loyal troops, forced the surrender of the Bastille, and, on 4 December, murdered 4 of the council of 10 and imprisoned most of the rest. By the time that the duke left Paris on 11 December 1591, the *parlement* had approved his actions and the *Sixteen* had been dismantled.

For the Duke of Mayenne, this was a victory, but not one that he dared to exploit. Members of the *Sixteen* continued to criticise his leadership with increasing vehemence until the fall of Paris in 1594. Whatever its faults, the propaganda and organisation of the *Sixteen* had acted as a unifying force among Catholics, capable of encouraging devotion and inspiring zeal. Without the *Sixteen*, Mayenne possessed no alternative in governing Paris but to turn to those *politiques* who became increasingly convinced of the necessity of a negotiated settlement with Henri IV.

The history of the Union in Paris is well known; that of its provincial counterparts in Amiens, Rouen, Nantes, Toulouse and the other Catholic cities of France remains to be properly investigated.[95] They all established councils which, in their infancy at least, were supposed to reflect the various social groups in these cities. As in Paris, they were vigorous in defence, tax-raising, and the organisation of municipal militias. In some cases, colourful local politicians became popular demagogues – Charles de Casaulx in Marseilles, Nicolas Godin in Bayeux, Etienne Tournier in Toulouse. Some of them were as socially divisive as the *Sixteen* in Paris; in Troyes, the Mayennist Philippe de Ver complained bitterly to the provincial governor of the libels and plots against him by the 'zealous Catholics' and the meeting was disrupted by a riot outside the governor's lodgings.[96] Some cities like Marseilles and St Malo exploited their maritime position to become truly independent republics, conducting their own foreign policy and recognising no superior authority from Paris or from the Duke of Mayenne.[97] In others, the provincial military governors appointed by the Duke of Mayenne suppressed the provincial councils when they became a menace to their authority and, in Dijon, Toulouse and Rouen their existence was relatively short-lived, although they could be resurrected, as in Lyons, when the absence of the governor or a lively hatred of military rule provided renewed support for their activity.[98] The confused politics of these provincial cities, many of them under siege from royalist forces as Paris was, is a true reflection of the Holy Union's transformation into a series of factions and parties.

ELECTIVE KINGSHIP

In 1589 and 1590, the candidate of the League for the kingship of France was clear; it was Charles, Cardinal of Bourbon. If, in theory, his claims to the throne were as good as, or better, than those of Henri IV, in practice his eligibility was poorer. The League preachers vaunted him as a new Melchisadech, a mighty warrior and priest-king, but, in fact, he cut a less impressive figure, an octogenarian, already known for his vacillation and love of the quiet life. He was also a closely guarded prisoner of Henri IV. League forces never attempted to release him and he died in his bed on 8 May 1591.

League lawyers had, in fact, before his death, already begun to investigate the precedents for electing a new king. They were not as scarce as proponents of the absolute French monarchy presumed, especially in the early history of the Frankish monarchy, as François Hotman had shown.[99] The problems in electing a king were not, therefore, theoretical, but practical ones. Firstly, the suggestion of an election enhanced the fears among Catholics that the League would establish a permanently elective monarchy or even a republic. As a Parisian attorney (and friend of Estoile) lamented in public in October 1589: 'Our civil disorder and factions have opened the door to a crowd of corrupt little men who, with effrontery, have attacked authority with such licence and audacity that those who have not seen it would not believe it. In so doing, they have wanted to jump from a monarchy to a democracy.'

There was an additional problem. This was the Spanish demands made of the League. Spanish influence strengthened during the siege of Paris. A new Spanish ambassador in Paris, Don Diego de Ibarra, arrived in January 1591 with instructions on how to exert it.[100] Spain must sustain Paris and the *Sixteen* and assist the Catholic princes to elect a Catholic king. Spanish agents should 'insinuate cleverly' the rights of the Infanta to the French throne and suggest that troops and cash from Spain were contingent on the marriage of the Spanish Infanta to whoever was chosen as king. The Salic law, the ambassador's instructions continued, 'was a pure invention . . . as the most learned and discerning of their lawyers recognise'. Election should take place in the *parlement* of Paris which would also ratify the marriage, for it would be too lengthy and disruptive to hold an estates general in the midst of war. Spain's compensation for the 'great expense' she had undertaken would consist of the city of Cambrai, the repayment of all her expenses, some guarantee ports and strongholds on the Channel coast and in Flanders.

This eliminated many candidates immediately from the election since they were, like the Duke of Mayenne, already married. Others, such as the Duke of Savoy, were ruled out as too unpopular. This left two serious candidates – the son of the Duke of Lorraine, the Count of Zweibrücken (Deux-Ponts); and Charles, son of Henri, Duke of Guise. Charles had been imprisoned ever since his father's murder at Blois but he managed to evade his captors in August 1591. He swiftly became the darling of the *Sixteen* and the candidate with Spanish support. Philip II sent a Franciscan friar round the towns of the League and the resulting reports of the popularity of the young duke were most encouraging.[101] But Mayenne remained implacably hostile to his cousin's candidature. The removal of the *Sixteen* from Paris was certainly one of his attempts to prevent them from supporting the young Duke of Guise in any forthcoming election or estates general.

The issue paralysed the League and this was a discernible fact at a meeting of its leaders in Picardy for Christmas, 1591. Their discussions had an undeniable element of pantomime to them.[102] The Duke of Mayenne, an old dame, equivocated on everything except his debts, his rights, those of his house, his province and his kingdom (in that order). The young prince charming, Charles of Guise, refused to talk to his uncle and complained of his obstructiveness. The Duke of Parma could scarcely comprehend the 'great jealousies' of Mayenne, let alone satisfy his importunate demands for cash. The Spanish ambassador wanted Charles of Guise elected as king without any delay. Mayenne's advisor, *président* Jeannin from the *parlement* of Dijon, told him that it had to be done with the consent of the princes. This would, he added, be expensive in terms of 'gratifications' to them. The meeting turned into a dialogue of the deaf. Worse, its divisions were quickly known in the Navarre camp. From the moment when Mendoza's diplomatic baggage was captured in January 1591, diplomatic correspondence between the cities, princes and foreign powers behind the League was regularly captured by Navarre.[103] His cryptographer, Choirin, was unequalled in Europe for his powers to crack codes and the most intimate details of League politics were quickly open to Navarre for his exploitation.[104]

Mayenne spent the whole of 1592 in trying to hold 'what remains of our party' together, at least until the moment when he had extracted favourable terms from Spain in return for his support for Guise's candidature. The problem was that Mayenne's demands were massive and, the longer he delayed the estates general, the less time lay on the side of the League and the more unpopular he became. In October 1592, the Bishop of Senlis wrote from Paris that their protector was 'held in derision'; that his timidity and 'nonchalance' had lost the war.[105] The people were 'miserable, full of rumour, discontent and impatient' for peace. When the estates general opened on 26 January 1593 this dissatisfaction turned to open criticism. Mayenne's opening speech was a poor performance, inaudible to many delegates.[106] Others missed his speech because the royalists frustrated their passage to the estates general.[107] It was a rump assembly which finally opened indirect negotiations at Suresnes near Paris with the forces of Henri IV on 21 April 1593 and which produced the truce which enabled the king to enter Paris the following year on 23 March 1594. In the meantime, Henri had been crowned at Chartres, and the failure of the League to find a credible alternative candidate for the kingship had made the task of winning their disaffected elements to his side easier.

HENRI IV AND THE PACIFICATION OF THE LEAGUE

The League was evidently responsible for its own collapse. Henri IV's contribution lay less in providing a decisive military victory than in ensuring that, by a combination of finance, fear and favour, the League's defeat was reasonably complete. Militarily speaking, Henri IV's victories provided propaganda, rather than strategic, advantages. Although his sieges had a debilitating effect on the League, they also wore down his own strength and financial resources. He had to raise the sieges on Paris and Rouen. His victory at Arques was important in that it prevented the king being forced to leave the important province of Normandy and it stimulated morale, especially in England. The victory at Ivry was not exploited, save in propaganda. He never confronted the forces of Spain under the Duke of Parma. He gained no major military victories in 1593–94, and all the major cities were secured by negotiations, rather than by force of arms. In 1595, his military campaigns in Burgundy were among the most successful in the wars of the League but the cities of Marseilles, Toulouse and the provinces of Provence and Brittany still remained

unsubjected. They would later accept Henri IV as a king by a show
of force and the exercise of diplomacy.

The various treaties of pacification with League towns and princes
were negotiated by the king's councillors and masters of requests,
and they display the skills of Sully, Villeroy, Bellièvre, as well as
Méric de Vic and other commissioners.[108] They deserve closer scru-
tiny than they have generally received.[109] Towns were offered the
confirmation of their privileges, the exclusion of Calvinist worship,
an amnesty for all seditious offences, the accommodation of rivals
for municipal offices and the writing-off (by forgoing their *taille* over
a specified period) of their huge debts. Nobles and provincial governors were offered sizeable pensions, gratifications for their close servants and clienteles, and the promise of offices and posts. Not all their
demands could be satisfied. Mayenne originally demanded a full and
embracing pardon for himself and all his servants and also the
exclusion of Calvinism from his province of Burgundy, the heredity
in perpetuum of the provincial governorship there, six *places de sûreté*
garrisoned with three companies of cavalry at the king's expense and
the rights to nominate to all the ecclesiastical and royal posts of the
province.[110] Not surprisingly, Henri IV's reply was that these
demands were 'so extraordinary and without precedent' that they
would render Mayenne 'absolute seigneur' in Burgundy at the
expense of loyal servants to the king.[111] Eventually, the private demands of the treaty of Folembray, agreed on 24 January 1596,
accepted rather less than this, but very substantial concessions were
granted to him.[112] The costs of these treaties were enormous –
900,000 *écus* to the Duke of Lorraine, 250,000 *écus* to Marshal La
Châtre for the strongholds at Orleans and Bourges, 492,800 *écus* to
Marshal de Brissac in Paris . . . as Henri IV ruefully said to one of his
secretaries, he had purchased, rather than procured their loyalties
(*pas rendu, vendu . . .*).[113]

The operation had required tact and persuasiveness and, in his
propaganda, Henri IV's efforts eventually matched those of the
League. In the royal centre of Tours, processions on New Year's Day
in 1590 ridiculed the League in Paris while the official printers
announced the king's victories to the royalist corporations
throughout France.[114] Some pamphleteers expounded (on traditional
lines) the absolute powers of the king. More frequently, they stressed
his personal qualities; his chivalry, concern for the poor, his patriotism and his courage. Had not a 'surge of loyalty' inspired the troops
to victory at Ivry? Did not that victory (they said) show that the king
had God's blessing? Had he not prevented the sack of Chartres to
spare the poor? Had he not (they argued) raised the siege of Paris
to avoid unnecessary suffering? They compared Henri III, the stay-
at-home king (*roi casanier*) to Henri IV, the warrior monarch (*roi
guerrier*).[115] For the first time, images of the king were used with an

overt political aim and to a wide audience.[116] Portraits of him, sometimes in a distinctive velour hat, were sold in the boulevards of the Latin quarter of Paris while the League pursued its final vendetta against Mayenne, circulated round the provinces and even in Venice. The reductions of towns to royal control were used as an opportunity for impressive displays of royalism. The royal entries to Paris, Amiens, Lyons and Rouen were carefully stage-managed affairs. The *joyeuse entrée* into Paris was particularly ingenious, for parts of the capital (notably the Sorbonne) were unenthusiastic about the royal entry.[117] But the careful attention to forms, the procession to the cathedral Notre Dame, the healing for scrofula (600 were supposed to have been cured), all had an effect.

The propaganda drew on old, well-established themes in French literature and history, endowing the king with the attributes of a Gallic Hercules in a display of elementary patriotism.[118] Henri IV was a king by the Salic law, the natural law of France. He was our 'good, true and natural king who is extracted from our blood'. It was argued that, if France had been an elective monarchy, the majority of France would, indeed, have chosen him as king. An extension of the same argument accused the League as being the abject servant of foreigners – Philip II and the 'Spanish rabbi', the Pope. Anti-Spanish sentiments were easily aroused in a country which had spent most of the century fighting the Habsburgs. The royal conversion to Catholicism was a powerful weapon in the hands of his pamphleteers too. By 1591, the League was already so concerned at the possibility that, under the influence of the papal legate, Cardinal Cajetan, the Sorbonne had decreed that anyone who even advocated negotiations with the king to convert him would be automatically excommunicated and that, even if Henri IV announced his intention to abjure, he would not be accepted back to the faith.[119] This decree was still in force when on 25 July 1593 came the announcement of the royal abjuration, delicately timed to gain propaganda effect, embarrass the estates general of the League and encourage the negotiations for a truce at Suresnes.

Above all, Henri IV played on the desires for peace. The propagandists tempted their readers with the image of a day when Henri IV would be recognised everywhere as king and the 'hideous face of France's desolation would be changed to joy and laughter, and all these storms dispersed by a beautiful sun which will bring us a day of contentment and liberty'.[120] The promises of the benefits of peace to each estate of the realm were quite specific. They tempted the peasant with the prospect of a safe harvest, the merchant with a profitable trade and the scholar with a renaissance of the arts. This contrasted with the antagonisms of the League which appeared in their written works and which were quickly exploited by the royalists. Nowhere is this better demonstrated than in the pamphlet which has been described as the 'last will and testament of the League'. the *Dialogue between the Noble and the Townsman*. Generally considered to have been written in the aftermath of Henri IV's conversion, it has the intense and sometimes desperate clarity of defeat and disillusionment.[121] By the end of the year, it was republished with a few amendments by the royalists to advertise their adversary's low morale. It was even reproduced in verse form with a coloured engraving on the front which advertised the royal cause.[122] In the original pamphlet, the *Manant* (zealot, League Parisian) meets the *Maheustre* (the *politique* nobleman) outside the walls of Paris. The *Manant* berates the nobleman and all the other grandees for abandoning the cause of justice, piety and purity. The nobility have lost their privileged position, he argues, by their treachery to the faith. In return, the *Maheustre* exposes the divisions of the League, through which France is being dismembered to satisfy individual ambitions. The work ends with a stark series of questions which pull away the comfortable idealism of the zealot; 'Where is your popular support? Who are your allies? Who is your king? How do you know you can trust him?' To each of these questions, the *Manant* can only whimper, pathetically, 'Dieu, dieu, dieu. . . .'[123]

All these themes in Henri IV's propaganda appear in a work produced at about the same time and which has become the most famous political satire in the history of France. Called the *Pleasant Satire or the Efficacy of Catholicon*, it was a composite work by several *politique* Parisians.[124] Manuscripts of an early version circulated in March 1593. It was a brilliant work – biting, merciless, humorous and astute. In it, the differences between public and private motives of the League supporters were brutally exposed. The scene was the estates general of the League. Each of the speakers before the estates was fed a Spanish wonder drug called 'Catholicon', composed of tablets like doubloons, which made them speak the truth rather than mouth the platitudes of the Catholic cause. One by one in the satire, the Duke of Mayenne, the Spanish ambassador, the League zealot from Lyons, the papal legate and the swaggering nobleman stand on the rostrum, larger than life, and reveal their real and sordid motives for supporting the League. Each both betrays and ridicules the ideals that he was supposed to have fought for. Only one delegate, the *politique* d'Aubray, presented the sober cause; that of peace, justice, the realm and the king. Monstrously pleased with the work, Henri IV hastened to sponsor its publication.

The defeat of the League appeared to be final and complete, but the appearance was deceptive. Substantial public burning of pamphlets and documents of the League were organised on the Place Maubert and elsewhere after the king's entry to Paris, but it could not destroy League mentalities. The king conducted no witch-hunt against his former adversaries; 'oubli et pardon' was said to have been his motto. The promises he had given, therefore, had to be sustained if the League was not to be renewed. League sentiments remained for at least another decade for Spain to foster and cultivate when it chose to. But Henri IV had demonstrated that every Catholic had his price. His propaganda had proved that, while the aims of the League were laudable in themselves, they were not worth the cost of establishing a new tyranny. He had proved that political stability was, in some senses, a worthy objective and could be gained on the basis of established institutions and laws. Elective monarchy, representative institutions, provincial separatism, noble factions had been proved doubly wanting by *both* Catholics *and* Protestants. The rest of the reign would be devoted to attempting to confirm the benefits which could accompany stability.

REFERENCES AND NOTES

1. L. Davillé, 1909, pp. 41–82.
2. The declaration of Péronne because this was where the Catholic League of 1576 had been pronounced. In fact, the declaration in 1585 was made from Reims and then published in another version from Lyons in June 1585 (*ML*, Vol. I, pp. 56–62). LN, No. 1089. Cf. LN 1100.
3. E. Pasquier, **1966**, p. 396.
4. Cromé, **1977**. Cromé's biography is given on pp. 24–7. This authorship, based on testimony by Estoile and Cayet, is now widely accepted.
5. 'Le procès verbal d'un nommé Nicolas Poulain, lieutenant de la prévosté de l'Isle de France . . .', *Arch. cur. de l'hist. de France*, Vol. XI, pp. 289–323 (cited as Poulain).
6. Cromé, **1977**, p. 95.
7. Barnavi, 1980, pp. 20–1 *et seq.* for further biographical details.
8. *Ibid.*
9. Poulain, pp. 289–90.
10. Cromé, **1977**, p. 65.   C. Valois, **1914**, p. 125.
11. Poulain, pp. 294–5, 306.
12. Poulain, pp. 293–5; C. Valois, **1914**, pp. 123–5.
13. D. Pallier, 1976, ch. ii.
14. Estoile, **1943**, p. 626.
15. D. Pallier, 1976, p. 62; Cayet, p. 22.
16.

Beyond endurance is	The Bourbon race
The Lorraine League	Gives peace to France
Their hands encompass	The defence of the state
The weapon which kills us	Is the Protestant religion

17. D. Pallier, 1976, pp. 63–9.   De Thou, *HU*, Vol. IX, pp. 69–70.   F. J. Baumgartner, 1976, pp. 71–4. Dorléan's diary reveals his interests in, if not his accurate knowledge of, English Catholic affairs. I have used

the abridged edition in *Arch. cur. de l'hist. de France*, Vol. XI, pp. 111, etc.

18. Cayet, p. 22.
19. *Arch. cur. de l'hist. de France*, Vol. XI, pp. 112–212, esp. pp. 156–176. This volume also includes the reply to the work by Du Plessis-Mornay.
20. Estoile, **1943**, pp. 507–8, 511–2.
21. D. Pallier, 1976, pp. 66–7. C. Valois, **1914**, pp. 147–8.
22. Estoile, **1943**, p. 508.
23. De Thou, *HU*, Vol. IX, p. 270. Estoile, **1943**, pp. 497–8, 500, 514–17.
24. De Thou, *HU*, Vol. ix, pp. 654–5; Estoile, **1943**, pp. 499, 508–9. F. Yates, 1954, pp. 215–70.
25. Estoile, **1943**, p. 508. A. Lebigre, 1980. The influence of the *curés* was remarked on by Pigafetta and Cornejo during the siege of 1590. Cf. C. Valois, **1914**, pp. 134–8.
26. Estoile, **1943**, pp. 502–3.
27. E. Pasquier, **1966**, p. 283.
28. Estoile, **1943**, pp. 509–10. For Boucher, see *DBF*, Vol. VI, col. 1207. Cf. C. Valois, **1914**, pp. 151–72.
29. Estoile, **1943**, pp. 502–3. A copy of the sermon exists in *B. Institut MS Godefroy* 288, fol. 35, etc.
30. *Revue rétrospective*, **1834**, pp. 267–77. Cf. C. Labitte, 1849.
31. For the taxation of Paris, P. Robiquet, 1886, p. 47 *et seq*. The registers of the town of Paris (Vol. IX, pp. 16–17, 53–4, etc.) provide a full conspectus of the fiscal demands on the city. Cf. F. J. Baumgartner, 1976, pp. 32–3. *ML*, Vol. I, pp. 199–201. For the city militia, G. Picot, 1874, pp. 132–66, esp. pp. 142–3. Estoile, **1943**, pp. 376–7, 396, 489.
32. E. Barnavi, 1980, p. 15. Cf. Cayet, p. 30 – 'This innovation of creating offices served as a pretext for the League and the *Sixteen* to turn an infinite number of lesser people from obedience to the King'. Estoile, **1943**, pp. 389–90 for the creations of June 1586.
33. Estoile, **1943**, pp. 449–50.
34. *Ibid.*, pp. 452–3, 467. They had also gone on strike in May 1580 over a similar issue.
35. B. Schnapper, 1957, pp. 151–72.
36. Estoile, **1943**, pp. 491–2.
37. *Ibid.*, pp. 482–3.
38. There is no overall study of the merchants in Paris although one is in preparation. See R. Descimon, 1982, pp. 89–90, who stresses that, as with the Huguenots in 1562, it was the merchants and professionals of the *secondary* rank that were most attracted to political activity in 1588. For a social study of one group of importance in the League, J-P. Chadourne, 1969, pp. 17–25.
39. *Arch. cur. de l'hist. de France*, Vol. XI, p. 141.
40. *Cal SP For*, Vol. XX, p. 603.
41. *Ibid.*, Vol. XXI, p. 6.
42. E. Pasquier, **1966**, pp. 252–3. Estoile, **1943**, pp. 451–2.
43. A rough sketch of court itinerary is as follows:

1585: most of the court at Paris all year until Nov. 15.

1586: court in Paris from Jan–June and Sep–Nov.

1587: court in Paris from Jan–June and Aug–Dec.

1588: court in Paris from Jan–May. King leaves at the Day of Barricades, but queen and queen mother stay in the capital.

44. Poulain, pp. 292–9. The first plot may have taken place on 7 July 1586, but the evidence is not incontrovertible. First definite plot is from October 1586 (*BN MS It* 1735, pp. 305–7).

45. The Duke of Mayenne had returned from an indifferent campaign in Gascony and was expected to support it. Poulain, pp. 298–9. LN, No. 1097. Estoile, **1943**, p. 485.

46. Poulain, pp. 298–9. *BN MS It* 1736, pp. 20–1 (16 Mar. 1587).

47. Other plots were to have taken place in July 1587, Sep. 1587 and Feb. 1588. The fears of the *Sixteen* are clear in Poulain, pp. 304–5 and 310–19. The names of many of the *Sixteen* were revealed in the publication, *La bibliothèque de madame de Montpensier* in c. Dec. 1587 (Estoile, **1943**, pp. 534–8).

48. Events of the Day of Barricades are carefully reported in the various accounts of *Revue rétrospective*, **1834** (Vol. IV), *Arch. cur. de l'hist. de France* (Vol. XI). C. Valois, **1914**, p. 205. Also H. C. Davila, **1647**, pp. 685 *et seq.*

49. There is no study of the clientele of members of the House of Guise. The *rentes* and debts of the Duke of Guise in *BN MS Fr* 8180 give the only impression easily available to date. For the view that the Duke of Guise instigated the Day of Barricades, see P. Robiquet, 1886, ch. ix, who echoes the views of Michelet's *Histoire de France*, 2nd edn, 19 vols, 1876–78.

50. Poulain, pp. 290–1, 307. Further details on Maineville in E. Barnavi, 1980, pp. 90–2. Cf. de Thou, *HU*, Vol. IX, p. 65.

51. Poulain, pp. 291–2.

52. *Ibid.*, p. 307.

53. H. C. Davila, **1647**, pp. 680–2. C. Valois, **1914**, pp. 199–207.

54. C. Valois, **1914**, p. 203.

55. D. Lamar Jensen, 1964, pp. 109–14; 1968, pp. 205–21. E. H. Dickerman, 1976, pp. 19–24. The only direct reference to a meeting between the *Sixteen* and the Spanish ambassador before May 1588 is in a despatch of 1 July 1587, but this reference is ambiguous and other evidence cited by Jensen is misleading.

56. Poulain, p. 295, and E. H. Dickerman, *op. cit.*, n. 55.

57. *Arch. Simancas* K 1568, fol. 31, etc. used by G. Mattingly for his account of the Day of Barricades in 1959, pp. 218–44. Cf. A. Viñas, 1939, pp. 514–33.

58. Estoile, **1948**, pp. 147–8, describes Ameline as an 'homme de menée et d'entendement'. He disguised himself as a Jesuit, a merchant or a courtier, to suit the people he was trying to attract.

59. In Rouen, P. Benedict, 1981, pp. 169 *et seq.*

60. Cayet, pp. 34–8. Cf. another project in *BN MS Clairambault* 357, fol. 146. The curious book *Remonstrance aux Trois Estats de la France* (Paris, 1586) by the lawyer, François le Breton (1549–86) also

contains what might be seen as political ideas of the League. Le Breton, who was executed in Paris for the 'sedition' in the book, became a hero to the *Sixteen*. F. J. Baumgartner, 1976, pp. 76–9. D. Pallier, p. 64. De Thou, *HU*, Vol. IX, p. 624. Le Breton's fate has been seen as the effect of increasing efforts by the king to control the press.

61. H. Drouot, 1937a, Vol. I, pp. 134–6.
62. Estoile, **1875–96**, Vol. IV, p. vi.
63. Henri III complained to the Paris municipality on 10 Sept. 1588 of their activities in circulating hostile pamphlets. He mentioned the despatch of Antoine Hotman to Brittany to the estates (*Mémoires de Nevers*, **1665**, Vol. I, pp. 744–5; *BN MS Fr n.a.* 2745, fol. 235). The historian J-A. de Thou was sent to Normandy by the king and Rouen was especially favourably treated by the king (de Thou, *HU*, Vol. IX, pp. 305–22; P. Benedict, 1981, pp. 174–5). Among the pamphlets, Palma Cayet (p. 63) thought that N. Rolland's *Remonstrance très humble* was very important for provincial delegates (D. Pallier 1976, p. 269). Another pamphlet, the *Discours sur la procédure* . . . (n.p. 1588, in LN 1295) gives details of the 'monopolies and gerrymandering' of elections to the estates.
64. There is no modern study of the estates of 1588. See G. Picot, 1888, Vol. III, pp. 370 *et seq*. E. Pasquier, **1966**, p. 331. M. Orlea 1980, p. 102 refers to the delegates coming with copies of the Paris *cahier*.
65. E. Barnavi, **1976–7**, pp. 81–154. Elections from Paris in A. Taillandier, 1845–46, pp. 422–59.
66. Estoile, **1943**, pp. 577–9. G. Picot, *op. cit.*, n. 64.
67. *Revue retrospective*, **1834**, Vol. III, pp. 433–55.
68. Estoile, **1943**, pp. 582–3.
69. P. Benedict, 1981, p. 178. For Jacques Commolet, see C. Sommervögel and Bäcker, 1892–1919, Vol. II, 1351–2.
70. D. Pallier, 1976, pp. 69–83; F. J. Baumgartner, 1976, ch. v. C. Reure, 1897, pp. 161–88; 1898, pp. 513–15. K. Cameron, 1978. Examples in *LN* 1540, 1557, 1597, 1611, etc.
71. E. Saulnier, **1913**, p. 25. Estoile, **1943**, pp. 611–12, 614–15.
72. *Ibid.*, pp. 610–11.
73. *De juste Henrici Tertii abdicationi* . . . (Paris, 1589, *BL* 283, b 10). F. J. Baumgartner, 1976, pp. 126–44. C. Labitte, **1849** pp. 137–8. There are detectable passages taken from the *Francogallia* and the *Vindicae contra Tyrannos*.
74. E. Barnavi, 1980, pp. 132–6. Estoile, **1943**, pp. 616–17. Cromé, **1977**, p. 99. A. Bernard, **1842**, preface. LN, No. 1544.
75. LN, No. 1569. Estoile, **1943**, pp. 619–20. H. Drouot, 1937a, Vol. I, pp. 246–92.
76. Cayet, p. 46. The career of Barnabé Brisson, an interesting career lawyer, is outlined in P. Gambier, 1957. Edouard Molé came from a distinguished Parisian family of judges, related to the Hennequin, Marillac, Nicolay and Séguier.
77. Estoile, **1943**, pp. 618–19. *Infra*, p. 90.
78. Estoile, **1948**, p. 19. *Arch. cur. de l'hist. de France*, Vol. XII (1834),

pp. 384–95.   Cf. LN, Nos 1386 and 1664.   O. Ranum, 1980, pp. 63–82.

79.   *Le Manifeste de la France aux Parisiens* . . . (n.p. 1589, *BN* 8° Lb 341706). Also quoted in E. Barnavi, 1980, p. 144.

80.   *BN MS Fr n.a.* 8299, fols 7, 40, 205, 227v, 240v, etc.

81.   For example, Jean Du Val, forcibly removed from the city guard with 'plusieurs injures'.   Cf. Me Guillaume Goussault, *conseiller*, who was threatened with drowning and 'un poignard dans le sein' by his local city guard which invested his house.

82.   Estoile, **1943**, pp. 606–8, 636–7.

83.   Estoile, **1948**, pp. 68, 101.   E. Barnavi, 1980, p. 45 for Bussy's family background.

84.   Estoile, **1943**, pp. 616–17.   E. Barnavi, 1980, pp. 46, etc.

85.   *Ibid.*, pp. 141–4.

86.   *Coppie de la responce faite par un polytique de ceste ville de Paris* . . . (Paris, 1589, *BN* 8'Lb 34652), p. 3.   Cf. LN, No. 1547 for a pamphlet which tries to give a description of salient politique characteristics – shifty eyes, flattery, inconsistent actions, etc!

87.   Estoile, **1948**, p. 96.

88.   *Ibid.*, p. 97.

89.   *Premier et second advertissement des Catholiques anglois* (n.p. 1590, *BL* 1192, i 6), pp. 95–105.   Cf. F. J. Baumgartner, 1976, pp. 167–8.

90.   Most observers expected Paris to fall (H. de l'Epinois, 1886, p. 378).   A. Franklin, **1876**, p. 133.   F. Pigafetta, **1876**, p. 22 for estimates of deaths.   Latest estimates of population before the siege, A. Lozinski, 'L' accroissement de la population de Paris au XVIe siècle', *Srednie Veka*, Vol. XXXVII (1973), pp. 146–73.

91.   *ML* vol. IV, pp. 276–314.   Estoile, **1948**, pp. 68–72.

92.   Began in Nov. 1589 (LN, No. 1659).   The disaffection with Mayenne became more evident during the siege – F. Pigafetta, **1876**, p. 16.   Estoile, **1948**, p. 60, 106 (Apr. 1591).

93.   *Ibid.*, pp. 127–47.   Analysis of the list and the *Sixteen*'s position in E. Barnavi, 1980, pp. 205–14.

94.   *Ibid.*, pp. 212–14.

95.   Provincial councils in H. Drouot, 1951, pp. 415–33.   H. Hours, 1952, pp. 401–22.   R. R. Harding, 1978, p. 93.   For Rouen, P. Benedict, 1981, pp. 179–184; Toulouse, M. Greengrass, 1979, ch. ix. The cities in Burgundy are discussed in H. Drouot, 1937a.   For a preliminary sketch of possible lines of enquiry, P. Ascoli, 1977, pp. 15–37.

96.   Philippe de Ver in *BN MS Fr* 4019, fol. 47.   See also the events in Orleans in 1591 in F. Hauchecorne, 1970, pp. 267–78.

97.   St Malo, F. Juon des Longrais, *Inventaire sommaire des archives municipales de St Malo* (1914), pp. 110–20.   F. Braudel, 1973, Vol. I, pp. 1205–17.

98.   H. Hours, 1952, pp. 401–20.   J-H. Mariéjol, 1947, chs iv and v.   F. Rolle, 1865, inventory of registers BB 122–32. Royalist pamphlets did not hesitate to mention the *petits souverains* among the cities and provinces – e.g. de Thou, *HU*, Vol. XI, p. 614.   LN 1711 – 'combien de

petites tyrannies y naistront, combien de petites Républiques s'y formeront, & combien de villes se cantonneront?'

99. See above, p. 12.
100. *BN MS Fr* 3982, fols 222 *et seq*.
101. *Arch. Simancas* K1579, fol. 76.
102. *BN MS Fr* 3982, fols 224v', 228, 230. L. Van der Essen, 1933, ch. x.
103. D. Lamar Jensen, 1964, p. 212. Sully's capture of diplomatic papers, Sully, **1970**, pp. 330–5.
104. d'Aubigné, Vol. VIII, p. 202.
105. *BN MS Fr* 3983, fols 140–44; 3646, fols 133, 210v.
106. A. Bernard, **1842**, pp. 18, 377, 558.
107. *Ibid.*, pp. 45, 378, 559, 650.
108. See map 1 for dates of major towns' capitulations. Sully's negotiations with Villars in P. Benedict, 1981, pp. 227–8. Sully, **1970**, pp. 454–7. For Méric de Vic, see M. Greengrass, 1979, pp. 289–95. Also E. H. Dickerman, 1968 and R. Kierstead, 1968.
109. They were published together in BN, F 15927 in 1606. The secret treaties were not included. Copies of these are to be found in Devic and Vaissète **1872–1904** Vol. XII, cols 1533–64 (for Joyeuse); *BN MS Fr* 4019, fol. 360 (Mayenne), 399 (Merceour); *BN MS Fr* 3646, fol. 77 (Guise).
110. *BN MS Fr* 4019, fols 265v–270. n.d.
111. *Ibid.*, fol. 271v.
112. H. Drouot, 1937a, Vol. II, pp. 458–62.
113. Estoile, **1948**, p. 393.
114. D. Pallier, 1976, pp. 83–96. New Year's Day celebrations in Tours in *BN MS Fr* 4019, fol. 67.
115. Du Plessis-Mornay's contributions in *Du Plessis-Mornay, Mémoires*, **1824–25**, Vol. IV, pp. 356–65, 372–81, 391–406. LN 1537, 1578 1745, 1786–7; 1840. *ML*, Vol. IV, p. 211, etc.
116. F. Bardon, 1974.
117. Estoile, **1948**, pp. 387–403.
118. F. Bardon, 1974 (esp. illustrations). C. Vivanti, 1967, pp. 176–97. M-R-Jung, 1966.
119. Estoile, **1948**, pp. 35–7. Description of the conversion in *MS Fr* 4019, fol. 15v. F. J. Baumgartner, 1976, pp. 201–10.
120. F. Pithou, *Extraict d'un traicté* . . . (n.p. 1594) LN, No. 1929.
121. P. Ascoli, 1974, pp. 6–22. J. H. M. Salmon, 1975, pp. 57–88. Cromé, **1977**, pp. 9–41.
122. Estoile, **1888**, Vol. IV, pp. 300–4.
123. Cromé, **1977**, pp. 210–11.
124. The provenance of the *Satyre Menippée* was finally elucidated by Charles Read in the 1876 edition (pp. i–xxiii). The notes to the 1726 Ratisbon edition render it still fundamental.

Chapter 3

HUGUENOTS UNDER THE LAW

Despite thirty years of civil war, the Huguenots had become an even smaller minority in the kingdom. At the time of the edict of Nantes in 1598, a census undertaken by the national synod at Montpellier found that, excluding Béarn and Navarre, there were 759 fully established churches (257 of which were attached to manors on the estates of Huguenot gentlemen) served by a total of about 800 ministers. This would indicate that Protestantism was the religion of between 1 and 2 million people in France or less than 10 per cent of the population. Even in the Midi, some Huguenot communities did not survive the wars and others were left depleted by apostasy.[1] Yet it was in this region that the English foreign traveller in the 1590s, Edwin Sandys, noticed that they had their greatest support.[2] But there were other important enclaves either within or close to France whose importance had grown as civil wars and migration to safer parts took effect. Orange, Navarre, Sedan, Metz, Gex and the Channel Islands all became part of the geo-political strengths of the Huguenot movement which the civil wars had, in some ways, strengthened. In addition, the Huguenots helped to put Henri IV on the throne and they expected some rewards.

The Protestants reacted like most minorities under threat. By the end of the civil wars, the ultimate implications of their ideology were forgotten. They ceased to envisage a different society for the rest of France and concentrated on their own position within the existing society. In some respects they shared the political assumptions of Catholic France and their political assembly angrily dismissed the peasant rebels (*Croquants*) in 1594 who approached them for assistance.[3] They had formed an exaggerated respect for the protection afforded by laws. The literate laity of their churches looked to a written document, guaranteed by God, Providence and a powerful protector, to provide their ultimate security. Despite their internal disagreements, the Huguenots were united in their belief that their salvation lay in some form of edict declaring their rights and guaranteeing their freedoms.

The relationships with the princes of the blood who served as their protectors were frequently strained and uneasy ones. Henri of Navarre was their leader for twelve years before he came to the throne in 1589 but he was still not trusted in the movement. This was despite the fact that he was a major figure in French politics whose seigneurial authority was coterminous with Huguenot influence in many regions. He was sovereign in Navarre and Béarn and could call on 300 gentlemen and 6,000 foot to serve him from those territories. Elsewhere, south of the Loire he had numerous counties and the duchy of Albret (see Map 1). In the county of Armagnac alone 1,800 fiefs owed him homage. Even north of the Loire, he was Duke of Vermandois and Beaumont, Count of Marly and Viscount of Châteauneuf en Thumerois.[4] In addition, he had inherited the provincial governorship of the province of Guyenne which, in peace-time, entitled him to a royal company of cavalry and a natural precedence over Catholic and Protestant in a substantial region of south-west France. In practice, he shared this authority with a royal lieutenant in the province but with the careful, shrewd and prudent Norman captain Jacques de Matignon as lieutenant from 1581, Navarre enjoyed friendship and cooperation. Between them, they ruled Gascony.[5]

Yet the Huguenots felt they had good grounds for distrusting their protector. His father had not protected them in 1561–62 and he had entrusted the education of his son to a succession of tutors of a variety of religious persuasions. Although Henri of Navarre spent eight years in the company of his mother, Jeanne d'Albret, a committed Huguenot, within three months of her death and firm will entreating him to remain true to his Protestantism he had married a Catholic (a marriage she had only reluctantly consented to in April 1572) and abjured his Huguenot faith.[6] When he escaped from court in 1576, he renounced this abjuration as a recantation extracted by force, and therefore null; but he quickly proceeded to give some grounds for believing that his Huguenot sympathies lacked a certain zealotry. In 1577, he readily accepted the edict of pacification and tried to enforce it in the government of Guyenne as well as in Languedoc and Dauphiné.[7] His entourage and friendships included many Catholics like Michel de Montaigne, the moderate Catholic judge from Bordeaux, Arnaud du Ferrier, his chancellor in Navarre, or the Viscount of Lavardin, Sully's patron at the Gascon's court.[8] Among the Protestants, he befriended the unorthodox like the frank and impartial historian La Popelinière and, at a later stage, the irenical minister, Jean de Serres.[9] At various times, Navarre's court attracted the reprehension of pastors and consistory and even Madame de Mornay was told to dress more modestly by the Protestants of Montauban in 1584.[10] Navarre's well-publicised, amorous escapades did little to endear him to the upright Huguenots of his party: still less did his proposals to hold a national council to settle the question of religion. He considered it for his ancestral lands in Béarn. He demanded the calling of a 'free and legitimate' council in March 1585 to settle the religious wars. He repeated his suggestion to the estates general at Blois in March 1589. Force, he told them, had achieved nothing. He had himself abjured, 'a dagger at his throat' but without any success in his case. He and his followers had endured the assaults of ten armies in the preceding four years but they still stood firm. There was, however, a peaceful course which could be followed, namely, the convening of a free council. 'Instruct me', he invited them, 'I am not ideologically motivated.' Truth, he claimed, would be embraced, wherever it was found to be. The interests of the state would be put above his own personal interests. In the meantime, he offered the widest possible toleration in religious matters in the areas under his control.[11]

The suspicions aroused by Navarre's protectorship and the varying attitudes within the Huguenot movement at large were aired in public at the large political assembly summoned to La Rochelle in December 1588. In his opening remarks, Navarre complained of the suspicions that his actions attracted from his co-religionists. But this did not deter the delegates from engaging in a detailed critique of his diplomacy and military strategy (especially after the battle of Coutras) as well as his financial administration. Navarre had to swear to observe the confession of faith, accept a larger, nominated, *conseil de surveillance* and agree to receive nominations for all financial posts in the Huguenot administration from the movement and only appoint those whom they themselves had put forward.[12] In return, the assembly promised him its full military support against the Catholic League. But Madame de Mornay had overheard one of the deputies say: 'Now is the time to make kings into serfs and slaves' and the comparisons between the estates general at Blois and the assembly at La Rochelle were evident to all contemporaries. Once the assembly was over, Henri of Navarre confided in Madame Gramont (*La Belle Corisande*), 'If they hold another assembly I shall go mad.' Even the opportunity to put a king on the throne had not, therefore, united the Huguenots behind his leadership.[13]

Of course, the King of Navarre enjoyed the support of his councillors and close servants – men such as Sully, his secretary Raymond de Viçose, or his household minister, Claude Sommain Clairville.[14] Aware of the need to win Catholics over to their side, they thought that the edict of pacification in 1577 provided a sufficient guarantee of Huguenot freedoms providing that it was adequately enforced. They ignored the demands for Huguenot separatism or, as Sully later described it, 'the kind of popular and Republican state like the Low Countries'.[15] But, despite Navarre's attempts to influence delegates from the south-west, these sentiments were not very well represented in the political assemblies except among the contingent of Huguenot judges and lawyers.[16] Instead there were a group of pastors and convinced lay Huguenots who concentrated on religious demands and were less interested in securing political privileges. They regarded peace as an essential prerequisite to the rebuilding of the Huguenot churches, the re-education of its clergy and the refounding of a proper church organisation. They looked to a Huguenot king, rather than a Huguenot cause, to sponsor new universities and remunerate their pastors. Philippe Du Plessis-Mornay, the prominent Calvinist theologian, scholar and political advisor to Navarre since 1581, was a leader and characteristic figure in this group. His reaction to the behaviour of the assembly at La Rochelle was to remind Navarre of the importance of patronage and management in the cause – 'All the fools are not on one side only' he advised him.[17] Immediately after the accession, he wrote to prominent members of the opposition to Navarre to try to persuade them to 'set their hand to this crown of thorns and turn it into a crown of lilies'.[18]

The more volatile and opposing elements came, primarily, from the Huguenot aristocrats. Henri, Viscount of Turenne, his kinsman Louis de la Trémouille, and François Châtillon headed a group of Huguenot nobles and captains who were less interested in peace or in Huguenot welfare, conceived in narrowly religious terms, than in preserving the Huguenot constitution which enabled them to play an independent political part within the movement. Turenne, the seigneur of a large part of the upper Limousin, had been schooled in the malcontent world around the Duke of Anjou and boldly protested that 'in serving the public, I serve my own interests'.[19] He was a man of large ideas and La Trémouille was his close ally. Châtillon was a seigneur with a Genevan education and 'a great hope' as Du Plessis discreetly put it.[20] Together they planned to remove Navarre from the protectorship and replace him with a foreign prince (such as the Elector Palatine) to whom they would be lieutenants and, in practice, masters. Their influence in the Huguenot cause is difficult to determine but they had their nominees at the political assemblies of the period 1588–98, one of whom was (according to Sully) the Huguenot poet and soldier, Agrippa d'Aubigné.[21] They may even have encouraged individual churches and Protestant colloquies to petition Henri of Navarre for the redress of grievances.[22] Secondly, there were the zealots, leaderless and not always very influential. They included among their ranks, pastors of advanced opinions and some elders from the Protestant strongholds.[23] They were assisted by the political theorist and advisor to John Casimir of the Palatinate, Dr Beuttrich.[24] They wanted no concessions, and were unprepared to surrender any of the Huguenots' hard-won political independence and military strongholds. They resented Navarre's *tyrannie protectorale* and wanted to replace him. The zealots were never a majority at the political assemblies but they exercised an influence beyond their numerical strength, especially when the suspicions of Henri IV's motives were at their height in 1596–97.

THE LETTERS PATENT OF MANTES, JULY 1591

Huguenot suspicions began to increase from the moment of the king's accession. In August 1589, Henri IV was forced to make a declaration preserving Catholics in their posts and offering to sustain the Catholic religion in order to maintain important elements of the royal army loyal to him.[25] Already, Turenne and La Trémouille began persuading some Huguenot zealots at a synod to condemn the royal concessions and choose a new 'protector'. It was even rumoured that the king was about to desert the faith. The king promptly wrote to Du Plessis-Mornay to try to eradicate this dissension[26]:

> They say that I have dismissed officers of the religion . . . that the ministers are no longer paid; that the officials who are in charge of the enforcement of the truce [made with the royalists] have reinstated royal officers and the Roman Catholic religion . . . in brief that in matters of religion, justice and finance, conditions are worse now than they were when the deceased King was alive. . . . These are the rumours which are being sown with the intention that they will lead to the naming of a new protector. . . .'

And, in the following two years, Henri IV did his best to curtail political assemblies of the Huguenots at regional and national level and encouraged the Viscount of Turenne to serve with him in his army at the siege of Paris. Then, he despatched him on delicate missions to Protestant powers abroad to reduce his meddlesome influence at home.[27]

But this did not remove the legitimate fears of the more moderate Protestants like Du Plessis-Mornay or the royalist Huguenot lawyers at the assemblies. For it was undoubtedly the case that the legal position of the Huguenots in France was ill-defined and almost non-existent. The edicts against the Huguenots enacted in 1585 and 1588 were still in force, legally speaking. The Huguenots could look to no lawcourt in the realm for redress of grievances beyond those royal courts staffed with Catholics who supported Henri IV. It was to try to meet the most pressing demands of the Huguenot moderates that the king reluctantly issued his letters patent of Mantes on 4 July 1591 in which he revoked the edicts of 1585 and 1588.[28] The letters were drafted by Du Plessis-Mornay. In effect, they re-established the terms of the edict of pacification of 1577. Huguenots were given rights to worship in one place in each locality (*balliage*), on the estates of Huguenot gentlemen, and in eight garrison towns. It was agreed that the pastors would be paid by the king and that Protestants should be free to enter all offices. Bipartisan courts (*chambres de l'édit*) of the sort previously established in 1577 were to be reconvened to deal with cases involving Protestants. There was also a reference to a 'Holy and free council or some notable assembly' which would achieve a final settlement of all outstanding sectarian problems and instruct the king on the true religion.

The concessions of Mantes were only a palliative. They were not an edict and were never registered in the *parlement*. They were therefore ignored by the Catholics. The *parlement* of Paris, in exile at Tours, still required Huguenots to forfeit their estates (and convert to Catholicism) before taking up offices. It never allowed the establishment of a *chambre de l'édit*. Ministers of the faith went unpaid. It is a measure of Henri IV's unwillingness to alienate any potential support from moderate Catholics by appearing to favour the Huguenots that this was the only substantial measure that he was prepared to grant in their favour before 1598.

HENRI IV'S CONVERSION AND THE HUGUENOTS

The abjuration of the Huguenot faith by the king occurred without any consultation of the movement in conditions that could only be described as discourteous. There was a perfunctory meeting with some Huguenot pastors on the eve of the declaration on 24 July 1593. The declaration was made from St Denis, the tomb of the kings of France, and the symbolism was clear to contemporaries, namely, that only Catholic kings ever truly ruled the country. Protestant councillors had advised him of the dangers, but understood the necessities, of a conversion which would lead to the rapid dissolution of the League. Maximilien de Béthune (later Duke of Sully), provides an account of a conversation with the king in May 1593 which ran through the advantages and disadvantages of the move.[29] Sully advised the king that the bulk of Huguenot opinion would remain loyal to him. The only opposition would come, he said, from the zealots among the consistories and their ministers. There was a considerable hope that the support of Turenne and the other Protestant nobles could be retained. Turenne had been given the hand in matrimony of Charlotte de la Marck, the (disputed) heiress to the estates and title of the Duke of Bouillon. Bouillon was an important principality on the sensitive north-east frontier of France and a refuge for exiled French Huguenots. This and other royal favours, it was hoped, would prevent his exploiting a delicate position.

As it was, the manner of the conversion and its timing ensured that even moderate Huguenot opinion was alienated from the king. Du Plessis-Mornay had been detailed to convene a political assembly of the movement at Mantes in late July 1593. He did so with considerable skill, inviting distinguished foreign observers to the deliberations and arranging for the king to nominate some of the delegates (to save time, not to offend privileges, as the churches were disingenuously told).[30] In fact, the king announced his conversion before the assembly had convened, and thus removed the opportunity that Du Plessis may have been trying to open up, of a pliable Protestant body willing to accept what the king proposed for the future of the movement. Du Plessis-Mornay hastily left the court and the king had to utilise all his personal charms and appeals to past fidelity to persuade him to return and once again be the king's honest broker with the Protestants: 'I have loved you more than any other gentleman in my realm; I have spoken freely to you. . . . If you have some complaint against me you should let me hear. . . . I write only this once to see if you are obedient to me. Come; come. You shall not tarry. Come.'[31] Du Plessis' reply indicated that he felt that Turenne's fears, rather than his own loyalties, had been proven more prescient. There was a royal monopoly, a fear of the advisors who surrounded the king[32]:

> The people are saying that it was more tolerable to live under Henri III than it is to live under Your Majesty. It is no wonder that they are looking for a 'protector'. Patience and hope are on the wane. The people look for relief. If you wish to eliminate the desire for a 'protector', you must diminish its necessity. Listen to their demands; you know what they need and what they want.

In November 1593, the assembly summoned to Mantes finally began its deliberations. Its demands were expressed in its long, detailed, 109-clause *cahier* of remonstrances.[33] They wanted extensive guarantees for the rights of worship for Protestants, and included among these demands for payments of their garrisons and rights to hold public assemblies. They wanted certain royal offices of justice open to nomination by the Protestants, rather than just purchase by certain Protestant individuals. Henri IV treated the assembly with humiliating contempt, refusing to visit it, denying an audience to its deputies and (when they finally were allowed to see him) declining to give them any written replies or promises. The assembly at Mantes retired after two months in session, having achieved nothing.[34]

The reasons for this obstinacy are evident. The negotiations with the Pope over the precise terms for his conversion were still under way. No major Catholic city had yet succumbed to him. The king could therefore offer the Protestants his goodwill alone. The failure to extract more from him hurt the moderates in the movement most and opened the door to their more committed brethen. In 1594, there were further attempts to elect the Elector Palatine as a 'protector', attempts which came to nothing but which set the scene for increasing wrangling and bitterness in the years to 1598.

HENRI IV AND THE EDICT OF NANTES

Between 1594 and 1598, the Huguenots tightened up their provincial organisation. At the national assembly of Sainte-Foy, they arranged their provinces, councils and assemblies, along with the representation of laity and clergy in them.[35] Some elaborate contingency plans for mutual military protection were discussed and even Du Plessis-Mornay was moved to remark that the Huguenots were wasting their time in just discussing *religion*.[36] The legal position of the Huguenots became even more inextricably complicated too. Several treaties made with individual League cities contravened the letters patent of Mantes and the king did not lessen the confusion by asking everyone to obey the edicts of pacification, without specifying which ones he was meaning.[37] The Huguenots' national assemblies became more insistent and their increasing size and length of sessions are one way of measuring this. The one at Saumur in 1595 lasted two months and was attended by under fifty delegates. In the following year, that of Loudun lasted six months and many of the delegates were re-elected to it. In March 1597, the assemblies grew to 70–80 delegates and then over 200 who met at Châtellerault in June 1597. By this time, they were in almost constant session and threatening to sit until a new edict was published and also enforced in the provinces.[38]

The king used some of his most able moderate Catholic diplomats to negotiate with the assemblies – men like the historian Jacques-Auguste de Thou, Méricde Vic, Gaspard de Schomberg and the Protestant Soffrey de Calignon. But they were instructed not to undertake to give new guarantees to the Protestant movement. Royal insistence that no edict would be undertaken which appeared to be a surrender to weakness or which would be unacceptable to the *parlements* of France was vital at this moment. As Dr Sutherland has shown, this was despite the pressures on the king from the war with Spain, a war which Turenne may have persuaded the king, against his better judgement, to fight.[39] While Henri IV struggled to recapture Cambrai, La Fère and Amiens, La Trémouille and Turenne remained in Poitou and the Auvergne in calculated disregard for the king's repeated summons to his presence. Instead, they opened up negotiations through the Huguenot movement with foreign powers and Catholic malcontents like 'the prodigal son' (as the king called him) Charles d'Auvergne.[40] Many of the delegates attending the political assemblies were nobles and captains newly disbanded from the Protestant armies, clients of Turenne and La Trémouille. Through the menace of not paying their *taille*, the Huguenots forced Henri IV's negotiators at least to consider reviewing their legal and civil status and it was from this review that the edict of Nantes eventually emerged.

The pacification of Nantes was eventually signed in April 1598. The king, having recovered Amiens from the Spanish, opened negotiations for peace at Vervins and marched his large army towards the Loire, ostensibly to defeat the last remnants of the League in Brittany. In fact, the Huguenot deputies were greatly alarmed and hastened to accept the royal terms.[41] The pacification was not, in fact, one legal enactment but four. There was a public edict of ninety-two published articles, probably signed on 13 April 1598. This was followed by fifty-seven so-called 'secret articles' to accompany the registration of the edict as a schedule. These expanded on particular clauses in the general edict and dealt with exceptions. Finally there were two letters (*brevets*) from the king. The first of these, issued on 3 April, assigned 45,000 *écus* of crown revenue to the Protestant clergy for their salary. The second *brevet* (of 30 April) allowed the Huguenots 180,000 *écus* per year for some fifty military garrisons in Huguenot strongholds (*places de sûreté*) spread through western France, and through the Huguenot crescent of Languedoc to Dauphiné. In addition, it allowed them about 150 emergency forts (*places de refuge*) and 80 other forts which were to be maintained at their own expense (see Map 1).

In the preamble to the general edict, Henri walked a tightrope between his newfound Catholicism and newly deserted Protestant faith. He spoke of his desire to serve God, his military labours, his wish to see Christians united. Peace was his goal, he said, and he never mentioned a universal principle as vague as toleration; indeed, at one point, the edict specifically envisaged an eventual reconciliation of the two churches. The king assured Catholics of their security in wealth and the dominant religious faith in the kingdom. The basis of the general edict had already been laid in 1562, 1570 and, above all, in 1577, in the peace which Henri of Navarre had negotiated and supported. But several of its clauses were tightened up where legal cases had proved that guidelines in the edict needed to be more precise.[42]

A major part of the edict was devoted to 'the removal of past disorders', the attempt to erase sectarian memories. There was a full amnesty granted for crimes committed in the past. Ministers were enjoined not to preach seditious or scandalous sermons. Forced abjurations were forbidden. Exhumations of Huguenots from Catholic cemeteries were to be forbidden. The edict was robust in dealing with a range of sensitive issues between the two religions – religious buildings, ceremonies, feast days, funerals and marriages.

The basic ninety-two articles granted freedom of worship on a carefully restricted basis to the Protestants. Huguenot worship was allowed in three categories; firstly, on the estates of Huguenot gentlemen who wished to allow it (the so-called *culte privé*). Secondly, it was allowed at two places in each (*bailliage*) in the kingdom, to be decided by royal commissioners (this was called the *culte de permission*). Finally, rights to worship were allowed in every place where the Huguenots could prove that it had been openly practised in 1596 and 1597. This was called the *culte de concession*. These three categories had been established in the edict of pacification of 1570 and amplified in 1577. They allowed for considerable flexibility of interpretation and befitted the geo-political framework of the Huguenots, suiting, on the one hand, the gentry-based religion of Normandy, and on the other, the Huguenot communities of the Midi.

In addition, an important clause (clause 27) removed the religious qualification from the right to acquire or inherit any office in the kingdom. This too had been enunciated in the edict of pacification in 1577 and the letters patent of Mantes in 1591. But it had been badly enforced in reluctant *parlements* which frequently refused to accept Protestant office holders, sometimes on other grounds than the purely religious, but with that in mind. This clause was the least that the king could offer to satisfy the delegates of the political assemblies who were lawyers with expectations of royal service, or who could reasonably hope to obtain remunerative service in the royal financial administration. Even so, the Huguenots would require the continued good favour of the king and his council after the edict of Nantes to combat the prejudices against them among the royal, Catholic tribunals.[43]

The edict also established bipartisan chambers of the *parlements* to judge cases involving Protestants. The clauses relating to the appointment of judges, competence, method of appeal and payment of these tribunals were much more effective than those in 1577 (clauses 40–4, 49–52, 62). The *chambre de l'édit* for the province of Languedoc was already in session following the decree from Mantes and half its judges were Protestants. Other provinces had to wait until the edict of Nantes and, even then, the success of these legal bodies was dependent on continuous pressure from the council of state for the enforcement of the edict, for the *parlements* were adept at ignoring unpopular tribunals and refusing to send cases before them. Nevertheless, a certain case law and series of precedents did develop which was useful in dealing with sectarian problems at an individual and communal level. The lawyers and judges associated with the chambers on the Protestant side were those who became most committed to the success of the edict of Nantes and its enforcement.

Soffrey de Calignon in Languedoc and Charles du Cros in Dauphiné, for example, were powerful voices for moderation within the Huguenot movement whose position in the bipartisan chambers enabled them to speak out with additional authority.[44]

The so-called 'secret' articles were not a sinister invention and they were never intended to be kept a secret. They were an attached schedule of exemptions and additional clauses which attempted to harmonise the general articles of the edict of Nantes with specific promises made to individual towns like Paris or Toulouse, that they would never suffer heretic services within their walls and suburbs. Some of the clauses in the secret articles deal with the establishment of Protestant universities and the training of ministers, clauses which would not have been inappropriate in the general articles – the division between the two was not a clear and well-stated one. But the *brevets* were more important, in some ways the most important feature of the pacification. In them, Henri IV granted the Protestants a very limited measure of independent military and political status. The payment of ministers was assumed to be the king's responsibility (although this had already been accepted in principle in 1589).[45] The payment of the garrisons – the so-called 'guarantee clauses' – was given for a limited period of eight years from the date of publication of the edict in the *parlement* of Paris, but the troops were to be deployed in their various strengths according to royal instructions and their captains were to be appointed by the king, although the *brevet* conceded that this would be done with Protestant wishes taken into account. The *brevets* were confirmed in 1611 but withdrawn by Louis XIII in 1629 at the peace of Alais and, from that date, the Huguenots lost the main advantages that the edict had afforded them.

On the basis of these *brevets*, it has been claimed that the edict of Nantes created a 'state within a state'.[46] The claim is difficult to substantiate, given that the *brevets* were only issued as personal promises of an individual king and not binding on his successors. By paying for their churches and garrisons, the king bought their loyalties (as with the League) and bound them more closely to the monarchy rather than separating them from it. The main articles of the edict (clause 82) specifically prohibited the Protestant political assemblies at either a national or a regional level so that the 'united provinces of the Midi' was officially disbanded. In the secret articles, the colloquies and provincial synods were permitted but only for religious purpose. It is true that the Protestants were allowed the separate chambers of the *parlement* for their cases, but it was royal law that was enforced there (even in cases of matrimonial law, where the Huguenot rules of consanguinity were less strict than the Catholic ones). Royal Catholic judges were always present. Huguenots were still not allowed, even under the edict, to possess as a corporate entity, any school, hospital, church or consistory property. Protestant property in France was still only recognised as the property of an individual. In fact the whole tenor of the edict is not the extreme degree of independence that it granted to the Huguenots to live under their own law, but the degree of dependence which, in practice, it demanded of them, on the pleasure of the king.[47] In comparison with the modest freedoms granted to the Protestants in the religious sphere, the extensive cash payments, indemnities and exemptions from taxation granted to the League towns, not to mention their rights to worship the Catholic religion to the exclusion of any other, put *them* into the category of a 'state within a state' rather than the Protestants. At most, the edict made the Huguenots an 'estate' of the realm in a kingdom already generously endowed with 'estates', that is to say, groups protected by certain privileges. But in comparison with the other estates of France – the nobility, the *noblesse de robe*, or the clergy – the Huguenots remained an estate on the margins or confines of traditional French society and liable, despite the efforts of Henri IV and his government, to become more vulnerable.

HUGUENOTS UNDER THE LAW

Pronouncing the edict was the work of a month; enforcing it was that of a decade. Only the main body of it was to be registered in the lawcourts and it took ten dangerous months to push it through the *parlement* of Paris. For the first six months in 1598, Henri IV's regime brought only gentle pressure to bear on the judges. Then, in a succession of lectures, private conferences and scarcely veiled threats (which reveal the king's political style with great clarity) it was finally registered on 25 February 1599. He called the judges before him to a kind of informal *lit de justice* at the Louvre on 7 January 1599 and subjected them to a harangue of great force and finesse. He stressed that he was not an absolutist monarch demanding obedience without question: 'You see me in my study and I am speaking to you not in royal attire with cape and sword (like a prince addressing foreign ambassadors) but dressed like the father of a family, in his doublet, speaking frankly to his children.'[48] The contrast with the political style of his immediate predecessor could scarcely have been greater. He then stressed that pacification was his aim and that, as judges, their obedience was vital and stability was in their interests as well as his.

> I have made peace abroad, and I now wish to see it established internally. You must obey me if only because I am king and all my subjects owe me obedience, but especially those of my *parlement*. I

have restored the banished to their property; others have returned to the Catholic faith. If obedience was due to my predecessors, it is all the more due to me because I have established the state which was mine naturally by inheritance and conquest. The magistrates . . . would not be in their courts without me. . . .

He then tactfully, but firmly, reminded them of their past disloyalties and what had resulted from them:

I know that there are plots in the *parlement* and that seditious preachers are encouraged. . . . This is the road that led to the Barricades and the assassination of the late king. I am not going that way; I will strike at the roots of all factions and all seditious preaching, and those that support them will be hurt as well.

Then, warming to his theme, he rounded on the judges, told them he knew of all their plots and reminded them that he was an elder son of the Catholic Church now:

Those who refuse me this edict want war . . . you in your long robes are like the Capuchins who hide muskets under their cloaks. . . . You will be sorry for creating this trouble for me . . . my council finds this edict good and essential for my State – the Constable [Montmorency-Damville], the Chancellor, Bellièvre, Sancy and Silléry – I have acted with their advice and that of the dukes and peers. Not one of them would not call himself a protector of the Catholic religion and yet they have advised me to accept this edict.

Finally, he displayed some bare knuckles before dismissing the judges to go away and think about what he had told them and do what he asked of them.

There is a rumour in Paris that I am about to levy some Swiss or other troops to coerce you. If I did so, it would be justified, and with results, and would fit in with my previous actions. I was victorious at Amiens, thanks to the finance which you would not have granted me if I had not come to the *parlement* to demand it of you.[49] Necessity drives me to this edict. In times past, necessity has turned me into a soldier. . . . I am a king now and I speak as a king and wish to be obeyed!

In this plain and direct speech lay the stuff of the struggle for stability. On the one hand, a king and a regime, anxious to establish themselves as the guardians of stability, yet unwilling to obtain it by a demand for absolute obedience without coupling it with an appeal to the reality of things and a reference to the past failures and misfortunes. On the other hand, a powerful and independent corporation, collectively aware that past disorders had brought it great damage, yet unwilling to compromise on matters of principle to individual members despite the manifest reality of things. Principles and compromise, past history and present reality, law and its capacity to change things, personalities and their ability to persuade others that loyalty was part of obedience and brought rewards – all this was part of the equation. Even when they registered the edict, the *parlement* of Paris changed it. Article Two was modified to exclude the second *place de concession* from any episcopal town. Since most towns in France were episcopal towns, this effectively excluded the Huguenots from worshipping in any main town. The majority of the other *parlements* followed Paris a year later, but with an ill grace, each requiring stiff letters from the king. One *parlement*, that of Rouen, resisted a full registration until 1609.

Even when legally binding, the edict still had to take root on the ground. Commissioners were sent round the provinces in batches – each a well-chosen royalist with considerable diplomatic experience and authority; some were former Protestant officers and others Catholic masters of requests and magistrates. In provinces like Burgundy, they encountered opposition from the orthodox crypto-League Catholic estates.[50] The most difficult problems occurred with the siting of the *places de concession*, particularly in provinces of the north and east with their highly scattered Huguenot communities and League loyalties. In the whole of Picardy, only two sites for worship were initially established under the terms of the edict, although, even in 1650, there were nearly 10,000 Protestants in the province. Eventually, Henri IV had to give personal permission for other sites in Calais and Abbeville to modify the rigours of the edict. In neighbouring Champagne, the commissioners settled disputes between Huguenot communities, each of which wanted to be chosen as the *place de concession*. They also disallowed some communities who claimed that their clandestine existence in 1596 or 1597 justified their being permitted under the edict. There were repeated problems with the siting of churches in the suburbs of main towns. In Paris, the village of Ablon was eventually chosen and the Protestant temple was built in a street called (providentially, according to the Protestants) the *chemin des Bannis*.[51] Later, in 1606, the long distance from Paris to Ablon caused the government, under Sully's insistence, to move the church to Charenton, and thus to disregard the strict terms of the edict. In this, as in numerous other instances, the edict of Nantes was rendered a success because it was not enforced too rigidly on either side.

In some respects, therefore, the Huguenots were not so much under the edict as under the king's good favour, and Henri IV ensured that his own personal religious persuasions remained somewhat unclear. As he boasted, his religion was one of the great mysteries of Europe. In its public response to a series of religious issues after the edict, Henri IV's regime acted like a gently rolling boulder which, as it went, knocked out for itself a broader path. Each decision which favoured one side was paralleled by a similar decision for the other. If he supported the Jesuits' college at La Flèche, then he granted the Protestants their college at Die. If he accepted the Jesuits back into Paris, then he agreed to move the Protestant temple to Charenton. If he appointed the Jesuit Father Coton to be his confessor, then he made the Protestant theologian and controversialist, Pierre du Moulin, his almoner. Only occasionally did his personal predilection for attempting to unite the two faiths, perhaps under a national council or colloquy, appear on the surface; when it did (as in 1607–8) it was promptly rejected by both sides as apostasy.[52] The notable royal tact helped the regime too. Henri IV remembered past loyalties and forgot past wrongs. He ensured that Protestants – even the zealot Agrippa d'Aubigné – were welcome at his newly established court. Protestants who abjured (following the example set by the king) were not given such special preference by the king as to give offence to their former co-religionists.[53] In the management of the Huguenot grandees, he displayed the combination of tact and firmness which characterised all his relations with the nobility (see below ch. 6). It was partly as a result of his achievement that the Protestant aristocrats – Lesdiguières in Dauphiné, La Trémouille in Poitou – did not associate themselves with Huguenot zealots in the decade after Henri IV's death. He also discontinued the meddlesome influence of aristocratic Huguenot ladies who proselytised for the faith without care for the political consequences. Madame de Condé remained permanently incarcerated and the king's sister, Catherine de Bourbon, was put under considerable pressure to follow the king's apostasy. That she did not was some reassurance to the Protestants although her influence at court was not great.

In a wider context, the government used Protestant talents in court and administration. Sully's Arsenal employed Huguenot artillery experts like Gillot and treasurers like Claude Arnauld. His financial ministry enjoyed the support of Protestant bankers like the Tallemand family and the Héroard.[54] The court physicians – the most famous of whom was Théodore Turquet de Mayerne, later a physician to James I, who appreciated his irenicism – were mainly Protestants.[55] Henri's châteaux were reconstructed by representatives from the dynasties of Huguenot architects, such as Salomon de la Brosse (1562–1624) and J. Androuet du Cerceau. Inside, côteries of Huguenot decorators and artists provided their décor. Protestant engravers provided the drawings for emblematic coins at the royal mints.[56] And it would only be a small exaggeration to say that Paris was reconstructed with the assistance of the Huguenots whom the city had spent two generations trying to expel. Though purveyors to the court, these Protestants still retained a mental view distinct from it as a result of their religion and their background. Their puritanism and their distrust of court mentalities would never make them completely at home there, not even Sully. But their presence provided a distinctive flavour to the first Bourbon's court. They curtailed the elaborate baroque tendencies of Henri III's court. They supported French culture as opposed to Italianate influences. They helped to develop French classicism as the expression of beauty through ordered, yet simple, classical proportion. In their propaganda, they stressed that the court played a positive part in achieving peace through royal beneficence and through obedience to the law.

In some respects, the edict of Nantes completed the process of shaping Huguenotism into a marginal religion in France. By placing their temples on the margins of French cities it indicated their position in French society at large. In some cities, the Protestants gained some new adherents. In Rouen, where the Protestants finally settled in one locality (before that, they had behaved like their emblem, the ark, and floated from one place to another during the civil wars) and gained the adhesion of a prominent merchant family, the Legendre. In Caen, the church also settled down, although the new temple was not built there until 1611.[57] In Paris, a number of resolute Protestants took advantage of the brisk trade in offices and invested there. Some, like Gilles de Maupeou, an intendant of finances and grandfather to Louis XIV's ill-fated financier Nicholas Fouquet, turned to Protestantism to secure Sully's patronage.[58] Sully certainly advanced Protestants in the provincial administration of roads, bridges and artillery wherever possible. Even Mère Angélique – who would become a kind of spiritual St Theresa to many Parisian magistrates – briefly found refuge in La Rochelle in 1607–8. In the Midi, despite some abjurations in traditionally strong Huguenot cities like Montpellier, Protestantism remained alive and vigorous under the edict of Nantes so that, in 1621, the complete royal administration and the towns in at least three dioceses of the Midi deserted to the Huguenot rebel cause. It was the decade of the 1620s which would prove the test of fire for French Protestantism.

But an edict could not change people's minds. The old venomous sectarianism remained in people's language and memories. A police officer, one of the *massacreurs* of 1572 perhaps, was astonished to find himself in one of his own cells in 1598 for calling someone a Huguenot dog. In 1605, there was an outbreak of sectarian disorders in Paris caused by some student handbills.[59] The Duke of La Force warned his wife of another St Bartholomew's Day massacre as a possibility. After the construction of the temple at Charenton in the suburbs of Paris, the consistory court was obliged to cover the classical marble frontage of the new building with plaster in order to remove the offensive slogans which had been painted there.[60] The temple was in fact destroyed by arson in a street riot in 1622, but it is easy to imagine that such destruction might have occurred a decade earlier in the weeks of tension leading to Henri IV's assassination.[61]

There was a sense in which it was important that religious debate and controversy continued, for this meant that neither side had gained a decisive victory, and so long as that was the case, there was hope on both sides. Henri IV never destroyed these hopes. In practice, he allowed the Huguenot political assemblies to meet with his permission. Attempts to find a new 'protector' went on, but Bouillon was discredited after the Biron revolt in 1602 and James I of England (on whom they centred their hopes) refused to entertain any such seditious notions. So the assemblies became something of a valuable sounding board where Protestant zealots could let off steam and royal commissioners and Protestant moderates argue the benefits of royal rule and peace. All this, of course, would change once a government in Paris appeared to threaten Protestant rights on every side and when Bouillon and a foreign alliance once more provided the Huguenot zealots with a platform. In one respect, attitudes changed dramatically, notably those on political thought and the nature of political responsibility. Among the professors at Saumur there was something of a monarchical cult, for they were well aware that only a strong and independent king could have achieved the edict of Nantes.[62] It was left to a Scot, Robert Boyd, to argue the case for the *mutua obligatio* among princes and people.[63] By 1620–21, even this had disappeared all but completely. And, in any case, Henri IV's regime did not deny the reality of a mutual obligation. At every turn, royal spokesmen emphasised that the king took his responsibilities to his people more seriously than anything else. Turenne, among many others, had found it difficult to argue against the royal spokesman, sent to him in 1594–95, who openly said that nothing was more pernicious than princes who believed that they could legitimately use an absolute authority over their subjects and servants as though kings were gods.[64] A belief in 'sovereign power' was clearly nonsense, Ségur Pardaillan continued, because no one could, because of his corrupt nature, render up everything to his sovereign. But, because a prince and his people were mortals, this was not a reason for not 'loving, serving and revering' them. Princes had to inspire a 'true sense of goodly affections' and 'good words' were not enough for that. Was not the edict of Nantes, later royal negotiators argued to Huguenots at court, a sign that Henri IV recognised his obligations towards his former co-religionists?

So the 'universal quarrel', as James I called it, went on. Towns like Nîmes, Orange, Die and Montélimar arranged their own municipal disputations to acquire a little brief glory in it. The provincial printing centres still echoed to the debates and pamphlets of the sectarian past – Lyons answering those produced in Geneva, Bordeaux answering those from Saumur.[65] The king only intervened occasionally to censor particularly obnoxious examples – those which touched on Antichrist, a particularly sensitive doctrine, or those plays which had a contemporary political message underneath their religious theme.[66] His promises – given in equal measure to both sides and equally tardily put into practice – encouraged hopes. Promises to allow the Jesuits back into the realm in 1599 (not performed until 1604); to accept the decrees of the Council of Trent (never enacted); promises to support the pastors with cash (always in arrears) and to accept deputies from the Protestants at his court (only on his approval) – all acted as useful tensions in France's delicately cantilevered state. With some justice, Henri IV could say – as he did to the English ambassador, Sir George Carew – that 'in according the factions of religion, or at least in containing of them in peace the one with the other . . . il pouvoit faire leçon a tous les autres Roys, *viz* He might read lecture to all other princes.'[67]

REFERENCES AND NOTES

1. J. Quick, **1692**, Vol. I, p. 198. Cf. E. Léonard, 1961, Vol. II, p. 169, whose arithmetic appears faulty.
2. E. Sandys, *Europae Speculae* (2nd edn, 1632) pp. 176–7: 'Neither is it very easy to proportion the parties, by reason they of the Religion are so scattered in all places. Yet in POICTOU they have almost all; in GASCOIGNIE one halfe; in LANGUEDOC, NORMANDY and other West maritime Provinces, a reasonable strong part; as likewise in sundry mediterran, of which DELFINAT the chief. But whatsoever be the proportion of their number to their opposite, which is manifoldly superior, not one to twenty; their strength is such as their warres have witnessed. . . .'
3. d'Aubigné, Vol. IX, p. 123.
4. *Du Plessis-Mornay, Mémoires*, **1824–25,** Vol. I, pp. 183–196 presents a full statement of Navarre's seigneurial authority. J. Russell Major, 1981, discusses his income, pp. 25–7 and mortgaged estates for the Protestant cause, pp. 32–5.
5. R. G. Tait, 1977. S. H. Ehrman, 1936 Vol. I, pp. 600–44 and *Catherine de Médicis, Lettres*, **1880–1909**, Vol. VII, passim for Navarre's dislike and quarrels with Matignon's predecessor until 1581.
6. N. Roelker, 1968, pp. 395–410.
7. *Catherine de Médicis, Lettres*, **1880–1909**, Vol. VI, pp. 249, 260, etc.
8. Jean III de Beaumanoir, Marquis de Lavardin, see Sully, **1970**, p. 39. Arnaud du Ferrier, *supra*, p. 26 Michel de Montaigne, see F. S. Brown, *Religious and Political Conservatism in the Essais of Montaigne* Droz, Geneva, 1963.
9. G. W. Sypher, 1963, pp. 43–5; W. B. Patterson, 1975, pp. 223–44. Other moderate Protestants in his service included his masters of requests Michel Hurault and Jean de Sponde.
10. L. Crump, 1926, ch. viii.
11. W. B. Patterson, 1972, pp. 247–52. *Lettre du roy de Navarre aux*

Trois Estats de ce royaume . . . Châtelleraut, 4 Mar. 1589 (n.p. 1589, LN No. 1537).

12. L. Anquez, 1859, pp. 38–51. *Procès-verbal* in *BN MS Fr nouv acq.*, 7191, fols 112–64.

13. *Henri IV, lettres*, Vol. II, p. 411–12.

14. D. J. Buisseret, 1966, pp. 28–31. Genealogy and additional details of his career are to be found in the Romane Musculus dossiers in the municipal library of Toulouse. For Clairville, Haag/Bordier, Vol. IV.

15. Sully, **1970**, p. 493.

16. Perhaps a third of the assembly were lawyers – see J. Airo-Farulla, 1975, p. 504.

17. Quoted in L. Anquez, 1859, p. 48.

18. *Du Plessis-Mornay, Mémoires*, **1824–25**, Vol. IV, p. 402 (18 Aug. 1589).

19. Quoted in N. M. Sutherland, 1980, p. 288.

20. J. Laborde, 1886, p. 229.

21. Sully, **1970**, p. 493. Other Huguenot gentry mentioned as among the zealots were Augustin de Constant, seigneur de Rebecque, a frequent delegate from northern France to the assemblies; Odet de La Noue, sieur de Téligny son of François de La Noue, who negotiated Turenne's marriage to the Duchess of Bouillon in 1591. Also Georges II Clermont d'Amboise, who expressed himself willing to endorse the opinions of the zealots in the assembly 'with his blood'.

22. M. Lamet, 1979, p. 431; M. Greengrass, 1979, pp. 248–9.

23. For example, Jean Rochelle, sieur du Coudray, town councillor of La Rochelle, who served as secretary to many of the assemblies.

24. *Allgemeine Deutsche Biographie*, Leipzig, 60 vols, 1875–77, Vol. II, p. 593 for further details.

25. N. M. Sutherland, 1980, pp. 291–4. Isambert, Vol. XV, pp. 3–5. Poirson, 1862, Vol. I, pp. 25–35; LN, Nos 1507, 1519, 1578. This followed from the truce between Henri III and Henri IV in April 1589, the terms of which were themselves the subject of confusion and suspicion.

26. *Du Plessis-Mornay, Mémoires*, **1824–25**, Vol. IV, p. 427, N. M. Sutherland, 1980, pp. 294–5.

27. N. M. Sutherland, 1980, pp. 295–7 and H. Lloyd, *The Rouen Campaign 1590–2*, Oxford U.P. 1973, pp. 30–48.

28. A Stegmann, **1979**, pp. 224–6. N. M. Sutherland, 1980, pp. 295–6.

29. Sully, **1970**, pp. 335–9.

30. *Du Plessis-Mornay, Mémoires*, **1824–25**, Vol. V, pp. 451, etc. d'Aubigné, Vol. IX, p. 85. See also J. Faurey, 1903, ch. 1.

31. *Henri IV Lettres*, Vol. IV, p. 5 (7 Aug. 1593).

32. *Du Plessis-Mornay, Mémoires*, **1824–25**, Vol. V, pp. 510–12.

33. This magnificent *cahier* remains unpublished in *BN MS Dupuy* 213.

34. L. Anquez, 1859, pp. 61, etc.

35. *Ibid.*, and d'Aubigné, Vol. IX, p. 85.

36. *Du Plessis-Mornay, Mémoires*. **1824–25**, Vol. V, pp. 510–12.

37. Fontanon, Vol. IV, p. 360 (15 Nov. 1594).

38. N. M. Sutherland, 1980, p. 323.

39. *Ibid.*, pp. 308–20.

40. *Ibid.*, p. 321; also M. Greengrass, 1981, pp. 336–7; Estoile, **1948**, p. 504.
41. d'Aubigné, Vol. IX, p. 281.
42. For example, clauses v (Protestant fortresses), xviii (forced baptisms), xxviii (burial grounds), etc.
43. J. Airo-Farulla, 1975, pp. 510–12.
44. The point is made in F. Garrisson, 1950, for both the commissioners of the edict and the chambers.
45. These had already been accepted by Henri III in April 1589.
46. E. Lavisse, 1904, Vol. VI, p. 423.
47. Points all made in C. Benoist, 1900, and reviewed in D. Ligou, 1968, pp. 20–2.
48. Estoile, **1948**, pp. 555–6.
49. A Chamberland, 1904, explains this reference, *Infra*, p. 96.
50. J. Proudhon, 1959, pp. 225–49. D. Ligou, 1968, pp. 23–5.
51. J. Pannier, 1911, pp. 101 *et seq.*
52. W. B. Patterson, 1975, pp. 223–44. Estoile, **1958**, pp. 271–2. François Hotman's son, Jean Hotman de Villiers, a diplomat, was much involved in the proposals of 1606–7.
53. When the treasurer Sancy converted to Catholicism in 1597 he wept before the papal legate and Henri IV remarked that he should have worn a turban (Estoile, **1948**, p. 504). *Ibid.*, pp. 603–4 for the king's wry comments on the conversion of a Normandy gentleman and the *intendant de finance*, Gilles de Maupeou.
54. J. Pannier, 1911, pp. 180–7; B. Barbiche, 1978, p. 191.
55. R. Mousnier, 1970, pp. 57–60. His father, Louis Turquet de Mayerne, wrote an interesting work of political economy which reflected the more fluid social structure of the French Midi.
56. R. Coope, 1972.
57. P. Benedict, 1981, pp. 230–2. M. S. Lamet, 1979, pp. 439–40.
58. G. de Maupeou, 1959, pp. 120–37; see also n. 53 above.
59. Estoile, **1948**, p. 170. This was at the time of St Bartholomew and also just after the date when Huguenots had to surrender some of their *places de sûreté*.
60. J. Pannier, 1911, pp. 454–61.
61. *Ibid.*, pp. 544–61.
62. H. Kretzer, 1977, pp. 54–75.
63. Boyd was professor at Saumur from 1608–14. His commentary on the Epistle to the Ephesians was later published by André Rivet in 1652.
64. Sully, **1970**, pp. 508–19.
65. Pierre du Moulin, the principal Protestant controversialist is treated in L. Rimbault, 1966, esp. pp. 26–61. For provincial disputations, see M. S. Lamet, 1979, pp. 433–6 (Caen); P. Koch, 1940, pp. 9–21 (Nîmes); P. Joutard, 1976, pp. 26–31 (Lyons); L. Desgraves, 1960, pp. xvi–xxxii and bibliographical descriptions (La Rochelle).
66. A. Soman, 1973, pp. 273–88.
67. G. Carew, **1749**, p. 441.

Chapter 4

FINANCIAL RECOVERY

THE SECRET OF FINANCE

French royal finances were a complex arcanum in the *ancien régime*. Few were privy to its secrets, perhaps only the intendants of finance who advised a council of *surintendant* of finances which, in turn, was responsible to the privy council. Each year, the intendants drew up a draft budget in August. When the king had approved it, the main tax, the *taille*, was repartitioned among the financial regions with the assistance of regional treasurers. In sixteen regions (*généralités*) they supervised local officials called *élus* spread through 140 *élections* which in turn saw the apportionment of the tax among 23,200 parishes in the *pays d'élection*.[1] There were also five 'small generalities' in the provinces of Burgundy, Provence, Languedoc and Dauphiné – small because the amount of revenue they collected was much smaller than the others in comparison with the geographical size of their regions. In some provinces (Brittany, Dauphiné and Normandy), *élus* or other royal officials oversaw the apportionment and collection of *taille*. In others (Languedoc, Provence and Burgundy), officials appointed by local representative assemblies did the job. Here, these assemblies retained a degree of authority over how much tax was collected and these were the true *pays d'états*. All the details of repartition and collection were supposed to be kept secret and were eventually incorporated into the royal budget (the *état du roi*) which was presented to the privy council in January each year.[2] Most other sources of revenue – indirect taxes, customs, *gabelles* (the tax on the sale of salt in various regions of France) – were the subject of individual contracts with tax farmers which were handled by the intendants of finance. Sales of royal office were undertaken in a similar way with revenues being handled by a special treasurer. The secrecy was regarded as essential to the king's credit-worthiness. Pressures to reveal the royal budget from estates general were bound to be treated with suspicion and unlikely to achieve a favourable result. Any reform of royal finance, as a result had to come from within. The suspicion of corrupt practices remained deeply ingrained among those who were not a party to its secrets. The author of the *Secret of the Finances* (1581) supported the demands of the provincial estates for greater public accountability and threatened to reveal the names of 214 families who had grown immensely rich from the profits of royal financial administration and tax farming.[3]

The financial system had not collapsed during the civil wars but it had proved hopelessly inadequate to meet royal demands.[4] Civil war cut the king's income from the *taille* and, at the same time, increased his military expenditure. The king had to borrow money and, once peace came, was required to attempt to liquidate the debts at a time when it was politically imprudent to increase taxation. By 1588, when the king was forced to present a budgetary statement to the estates general, he declared a capital debt of 138 million *livres* and a deficit of 12 million *livres* on that year's income.[5] Among the public debt, contemporaries included the mortgaged royal domains and forests, much of which had been alienated by 1560. They also included the *rentes* and other public debts to foreign powers. By 1588, the French king was owing money to Elizabeth I, many German princes, the Grand Duke of Tuscany and the Swiss cantons. There was also a debt of about 1.8 million *livres* on Lyons, some of it originating before the civil wars began. There were also many loans from Italian financiers still outstanding. Even the crown jewels were mortgaged to Orazio Rucellai, to whom the king owed in 1589 over a quarter of a million *livres*.[6]

There was a surrealist quality to French finances by this date which it is as difficult for historians to interpret as it was for contemporaries to accept. It was undoubtedly the case that the levels of extraordinary taxation had risen substantially in the reign of Henri III, but so had the debts. Contemporaries tended to ignore the effects of inflation and to regard the discrepancy as the results of corruption. They also did not include the creation of offices, their sale and resale, as part of royal borrowing. although it was a process intimately connected with the national debt. It offered an immediate, additional source of revenue, but, in the longer term, the payment of salaries to them constituted another kind of interest charged to the revenue, even though the king regularly defaulted on their payment. In this mirror world, in which supernumerary offices were created to pay for debts, lay the origins of a dropsical administration which contemporaries readily saw as limp with malversation and apparently incapable of undertaking its own reform.

The *surintendant des finances* and the intendants were most vulnerable to the charge of corruption. François d'O, seigneur de Frênes and Maillebois (1551–94), was *surintendant* from 1578 to 1594 and widely held to have presided over a cabal of tax farmers, intendants and foreign financiers which diverted large sums of public money to private pockets.[7] When he died, his house in Paris was ransacked by angry Parisians claiming to be his creditors.[8] Royal treasurers, *trésoriers de l'épargne*. were also suspected of corruption because there was no public treasury and large supplies of money were thus stored in their private houses. The office of treasurer was an expensive one and attracted rich individuals to it because there was a handling charge on all cash which passed through the treasurers' hands as well as interest on all short-term loans.[9] A succession of treasurers required special royal immunity from investigation for alleged financial irregularities.[10] The popular belief in Paris of their corruptibility was strengthened by the discovery of a vast coin hoard under the floorboards of the study of Pierre Molan, the current royal treasurer, by the *Sixteen* in March 1589.[11] In 1597, Molan was the first to pay for his exemption from an inquiry into financial malpractice although, according to one senior government official, he was 'the most culpable'.[12] To members of the *chambre des comptes* in Paris, the chief auditing court of royal finances, corruption lay most evidently in the growth of the *comptants*, directives to the royal or provincial treasurers to disburse money without regard to the budget and for undisclosed purposes.[13] One of its judges went through selected years of the royal accounts to show how the use of *comptants* had grown dramatically in the course of Henri III's reign in order to provide cash gifts to favourites and financiers and destroying the reality of the budget.[14] In fact, this was bound to be disrupted in wartime and, in 1586, the distinction between ordinary and extraordinary revenue was dropped in order to release all available resources for the military effort.[15] In addition, mititary governors, provincial estates and towns levied taxes without royal authority on both royal and League regions. In November 1589 a royal edict – neither the first nor last of its kind – forbad the governors of towns from levying taxes for their garrisons without royal permission.[16] In April 1590, another prohibited all levies without proper royal authorisation. In January 1593, there was another effort to forbid this and all commanders were instructed not to seize royal funds which had been collected. In February 1593, taxation without royal permission was condemned in Brittany; in August illegal taxes on vineyards were prohibited.[17] These and many other expedients became part of the wartime financial burdens so that the secrets of finance threatened to lie close to the butt of a pistol.

ROYAL DEBTS AND THIER CONSEQUENCES (1589–96)

In a famous aphorism, Henri IV is supposed to have remarked that he ascended the throne as 'a King without a kingdom, a husband without a wife and a warrior without money'.[18] He needed the expertise of the royal financial administrators of his predecessor and he negotiated with François d'O in August 1589 for his loyalties and those of his financial circle.[19] As a resolved Catholic, an able soldier with an important following in Normandy and a vigorous financier, François d'O was able to extract considerable concessions from the new king and was responsible for the king's declaration of August 1589 whose leniency towards Catholics in royal office was so offensive to his co-religionists.[20] This was the first of a series of consequences to flow from the king's financial plight. In September 1589, he accepted the responsibility for paying for the debts of Henri III although he had no immediate means of satisfying these creditors.[21] This was an essential prerequisite for gaining further credit from them, since some of these debts were to the Elector Palatine (old Huguenot war debts which the king had underwritten in 1576) who was likely to be a major supplier of further foreign credit for the new king.[22] Similarly, it was vital to hold the English and Swiss to his alliance and not to alienate them by refusing to recognise their past credit to the monarchy. In a more general sense, it may have been important to try and preserve the myth that the French king would, unlike his Spanish counterpart, honour his international debts.

The king's military campaigns and objectives also became dominated by his financial position. His principal mercenary captain in 1587–89 had been François, Baron de Dompmartin with whom he reached a complex agreement on 14 August 1589 to raise 1,500 cavalry for the royal army in order to sustain it in the short term.[23] But, by December 1589, the king was already lamenting that nothing defeated him more than the failure of the revenue for his troops.[24] The victory at Ivry in March 1590 was not exploited because François d'O had to negotiate with the Swiss troops and satisfy their demands for pay. In September 1590, Henri IV was forced to lift the siege of Paris, not only because the Duke of Parma had reinforced the capital, but also because part of the royal army had 'broken'. Elizabeth I's envoy reported the disbanding of her own troops among others as 'so strange unto me as seeing of it I kanne scarce believe ytt'.[25] In July 1591, the siege of Noyon had to be abandoned in order to pay the remaining Swiss off and collect new forces raised by Christian of Anhalt from Germany. A year later, in July 1592, Anhalt was also threatening to retire as he was owed over 3 million *livres*. In March 1593, there were further problems with new contingents of Swiss –

the debts to Swiss cantons and colonels by this date were between 9 and 12 million *livres*. The English and Palatine governments had effectively refused to advance any further credit.[26] In 1595, the Burgundy campaign was halted because the Swiss refused to cross the Marne until their immediate demands were settled.[27]

Other consequences of royal indebtedness appear in a memorandum to the king in July 1591, probably prepared by François d'O at the camp of Epernay. The realm, it said, had suffered a 'great and cruel war' for three and a half years. The means to sustain it were exhausted. The domain was almost completely mortgaged; no further loans could be anticipated from towns, merchants or provincial estates with any reliability or on any scale. Even the *taille* was faltering in Normandy (which paid a disproportionately heavy burden of taxation) where 'a great proportion of the villages were either abandoned or half depopulated . . .'. Financial assistance from abroad was the only remaining resource. If the king's Protestant allies merely gave him 'general sweet talk' (*'belles parolles generalles'*) then he must consider conversion to the Catholic religion within six months as the only possible way of gaining a general truce and opening up new sources of revenue at home and abroad. Huguenots, then and later, advised him to exploit the wealth of the Catholic Church more vigorously, but there were clearly political dangers in alienating moderate Catholic opinion while, in many Huguenot areas, ecclesiastical wealth was already on lease to laymen.[28] Many bishoprics were also in Navarre's hands because the Papacy refused to confirm any of the king's nominations to them. So the king ignored the advice from both sides but, by March 1593, the financial position was desperate and François Dompmartin was trying to scrape together 50,000 *écus* from the Normandy receipts to meet the most immediate and pressing of the mercenary soldiers' demands and keep them in the field.[29] While the more immediate political considerations dominated the royal decision to convert, there is no doubt that financial pressure pushed him in the same direction.

The pacification of the League was not, in the short term, a great financial benefit. The enormous gratifications to League nobles and cities were very expensive for the royal treasury – how much they totalled depended on when the account was drawn up, because the money was not all paid out at once.[30] Sully's account in 1605 was of just over 32 million *livres*. Already in 1594, the scale of the *comptants* proved the enormous strains that these pensions placed on the royal financial administration. The pressures were increased by a string of arrears granting release or postponement from arrears of taxation which were unpaid.[31] In April 1594, these were applied generally so that all unpaid *tailles* and military levies for the years 1589–92 were cancelled in the loyal parts of the kingdom and a delay was granted for the payment of the *taille* in 1593.[32] The taxes levied on the French

Church were also abandoned for the years 1589–92.[33] The necessity
for these moves appeared in the peasant rebellions and popular
sedition in the south-west and increased resentments towards tax
collectors elsewhere. In the Paris region, tax receivers had to be
protected by a force of forty-five armed guards in January 1594.[34]
The search for expediencies to meet the royal debts continued so that
there were new and extensive sales of royal offices (including *alternats* –
those supernumerary positions where two men shared the same
office and its salary). Titles to nobility were sold in Normandy and
elsewhere. The *élus*, theoretically exempt from taxation, found themselves among those who paid revenues to the king. Other officers
were pressed for forced loans.[35] Inevitably, there were vigorous
protests from the *chambre des comptes* and the *parlement* in Paris
as well as among representative assemblies in the provinces.[36] In
Dauphiné, the first royal levy to be raised without the consent of the
estates began in 1594, while the estates of Normandy were also not
called in that year.[37] The problems of Henri III's reign appeared to
be repeating themselves.

Like his predecessor Henri IV publicly committed himself to
reform. Although he assumed Henri III's debts and inherited his
surintendant, Henri IV tried to distance himself from the court and
its supposed corruption. In fact, there was no court from March 1589,
when Henri III dismissed it, until at least 1598 and probably not
completely until the king's marriage to Marie de Médicis in 1600.[38]
When François d'O died in October 1594, the king placed the direction of finances into commission, appointing robust, reliable and
elderly military commanders like Montmorency-Damville, Schomberg and the Duke of Nevers to serve on it.[39] At the same time, the
council of finance was to observe strict budgetary propriety, to investigate every pension and assign it properly on the revenue, to ensure
that every imposition was properly authorised by royal commission,
and to record every creation of royal office with the name of the
individual who had bought it, for how much, and the amount of the
salary which was to be paid.[40]

The council of finance promptly began its work and, with the
assistance of its administrators like Pierre Forget de Fresnes
(1544–1610), Nicolas Harlay de Sancy and Pomponne de Bellièvre,
it ordered investigations into alienations of the royal domain, the sale
of ecclesiastical property, the salt farmers and the military levies. It
issued a general decree to regulate many aspects of tax collection.[41]
Provincial treasurers were asked to enumerate every extraordinary
tax levy and investigate the royal officials, their salaries and rights.
Efforts were made to ensure that all those who should pay tax,
actually did so and that villages whose tax had been reduced because
of wartime devastation were in fact the ones that had most suffered.
In fact, some provincial treasurers complained about the vigour of

these inquiries and suggested that some of them (notably that on usury) was itself being undertaken for fiscal motives.[42] They were afraid that they were preventing them from collecting essential revenues for the war against Spain. Henri IV's declaration of war against Spain in 1595 was financially, a disastrous step. The assistance expected from abroad by those who had advised him to undertake the war was small. Catholic powers in Italy, with the exception of the Duke of Tuscany, were unprepared to leave their Spanish tutelage without clear signs of the French king's ability to protect them.[43] Protestant powers did not trust him after his conversion. German princes and England offered virtually nothing while the Dutch and Swiss alone provided a loan and some troops.[44] Financial resources had to be found in France and, as a result, expedient finance quickly predominated over attempts at reform. Reductions in the *taille* for those areas worst hit in the civil wars were authorised but the threats to the lives of tax collectors increased. In 1596, the inhabitants of one Normandy village were accused of attacking and killing members of the armed guard sent to assist the receiver.[45] Attempts to reduce the interest paid to the *rentiers* in Paris produced a vigorous reaction in the *parlement* of Paris while attempts to introduce taxes on walled towns were blocked by the *cour des aides*.[46] Attempts to conduct outright sales of royal domain also ran into stiff resistance from constituted bodies, and representative assemblies in provinces like Normandy showed their ability to defend provincial rights as vigorously as they had done in 1579.[47]

Meanwhile, the war against Spain did not go well. The Spanish took Calais in April 1596 and threatened the whole of the province of Picardy. The siege of La Fère proved hard and expensive. The correspondence between Henri IV and his council of finance in the spring of 1596 is a long litany of complaints. To the Constable of France, Montmorency-Damville, he wrote in March: 'If my finances were well-regulated and I could pay my army and satisfy those who merit it such as the delegates of the [Swiss] League, nothing would be beyond me'.[48] To Bellièvre he demanded that a forced loan be accepted by the judges: 'I desire your reply in writing and that it be simply 'yes' or 'no' . . .'[49] Meanwhile, he wrote to Sully a letter, parts of which almost certainly were fabricated by its recipient in the surviving version, but whose tone may be authentic and represent the king's exasperations[50]:

> My shirts are torn, my trousers are worn out, my larder is often bare and, for two days, I have had to dine and eat out with others. My purveyors say that they can no longer feed me because they have received no money for the past six months. By this, you may judge whether I should be thus treated and whether I ought any longer to permit financiers and treasurers to let me die of hunger while they sit at well-laden and stocked tables. . . .

He was eventually forced, like his predecessor, to hold an assembly of notables. It was called, at extremely short notice, to Rouen for 31 August 1596; letters of invitation to participants and to constituted bodies of the polity were only issued on 25 July 1596. Henri IV was clearly anxious to avoid an estates general, believing that, as one of the members of his council of finances said: 'It was too dangerous to assemble the estates of France when the minds of those who attend are filled ... with factions, private interests and disobedience. . . .'[51] Eleven bishops, 26 nobles, 24 members of the sovereign courts, 18 treasurers attended as royal nominees. There were also deputies from fifteen towns who were present at the opening session of the assembly which, after many delays, began on 4 November with a speech from the king. In it, he promised that he had assembled them to follow their advice, and put himself in their tutelage.[52] It was remarked in Paris that Gabrielle d'Estrées, the royal mistress, who was hidden behind a tapestry to hear his speech, later expressed some surprise at his submissiveness. 'Ventre saint gris! It is true!' he is supposed to have replied, 'But I said it with my sword at my side.'[53]

Certainly this was an assembly for which there had been little time to prepare and whose principal task was to provide the king with a justification for raising more taxes. The council of finance came to the assembly with hastily drafted proposals which involved the reduction of pensions, interest on the *rentes* and salaries, with some additional revenues which spared the further sale of royal domain. Bellièvre proposed that a specific sum – 16.05 million *livres* – should be assigned on particular revenues and administered by a special 'Council of Good Order', perhaps nominated by the assembly of notables, in order to ensure the regular payment of the interest on the public debt. This would, he estimated, leave about 15 million *livres* free for the war efforts.[54] His calculations were almost certainly too optimistic and the council of finance was dissuaded from offering this version of the Great Contract of 1610, famous in English financial history, to the assembly of notables. Instead, the assembly was encouraged to investigate the numerous allegations of weaknesses in the French finances – the private levies of *daces*, or war time tolls, the numerous assignations on provincial receipts, the corruption of provincial treasurers (their *bureaux* were disbanded in September 1596). But, by 16 January 1597, the notables had still been unable to find the necessary financial savings or accept a new financial resource. Henri IV was desperate and on 10 January 1597 he had been forced to enter into a major new contract with Zamet and Cenami to advance almost 1.5 million *livres* to meet his immediate needs.[55] Therefore he recommended that the notables accept a 5 per cent sales tax (one *sol pour livre*) on all merchandise sold in towns. Two weeks later, the proposal was accepted and the assembly had submitted its ponderous advice to the king for his consideration. Many of their suggestions were laudable and reflected recommendations made previously in 1576 and 1588. The key question remained, as the Cardinal of Florence said, 'whether they could be put into practice.'[56]

This question was answered, in the short term, by the crisis raised by the Spanish capture of Amiens on 11 March 1597. This victory threatened Picardy and even Paris, encouraging others to take advantage of royal weaknesses. In addition to the Protestant malcontents, there were the Dukes of Tuscany, Savoy, Mercoeur and the Count of Auvergne. The amount of receipt anticipated from the sales tax was overestimated so that a new series of purely financial measures was quickly required. These included new offices in every lesser jurisdiction in the kingdom, the sale of nobility, the renewed sale of royal domain and forced loans on officials in Paris.[57] The predictable response came from the constituted bodies in France. The *chambre des comptes* in Paris refused to register some of the measures saying that it had heard too much about the king's necessity and not enough about the needs of others.[58] The *parlement* of Paris, in its meeting of 26 April 1597, proved even less sympathetic. They wanted the full implementation of all the reform demands presented to him at Rouen before they consented to anything. On 11 May, he went to the *parlement* to explain his financial difficulties personally and a series of important concessions were granted to win their loyalty.[59] He accepted the formation of a *chambre de justice* to investigate financial corruption – the fourth since 1574. He also agreed to set up a special council – a version of Bellièvre's 'Council of Good Order' – to administer the interest on the public debt. But these were palliatives, rather than reforms. The *chambre de justice* was abolished in July after it had extracted some money from royal financiers; the special council was never given any money to administer and it fell into disuse very rapidly, if it ever effectively met at all. By July 1597, the king was even abandoning the council of finances itself and approaching individual intendants of finance like Sublet d'Heudicourt, Saldaigne d'Incarville and Harlay de Sancy to provide him with revenue and financial management.

Henri IV never forgot these critical years. His sense of weakened authority is expressed in the recorded version of the speech he made before the *parlement* on 21 May 1597.[60] The failure of his council of finance, the insufficiency of mercenary armies without financial reserves to pay for them, the handling of royal debts in wartime, and the stubborn protectiveness of the constituted bodies were all important political lessons. The problem still remained of in what direction, and how, could financial reform be made to assist the exercise of political authority rather than being its endless, unhappy and destructive burden.

SULLY'S RISE TO POWER

Genuine financial recovery was out of the question so long as the monarch remained at war. It only began in earnest after 1598 and has always been associated with Henri IV's famous finance minister, Maximilien de Béthune, Baron (later, in 1606, Duke) of Sully. Born in December 1559, the son of an impoverished noble family which had just been converted to Protestantism, Sully claimed descent from the Counts of Flanders as well as affinities with the Houses of Horn and Montigny.[61] In fact, both his mother and second wife were *bourgeois*, although Sully carefully disguised the fact in his memoirs. In 1572, he became a 'client' to Henri of Navarre and followed him to Gascony at the age of sixteen in 1576. He rose through the Huguenot army and, by his fidelity to Henri IV and the respect in which he was held by Catholics (among whom he counted many friends and relatives), he became politically significant towards the end of the wars of the League. His first experiences with royal finances involved the fleecing of barges and merchants attempting to trade with Paris towards the end of the League.[62] Sully prided himself on one capture of 7,000 *écus* which he kept as a recompense for his own losses from his estates while in the king's service.[63]

From 1594, he was a reporter to the privy council and the king had him in mind (according to Sully) for the new council of finance, formed after François d'O's death on 25 November 1594.[64] In fact, he was not appointed to it and became, instead, one of the commissioners delegated by the council in 1595 and 1596 to go round the *élections* to conduct broad-ranging investigations of maladministration and corruption. Sully later exaggerated the success of his own mission (two generalities visited became four, four *receveurs* arrested became eight, 300,000 *écus* raised in revenue became 500,000 *écus* . . .), but it is clear that his ruthless zeal earned him the dislike of the provincial treasurers and the respect of the hard-pressed king.[65] Sully later pretended in his memoirs that, from this moment, he was the king's most respected councillor. In fact, he was still highly inexperienced in comparison with Bellièvre, Forget de Fresnes or Harlay de Sancy. He was a Protestant and they were Catholics; he was also much younger than they were. There was no doubt that he was a distinctive and rather unusual figure, a soldier-financier, a captain of the accounts. At the assembly of notables, the difference between Bellièvre's cautious, compromising and conciliatory approach and Sully's more brutal expedients for taxation was apparent.[66] It should not be drawn too strongly, for Sully and Bellièvre were both aware of the enormous difference between income and expenditure and the need to reconcile interested groups to the king when demanding extra taxation from them. It was undoubtedly the case, however, that after the assembly of notables and during the battle for the recovery of Amiens, Sully's fiscal expedients became imperative and his ruthlessness earned him the king's enduring confidence. In 1598, he was appointed superintendent of finances (*surintendant des finances*) and, thereafter, rapidly increased his authority.[67] He was named successively *grand voyer de France* (in charge of roads and bridges), *grand maître de l'artillerie* (in charge of artillery) and *surintendant des fortifications* (in charge of fortifications) in 1599.[68] After 1600, his authority grew at the expense of the council of finance which became merged with the king's council. Within the privy council, Sully became (with Bellièvre and Villeroy) a member of the king's inner cabinet. Villeroy was in charge of foreign affairs, and, after 1601, Bellièvre's authority as chancellor retreated to more narrowly legal matters leaving Sully as more of a master over internal policy.

Sully was the first to sing his own praises. After his resignation from Marie de Médicis' government in January 1611, he spent the next five years writing the first draft of his memoirs. He then decided to publish the first half of these in December 1638, spurred on by the success of Scipion Dupleix's work, *Henri IV*, in which his own role had been almost completely ignored, and also the publication of the letters of Cardinal d'Ossat and the memoirs of Villeroy, both of whom had been close to the Henrician cabinet.[69] The volumes appeared under a long title, generally abbreviated now to the *Economies royales*. They were composed with an artifical conceit as though his secretaries, Balthazar, Maignan, Moréli and others, were writing *aides-mémoire* to him ('In your travels you [Sully] met . . .', etc); in fact, it is clear that the work was carefully written and rewritten by Sully himself from his extensive annotations to successive drafts. Sully's oversight of the publication even extended to the importing of a printer to his *château* at Sully-sur-Loire to undertake the work under his own roof. To write his memoirs, Sully relied not just on a carefully organised archive of materials, but also on journals that he had dictated to his secretaries at various points in his public life and to which he refers at various points in the text. This did not prevent considerable degrees of exaggeration, special pleading and even falsification creeping into the *Economies royales*. Some passages were rewritten for later editions. As a result, the work requires careful historical use, but its record of Sully's energy, administrative zeal and grasp of affairs is not false. It is entirely typical of the man that, in a month's enforced isolation in his château at Rosny because of the plague in 1587, he should devote himself to drawing up a complete map of his house, gardens, plants and surrounding lands, making extracts from books on topics which currently interested him, and digging and completely replanting one of his orchards.[70]

Prudent husbandry of resources in the state (*mesnager* was his favourite word) was his great aim, and it is confirmed in his private papers which were deposited in the National Archives in Paris in 1955.[71] These reveal Sully's jackdaw eye for detail, his understanding of the budgetary mechanism, of accounting procedures, his imaginative use of statistics. He made personal copies of the royal budgets and codified and cross-referenced them with a key of over 2,000 symbols.[72] He compiled lists of the royal gifts and pensions as well as the household expenses as though it was his own estate that he was managing.[73] His inquiries ranged into legal intricacies and back to the malversation of the previous reign.[74] This is how the *Economies royales* described his activity on the commission in 1596[75]:

> You [Sully] forthwith (as was your custom) pursued all sorts of enquiries in the registers of the Council of State, the *parlements*, the *chambre des comptes*, *cour des aides* as well as from former secretaries of state (for those in office would reveal nothing), colleges of treasurers, treasurers at the exchequer and treasury, and in the books of ordinances, from which you made copies and drew up instructions and memoranda on state policy relating to finance so as to be able to administer this area with such rules and regulations . . . that the revenues of France might be so restored to their proper value, and royal taxes so well managed [mesnagez] and accounted for, that there would no longer be any misappropriation. In this, you laboured with assiduous care and diligence, night and day . . ..

Sully enjoyed the advantages of a long period in office and the support of a king who, as Carew remarked, had 'an economical faculty for looking into matters of profit'. Henri IV sustained Sully 'in all his rough courses which he hath taken for the increasing the revenues of the crown' and Carew added that the finance minister 'hath found great profit thereby himself'.[76] Sully's surviving correspondence, particularly with the provincial treasurers, provides ample evidence for this roughness; it also displays his firm grip on the financial administration and his acute political acumen.[77] Sully may have been wrong to imagine that he alone was capable of running the king's finances. He was not mistaken in believing that he brought to the task special skills and peculiar energies which indelibly stamped themselves on the reign of Henri IV.

FINANCIAL RECOVERY

Sully later told Sir George Carew that, when he came to the management of the revenues in 1598[78]:

he found . . . all things out of order, full of robbery of officers, full of confusion, no treasure, no munition, no furniture for the King's houses, and the crown, indebted three hundred millions: that is three millions of pounds sterling. Since that time . . . in February 1608, he had acquitted one hundred and thirty millions of that debt, redeeming the most part of the revenues of the crown that were mortgaged . . . [and] had brought good store of treasure into the Bastille, filled most of the arsenals with munition, [and] furnished most of the King's houses with rich tapestry . . ..

The latter part of this achievement was what most pleased the king. On 20 July 1602, the king decided (in the aftermath of the revolt of the Duke of Biron) to create a contingency fund 'to provide for the security, maintenance and conservation of the state' with a treasure stored in a strong room of the Bastille to which Sully kept one of the three keys.[79] Revenue was paid *comptant* to the treasury and, by 1605, it was a magnificent sight. Four large coffers contained pieces of eight and sixteen (*sols*) in 1,465 sacks, while a further 55 sacks were in another cabinet. Forty-two barrels also contained over 2,000 sacks in them. By this date, the treasure was about 3.4 million *livres*.[80] Despite the fact that over a million was withdrawn in 1606 for the army of Sedan, there were over 7 million *livres* in store by 1607.[81] When Henri IV died, there were still 5 millions in the store and just over 11 millions of budget surplus 'on hand' in provincial treasuries. A steady replenishment of arsenals also went on both in Paris and the provinces and Sir George Carew described the king promenading on the palisade between the Bastille and the Arsenal, boasting that 'none other hath such an alley to walk in, having at the one end thereof armour for 40,000 men ready prepared; and at the other end money to pay them, even to the end of a long war'.[82] There was an exaggeration here, since the events of 1610 would demonstrate how quickly treasure would be used up on the preparations for a campaign, but it was, nevertheless, an important demonstration to contemporaries at home and abroad that France had the means to mobilise military force very quickly if it was needed.

Underwriting the growth of this treasure was the 'undeclared bankruptcy' which Sully shrewdly and effectively negotiated without endangering France's future credit. Foreign debts were potentially the most dangerous ones and foreign governments were Henri IV's most powerful creditors. The Swiss (who were owed 35.8 million *livres* in 1598) expressed their resentments by threatening to arrest the French ambassador to the Leagues.[83] The Swiss troops were an essential part of the French royal army (the contract for them was renegotiated every five years) and the friendship of the Swiss cantons was essential to maintaining French influence in the Alps. In the Savoyard war, the French government accepted new terms for the Swiss troops and, in the treaty of Soleure on 20 October 1602, agreed to pay 1.2 million *livres* annually until the Swiss debt was entirely repaid.[84] It would have taken thirty years for this to happen but Swiss cantons and Switzer colonels were frequently not prepared to wait so long and many of them settled privately for a token repayment. In 1609, Marc Escher from Glaris, who had 13,050 *livres* of *rente* assigned to him and who had used every weapon of the creditor to extract the interest and principal of his debt, finally accepted 1,500 *livres*. He was later angered to learn that the difference between the *rente* and the payment he was given was transferred to the king's coffers in the Arsenal.[85] By 1607, the government in Paris thought that the debt to the Swiss was only 16.7 million *livres*, half what it had been in 1602. These private deals were sometimes not as unfair as they sounded because some of the original contracts had included payments substantially in excess of the soldiers or service received.[86] Even so, the financial stability of Henry IV's government in this, and other affairs, would rest on the impotence of its creditors.

Other debts with England and Tuscany were reduced in different ways. Henri IV once remarked to Elizabeth I that he wanted a speculative marriage with a dowry which would repay his debts. His engagement to Marie de Médicis in 1600 was a purely financial affair. Ferdinand I, Grand Duke of Tuscany, was owed 3.5 million *livres* by the king who hoped that the dowry would pay it all off. The grand duke was horrified at such a large dowry – even the Holy Roman Emperor would not have asked for so much. Eventually, by a contract drawn up on 7 March 1600, it was agreed that the grand duke should pay Henri IV 1 million *livres* with a further 800,000 *livres* accepted as debt repayment. The deal was a very favourable one to the French king (who had pushed the grand duke to act quickly by promising to marry his latest mistress, the Marquise of Verneuil, within six months if she became pregnant) and the outstanding debts of Tuscany were quietly ignored afterwards.[87] To the equally parsimonious English queen, the French debts of four million *livres* owed to her, with additional debts to London merchants which she had underwritten, were intolerable. Henri IV was an 'Antichrist of ingratitude' for failing to satisfy them. Trade restrictions were England's only method of reprisal.[88] Eventually, Sully negotiated a treaty in 1603 which allowed a third of France's subsidy to the Dutch to 'count' towards France's debt repayments to England. Whether the amounts that France paid to the United Provinces (3.05 million *livres* were expended over the next five years) satisfied the entire English debt was a matter of dispute between the two countries which was not settled until after 1610.[89] It is clear that subsidies to foreign allies, disguised as debt repayments in order to continue the war against Spain while remaining at peace officially, were a useful piece of diplomacy. Debts had, once more, been turned to political advantage.

The German princes were treated to the worst deal. Henri IV wrote to Prince Christian of Anhalt in 1599 that he was sure that the prince would understand his difficulties: 'Those who understand the ways of the world, know that it is not only very difficult, but even impossible to reestablish oneself after such a desperate affliction as our poor state has suffered'.[90] The Prince of Anhalt was accommodating, but, by 1602, his patience was running out. The Dutch, the English and the Swiss had all received compensation but the Germans, who had done the king's fighting, had received nothing.[91] It is hardly surprising that some German princes contemplated support for the Duke of Biron's revolt in 1602. In the years 1602–5, some German princes' debts were partially satisfied but the towns (with the exception of Strasbourg) received hardly anything and the Elector Palatine was kept waiting the longest.[92] This was condign punishment for the country whose Elector had encouraged French Protestants to look to him as their protector. If princes could not secure repayment of their debts, there was little chance that Italian financiers would succeed unless there were special circumstances to assist them. Orazio Rucellai held the French crown jewels but did not succeed in reaching a settlement for his debts. It was left to his heirs after 1606 to accept payment of half his debt as legitimately incurred by Henri III, and thus releasing the crown jewels for Henri IV. Other Italian financiers – among them the Bonvisi, Sardini and Capponi – died without their debts being repaid, and the Italian influence in royal and court credit thus declined from its pre-eminent position in the later sixteenth century. Only Zametti maintained his position, partly on the basis of the huge loans which he made in 1597–98 to sustain the king and partly because his political position at Henri IV's court was secure.[93] He was the king's gambling partner, a personal friend and also superintendant of the queen's household.

Internal debts were more easily dealt with. Firstly, there were the assignations on revenues for past debts incurred by the king. Treasurers had already been instructed not to accept any assignations from the past unless they were currently assigned on the revenue.[94] This led to a scramble for new assignations and pressure at the localities for quick payment of the old ones. Sully spoke of 'wailing, accompanied by all kinds of special pleading' by provincial governors and military captains.[95] Even the constable, Montmorency-Damville, whose financial position was bleak as a result of debts incurred in the wars, lamented that his 'little assignation' on a Languedoc revenue had been stopped. Sully promised him that he would receive a replacement assignation which would be worth something and the message for the future was a clear one. Assignations would be harder to get and more worth the having when you received one. Epernon, governor of Poitou and Saintonge, a man with a different political style from that of the constable, proposed to appropriate for his own purposes a particular levy in his own government in a proposal placed before the council. Sully tore it up, calling it a 'robbery'. The result was nearly a fight in council which Henri IV settled by supporting Sully very firmly.[96] A similar dispute occurred with the Count of Soissons, who threatened to have Sully assassinated unless his assignations for debts incurred in royal service were met. Thereafter, Sully maintained a noble bodyguard for his own protection. Other debts and pensions, promised to League aristocrats, were only satisfied in part and tardily. The Duke of Guise was still owed 5,000 *livres* in 1610 for a debt which should have been settled in 1596.[97] The Duke of Mayenne's debts were also not finally satisfied until 1611.[98] One of the first actions of the Regency of Marie de Médicis was to use the *comptants* to remedy these outstanding payments to League nobles.

A more difficult task was the liquidation of the *rentes*, since these creditors formed a sizeable part of the Parisian bourgeoisie and had already revealed their political influence. Sully's first aim was to discover the full extent of the king's liabilities and, in March 1599, a five-member commission was appointed to verify the *rentes* since 1560.[99] They identified over 36 million *livres* of *rentes* of which 7 million had been constituted as gifts of the crown, and had in fact never provided any revenue to the monarchy. By 1605, some *rentiers* had been paid no interest for seventeen years and the city provost estimated that the arrears on payments were over 60 million *livres*. Once the scale of the problem had been identified another commission produced, in 1604, a series of recommendations. They were that certain *rentes* should be automatically discontinued without compensation, especially the gifts. Interest should be reduced at varying rates, depending on how long the *rente* had been issued. The problem of arrears of interest would thus be ignored and a scheme to repurchase the *rentes* with compensation (for those that remained) would be instituted. There was a storm of protest at these proposals and a genuine fear that Paris would see disorders of the kind which had occurred in 1588. The city provost, François Miron, conducted an able campaign against them, arguing that they went against the king's promises in *parlement* in 1597, that they would lead to lawsuits and public disorder and that the only beneficiaries would be the financiers who had failed to provide the assigned revenues for the *rentiers*' interest in the past.[100] Miron seized the treasurer's house and insisted that, since *rentes* were contracts issued, officially, in the name of the provost and the city of Paris, it was *his* credit-worthiness which was being attacked. Some changes were made to proposals but they were not the ones that Miron wanted. As he ruefully observed, 'Kings cannot be constrained – only in so much as it pleases them – to pay debts to their subjects.'[101] He thus raised the sensitive issue of the *mutua obligatio* which was at the centre of the struggle for political stability. But, as the king said in another context, he wanted

Sully 'to increase his revenue and not to deliver justice'.[102]

Two other operations to liquidate debts led Sully into conflict with provincial authorities. One was the attempt to repurchase royal domain. In January 1603, letters of commission were sent to the treasurers, asking them to search out 'all sorts of means to accomplish the repurchase of our domain'.[103] In the following year, Sully proposed to establish a sinking fund, run by tax farmers, who, in return for the farming of certain revenues, would undertake to repurchase part of the alienated royal domain. The scheme met with systematic objections from the sovereign courts which were not without some justice on their side. Most of these proposed contracts would run for a long time, perhaps fifteen years or more which was 'a century . . . for peace and stability to last in a state as large as this one'. The tax farmers would be guaranteed against any losses but there were no ways of knowing how much domain they had redeemed if the contract was stopped before its termination. There would be endless legal cases. There was an attempt to involve provincial estates in the project, tempting them with the prospect that they could expect to pay less tax in the future if the king had a larger domain. Numerous contracts were issued after 1608 but, in the end, they would not make a great deal of difference to the king's overall financial position.[104] Next, Sully investigated municipal debts. Sometimes this was done as a result of a request from a town to raise additional revenue to pay the interest on their debts. At other times, it was done as a result of investigations by Sully's officials of roads and bridges. Many French towns had fallen into considerable indebtedness and, at Troyes, the mayor was arrested in 1602 by an angry creditor.[105] Progressively, Marseilles, Troyes, Bordeaux and many other cities were allowed to raise local taxes to remove their debts, even though some of them then devoted the proceeds to trying to repurchase some of their franchises from the king rather than amortise their debt.[106]

The main contours of Sully's financial achievement appear in Fig. 2. The principal feature is the shift from direct towards indirect taxation. The total levy from the *taille* decreased from 18 million *livres* in 1596 to an average of 15.85 million *livres* per year for the first decade of the new century. At the same time, Sully increased indirect taxation, the revenue from indirect taxes. This was supplemented after 1608 by significant returns from the *paulette* to the bureau of casual revenues (see below, p. 155–9). The rise in indirect taxation was not painless. Some of the increases came from more competitive farming of these taxes – in other words from tax farmers rather than the population at large.[107] But the main indirect tax, the *gabelles* or salt tax, was highly unequal in its repartition, and the area of heavy *gabelles* found itself burdened by increases in the price of salt and the quantities that each inhabitant was required to purchase. In 1601, the introduction of the sales tax of one *sol pour livre* (5 per cent) to certain towns produced riots. Those in Poitiers in May 1601 and Limoges in April 1602 had to be suppressed with vigour and the tax was then withdrawn.[108] But the increases in indirect taxation were psychologically shrewd. The income to the treasury was not being constantly eroded by the falling purchasing power of money. Increases in the *gabelles* redistributed wealth in this heavily unequal society, since the salt was bought by privileged and non-privileged alike. And during a period of falling prices, increased *gabelles* merely maintained old prices, so that the sense of an increased burden of taxation was not immediately perceived. Reductions in direct taxes diminished the strain on the financial machinery of the state and were immediately perceived as a generous recognition by the king that the demands of the peasants in the *Croquants* uprising had been comprehended.

Sully's budgets bear more relation to what was being actually levied. Unrealistic arrears of tax were written off in January 1598 and, in the following August, commissioners were despatched to the *pays d'élections* to conduct a vigorous and sustained campaign against corruption in the financial administration of the *tailles* and to reapportion the burden around villages where it was needed.[109] This *régalement* (or *ré-également*) was not a novelty – the process had been undertaken in 1567, 1578 and 1593 but it had never been so thorough, so well supported from the centre, or so determined to remove local opposition to investigation. Later, the privy council issued an authoritative edict in March 1600 which itemised and outlawed abuses in the *tailles*.[110] It was to become the most comprehensive statement of the proper procedures to be observed in the levy of *tailles* to appear in the *ancien régime*. Commissioners also interpreted the royal will to the *pays d'états*. In Brittany, for example, Sully remained in Nantes after the province finally submitted to Henri IV in May 1598. He dismissed the provincial treasurers and appointed two men more favourably disposed towards the king. When Sully left, he appointed his 'client' Gilles de Maupeou as a 'commissioner, deputed . . . for the direction of finance' for the province of Brittany.[111] Maupeou's achievement was enormous. He settled the arrears owed by former receivers of the province. He negotiated revenues from the provincial estates and limited their financial independence. In 1599 and 1600, he codified the tax farms in the province and began to investigate the municipal debts of Nantes.

Throughout his period in office, Sully inspired the provincial treasurers to a prompt despatch of their responsibilities. In December 1598, he suppressed the colleges (*bureaux*) and presidents of the provincial treasurers and, in November 1601, he carefully delineated their functions by royal edict.[112] To enforce his will, he sometimes threatened to suspend a whole generality of treasurers for failing to comply with royal requests. At other times, he hinted that wages would be curtailed or that they would be plagued with special enquiries. He demanded swift responses and this was how he addressed the treasurers in Caen in 1610 about the failure of a receiver to present his account to the council[113]:

> He [the receiver] should have presented them several months ago since it is sixteen months since he was in office. I do not know if you have checked his final accounts yet, but I can assure you that he has not presented them to the council. In this, I blame him for his negligence and would prefer to have evidence of your diligence in order to stimulate some in him . . . [Addition in Sully's handwriting]: Messieurs, Your negligence is a great disgrace to us; if you do not mend your ways, I shall inform the king and he will take the necessary action which assuredly will not be to your advantage. Give me a prompt reply. M. de Béthune, duc de Sully.

The result was that regional treasurers ceased to spend significant amounts of revenue outside the budget on their own authority.

At the same time, Sully tackled tax farmers ('the great destroyers of the kingdom's revenues' as he described them) and financiers ('great rich robbers') by holding specially constituted judicial inquiries (*chambres de justice*). They were held so often that they even appeared to become part of the normal institutions of the kingdom.[114] The first was established, as has been noted, on 8 May 1597, but it was suppressed a month later when the king, aware that he needed finance from any quarter to recover Amiens, accepted a 3.6 million *livres* gift from the financiers in return for a promise of a limited pardon. A similar judicial investigation began in August 1601 and lasted until September 1604, when Henri IV accepted the offer from two financiers of a 'loan' of 600,000 *livres* in return for an amnesty. Some royal officials refused to subscribe to the loan and they formed those to be investigated by a third inquiry from January 1605 to 1607. In March 1607, a fourth *chambre* was instituted which went vigorously to work, inculpating several of Sully's clients (particularly the treasurer, Etienne Puget and the war treasurer, Jean de Murat). Sully harangued the royal prosecutor of the tribunal, threatening to shut him in the Bastille. Two months later, Henri IV closed the investigation, requiring guilty officials to repay the funds they had embezzled. Over 1 million *livres* was involved but only a fraction of the money was ever recovered. Clearly, *chambres de justice* were used for a political, rather than a reforming, purpose. They were quite expensive, found it impossible to distinguish between important and insignificant cases of fraud and were reliant on the quality of information that came before them. But they were useful in persuading members of the sovereign courts that financiers as well as *rentiers* suffered alike from Sully's rough courses.

Lastly, Sully exercised a tight control on expenditure. As superintendent of buildings, artillery, roads and bridges, he was in control of major spending departments of state. In addition, he managed the king's privy purse. Expenditure on the court was not lavish. The queen was allowed to establish her own entourage between 1601 and 1605 and thereafter Henri IV refused to pander to her expensive tastes.[115] Military matters remained the main item, but were only a fraction of the costs of wartime expenditure. The *deniers comptants* were not abolished but used to pay pensions to the Dutch and the Huguenots, rather than gifts towards his favourites.[116] Sully periodically raged at the king's prodigality towards his preferred vices of mistresses and gambling. Neither were as politically damaging or costly as Henri III's *mignons* and neither threatened the budgetary surplus. Although deflationary in impact, the Bastille war-chest quickly restored the king's credit. Sully's accounts reckoned that the king was worth over 32.5 million *livres* in 1608; in bullion terms this was about 355 tons of silver. By comparison, the annual imports of silver from the New World Spain were about 350 tons a year during the decade. This perhaps explains why Sully could contemplate a trial of strength with Spain in 1610. Henri IV was more cautious, aware that the financial position was contiguous on political stability; Sully's difficulties in balancing the budget in 1611, given Marie de Médicis' higher expenditure, suggest that he was right to be prudent.[117] The next decade would demonstrate how vulnerable financial solvency could be to renewed political instability.

SULLY AND THE CONSTITUTION

Sully's vigorous political style created resentments within the official bodies of France, and these have led historians to argue that Sully was responsible for constitutional changes which made his period in office the prototype for ministerial absolutism in France as it was later practised under Cardinals Richelieu and Mazarin. In particular, it has been asserted that Sully used special commissioners like intendants in the government of provinces. He wanted to eliminate representative institutions in France. He trespassed in a permanently damaging way on the jurisdiction of the sovereign courts and he established a ministerial style of government.[118]

It is worth observing that Sully was not a fundamental political theorist. His style was more military and abrupt. When for instance, Turenne discussed Huguenot political aspirations with him, he dismissed him as incomprehensible.[119] Sully differed from his colleagues in the king's council in his political style, but not in his fundamental attitudes. Disagreements over the way to enforce royal authority came at the level of tactics, rather than of strategy. The chancellor, Pomponne de Bellièvre, was more cautious, 'an excellent negotiator' as Carew said, 'the treasurer of promises' as he was known.[120] He believed that it was better to recline in the new-found peace, rather than embark on any vigorous reconstruction of the administration in outlying provinces or among powerful institutions lest it awake old or slumbering sectarian hatreds. Sully, on the other hand, thought that, in order to prevent the recurrence of abuses, changes in government should be made while the memory of past disorders was fresh and could be exploited to advantage. The issue in debate was not the king's absolute authority in his state or the constitution which, since it was unwritten, would bend and sway before issues and personalities as it had done in the past. The issue between Sully and Bellièvre was how best to avoid future civil troubles. Stability, not absolutism was the question.

Sully certainly used commissioners frequently to regulate provincial problems, but this was not a novelty. From the beginning of the civil wars monarchs had resorted to commissioners to establish edicts of pacification, administer a royal army or investigate abuses in administration. The word 'intendant' was sometimes applied to these commissioners, as it was commonly applied to the overseers of great noble estates and fortunes, but these intendants were not the equivalent of the regular, permanent intendants established by Richelieu under the pressures of the Thirty Years War. They were never systematically employed in the *pays d'élection*. Their use was haphazard in the *pays d'états*.[121] Sully's attitude, as that of Richelieu after him, and that of the treasurers of France, was ambiguous. He was worried lest too many commissions damaged the ability of the treasurers to extract revenue. He wrote to the municipality of Rouen in 1603 that he had tried to revoke certain commissioners but that he had been overruled in council. In October 1607, he encouraged the treasurers of Burgundy to oppose an officious commissioner sent to their province.[122]

Both Henri IV and Sully mistrusted representative assemblies. The king's memories of the Protestant political assemblies were unhappily recent. Sully argued that provincial estates artificially protected some areas of the kingdom from taxation at the expense of the rest. He pointed out that opposition in the previous reign had taken root in the provincial estates. Social resentments in the popular risings during the League had focused on the provincial assemblies. Politically, financially and socially, they threatened future stability. Aristocratic governors of provinces, on the other hand, protected their representative assemblies, arguing that to remove them was to endanger provincial privileges (occasionally enshrined in old charters), and to invite renewed rebellion. The provincial estates claimed that they defended distant provinces, administered themselves cheaply and that to attack them was to threaten municipal privileges and generate lasting rancours which would lead to political instability.

The council of state was divided on the issue, aware of the strength of provincial feeling but suspicious of provincial privileges. Sully presented the case for introducing *élections* (officers to raise royal taxes) in those *pays d'états* without them, but this frequently became the basis for negotiating better revenue contributions to the exchequer. In Brittany, the only change occurred in the border when, in 1606, thirteen parishes on the march between Poitou and Brittany were finally declared an *élection*.[123] In Languedoc, the province was protected by the constable, Henri de Montmorency-Damville. Damville arranged for a written guarantee of its privileges in return for a large gift to the king in 1600 and again in 1604. After Damville retired from active politics in 1608, the province became more vulnerable and lost some of its considerable financial independence but retained its immunity from *élus*.[124] In Dauphiné, the levy of taxes without the consent of the estates had already begun before Sully came to power and the process was continued in a province where there was a bitter and long-running battle over the system of tax assessment between nobles and commoners.[125] To preserve the province in harmony, it was clearly important for the king to make a decision and enforce it on the province, while not alienating any social group in the process. This was almost impossible, and the decision was delayed until, on 2 March 1602, the king ordered his council to devote a fortnight to deciding the merits of the case. They eventually decided in favour of the nobles and royal office holders and against the delegates of the towns of Dauphiné. The provincial governor, Lesdiguières, was delighted, because this had been his advice. But the council proceeded cautiously in implementing its decision in order not to upset the third estate in a province uncomfortably close to the troubled Alpine region.

The issues were clearest in Guyenne and in the newly acquired small territories of Bugey, Bresse and Gex, adjacent to the province of Burgundy.[126] In Guyenne, Sully sent two commissioners to the province in 1602 to investigate 'the abuse and corruption of the province's finances since 1585' with a proposal to introduce *élections* in mind. The lieutenant of the province, Alphonse d'Ornano, alarmed at the disruptive effect of such 'novelties', sent his intendant, Raymond de Viçose, to the king and the chancellor, Bellièvre, to warn them of the possible unrest in the province. When the affair came before the privy council, Sully was absent and it was shelved while the commissioners were revoked. In 1604, Sully's position in council was stronger and the province's was weaker. Bouillon's conspiracy had not produced widespread revolt in the south-west. The divisions between towns and *plats pays*, evident during the

League, were still present in the locality. Sully exploited them and reintroduced his proposal for *élections*. A meeting of dubious legality of the estates of Guyenne was hastily convoked in the province and a deputy urgently despatched to Paris. Despite importunate letters from d'Ornano, and the diplomacy of Viçose, the council accepted the case for *élections* in Guyenne and the edict was passed. But the change was only introduced with great caution. The issue was suspended in 1605 for fear of popular sedition. *Elus* only began to collect taxes after the lieutenant d'Ornano had died in 1609. Personalities, the politics of a province, the facts of the case, all played a part in determining the survival of local representative institutions. The same conclusion holds for the treatment of town councils. Where there was clear evidence that municipal franchises had been used by political parties to gain power (as, for example, in Brittany), the government made strenuous efforts to curtail the number of elections and the size of the franchise.[127] Where elected town councils had clearly taken part in riots against the king (as in Limoges in 1602), there was also a clear case for restricting municipal constitutions.[128] But in towns like Rouen, where the local autonomy had been sustained by the *parlement* rather than by the town council, nothing was changed.[129]

Sully had some of the attributes of a minister of the Richelieu and Mazarin period. He tried to limit the authority of the sovereign courts, convinced that they had exceeded their constitutional position during the civil wars. He was particularly aggressive towards the *chambre des comptes*. A memorandum of 1601 listed the various abuses which he had discovered[130]:

> In Provence . . . the *chambre des comptes* orders expenditure on delegations, reimbursements, gifts and other expenses outside the royal budget. In Languedoc, the *parlement* sanctions the full payment of the *rentes*, not withstanding the fifty per cent reduction made by the budget . . . the *cour des aides* releases tax officials imprisoned by the treasurers and suspended from office for failing to pay their deposits. At Limoges, the *chambre des comptes* ordered in one year and on one account, expenditure of 10,000 *écus* not included in the royal budget on its own authority. In Normandy . . . the *cour des aides* at Rouen has given an order against the commissioners of the reorganisation (*régalement*) of the *taille* and instructed officials to pay no attention to them either now or in the future . . . In Paris . . . the *cour des aides* reverses all the judgements and ordinances issued by the commissioners for the *régalement* too . . ..

Sully demanded documents from the *chambre des comptes* in Paris which had never previously left the chamber. He also created his own clientele in the financial administration, and used it to restrict the privileged courts. This gave him something of a departmental base, but his loss of favour in 1611, removed his clientele, dismantled the department and allowed the sovereign courts to reinforce their position once more.

The most significant constitutional change was not directly the result of Sully's activity (although his own position reflected the change) and this was the growth in the importance of the privy council. A memorandum by Jérôme Luillier in 1606 for the keeper of the seals explained why it had happened.[131] The privy council was a child of the civil wars, beginning at the time of the departure of the chancellor, l'Hôpital, from office. The various edicts of pacification (which allowed appeals to the privy council), the inevitable bitterness of conflicts in a civil war, the 'factions and partialities' of the *parlements*, the legal chicanery of Morvilliers when he was chancellor, the treaties of pacification with the League (which also gave right of appeal to the privy council), and the insistence by tax farmers that their treaties contain a clause giving them right of appeal to the privy council in cases of legal dispute concerning their farm, all these resulted in the growing importance of the privy council. The growth was mirrored in the number of masters of requests (*maîtres des requêtes*) who prepared its briefs and carried out its decision. They would later provide the intendants in the provinces. By 1606, there were fifty-six or fourteen per quarter, of these expensive and well-paid posts. Luillier looked forward to the day when the reasons for the growth of privy council affairs would no longer apply and when the stability and harmony of French society would no longer require the incessant activity of the privy council. But the whole trend of French government and society was against that. The privy council was essential to the struggle for stability and, coordinated by ministers like Sully, it had a permanent place in the constitution of the Bourbon monarchy.

REFERENCES AND NOTES

1.   This is based on the widely known *Treatise of Finance* which used the budget of 1607. It was perhaps the first budget to have received such circulation (*BN MS Fr* 4020, fol. 355, etc). Cf. D. J. Buisseret, 1968, pp. 57–8.

2.   *Ibid.*, chs iii and iv. Cf. the *règlements* on the subject of the budget in *BN MS Fr* 16626 (Feb. 1571, May 1582, Apr. 1600).

3.   N. Froumenteau (pseud. N. Barnaud?), *Le secret des finances* (n.p. 1581, *BL* 283, c 14).

4.   M. Wolfe, 1972, chs vi and vii.

5.   R. J. Bonney, 1981, p. 34.

6.   B. Barbiche, 1978, pp. 80–2. *AN* 120, AP 34, fols 15–51.

7.   *BN MS Fr* 16626, fol. 150; the opinions of a later seventeenth-century

commentator. CF. P. Champion, 1939, pp. 521–6 and R. J. Bonney, 1981, p. 33.

8. Estoile, **1948**, pp. 433–4; Sully, **1970**, pp. 530–1. An indication of François d'O's wealth in Paris is to be found in the inventory of his Paris residence (*AN Minutier Centrale* LXXVIII, 156, 29 Oct. 1954).

9. R. J. Bonney, 1981, pp 10–12. Cf. *BN MS Fr* 16626, fol. 148.

10. *BN MS Fr* 16627, fol. 47 (*Règlement* on the *remonstrance* from the chambre des comptes in Paris on the discharge granted to François Sabatier in 1577 – which also refers to discharges for Pierre Molan and Jean de Baillon in 1563 and 1565.

11. Estoile, **1943**, pp. 618–19, 647.

12. Estoile, **1948**, p. 504. A. Chamberland, 1904, pp. 40–2.

13. For the history of the *comptants* generally, see H. Michaud, 1972, pp. 87–150; F. Bayard, 1974, pp. 1–27; R. J. Bonney, 1976, pp. 825–36.

14. *BN MS Dupuy* 848, fols. 52 *et seq.* from which the following account is drawn:

Date	Amount of comptants	Additional comments
1523–25	6,000 *livres*	
1525–26	42,758 *livres*	Imprisonment of François I in Spain.
1530	1,277 *livres*	
1540	437,117 *livres*	Of which 417,000 *livres* set aside for a contingency fund – 'c'est le vraye usage des comptants'.
1545	8,950 *livres*	
1550	13,452 *livres*	With 93,881 *livres* to the contingency funds.
1558	16,200 *livres*	
1563	12,531 *livres*	
1570	37,127 *livres*	
1576	538,001 *livres*	Divided into two accounts – 'par rolles' and 'par acquits patents'. 'Icy l'on commence à voir l'exces et l'abus desd. comptants.'
1581	11,774,283 *livres* (account in *écus*)	*Remonstrance* from the *chambre des comptes* – year of Epernon and Joyeuse marriages.
1587	3,662,850 *livres* (account in *écus*)	
1589	45,752 *livres*	
1594	13,200,000 *livres*	'y sont comprins les Reductions des villes et les compositions avec ceulx de la Ligue . . . .'

15. *BN MS Fr* 16627, fol. 49 (Letters patent, Paris, 16 Mar. 1587).

16. Isambert, Vol. xv, p. 10.

17. *Ibid.*, p. 20. Valois, Vol. I, Nos 23, 118, 119, etc. See, generally, M. Wolfe, 1972, pp. 213–16.
18. S. H. Ehrman, 1936, Vol. I, p. xxxix, quoted in R. J. Bonney, 1981. Dr Bonney's definitive study of the king's debts has been drawn on heavily for parts of this chapter.
19. A. Poirson, 1862–65, Vol. I, p. 19–31.
20. See above, p. 72.
21. R. J. Bonney, 1981, pp. 34–5. On 24 Aug. 1589, Henri IV accepted Henri III's debts to the Duke of Württemberg and the Count of Montbéliard, in return for new loan arrangements (*BN MS Fr* 4019, fol. 36).
22. See *BN MS Dupuy* 848, fol. 270 (Estat au vray des sommes de deniers deues par le Roy au prince palatin . . .).
23. L. Anquez, 1887, pp. 52–4, 206–20.
24. *Henri IV, Letters*, Vol. III, pp. 107–8.
25. J. B. Black, 1914, p. 27.
26. R. J. Bonney, 1981, pp. 36–7. J. B. Black, 1914, pp. 70 *et seq*. The Palatinate began charging high rates of interest; its last major loan was on 10 Apr. 1592.
27. R. J. Bonney, 1981, p. 35.
28. For example, the memorandum in *BN MS Fr* 16626, fol. 136.
29. *BN MS Fr* 10839, fol. 40.
30. The figure of 32 million *livres* comes from Sully's memoirs (Sully, **1881**, Vol. XVII, pp. 28–30). A. Poirson, 1862–65, Vol. I, pp. 660–9 compared this with other accounts. Lavisse, Vol. VI, pt. ii, p. 53 thought the figure of 32 millions an inflated one and so does M. Wolfe, 1972, p. 221.
31. In the year 1594, just over 200 surviving decrees of the council granted tax relief to inhabitants – Valois, Vol. I, Nos 342–1873.
32. Valois, Vol. I, Nos 693, 701, 726, etc.
33. *Ibid.*, Nos 1044, 1095, 1536, etc.
34. J. Russell Major, 1974, p. 6.
35. Valois, Vol. I, Nos 1544, 2499, 1857, 2058, 2694, 2842–6, etc. R. Mousnier, 1971, pp. 132, 135.
36. Valois, Vol. I, Nos 883, 2251, 2515, 2606, 2713, etc. J. Russell Major, 1974, p. 7. A. Poirson, 1862–65, Vol. I, pp. 105–8, 117–20.
37. L. Scott Van Doren, 1975, pp. 36–48. J. Russell Major, 1974, p. 6.
38. *Ibid.*, pp. 7–10.
39. *BN MS Fr* 16626, fol. 20 (27 Nov. 1594, St Germain-en-Laye); R. J. Bonney, 1981, p. 44.
40. *BN MS Fr* 16626, fols 22–3.
41. J. Russell Major, 1974, p. 9. R. Mousnier, 1971, pp. 151, 157 for reform of offices which it undertook. *DBF*, Vol. XIII, cols 480–1 for Forget de Fresnes, an important royal pamphleteer, negotiator and financial administrator.
42. *BN MS Fr* 3447, fol. 60 (*remonstrances* to the *conseil des finances*, 26 Mar. 1596).
43. A. Poirson, 1862–65, Vol. II, p. 168. Lavisse, *Histoire de France*, Vol. VI, pt i, pp. 408–9.
44. J. B. Black, 1914, pp. 103–7; R. J. Bonney, 1981, pp, 37–8.

45. Valois, Vol. I, No. 3128 (30 Nov. 1596 – village of Touquette near Lisieux).
46. *Revue Henri IV*, Vol. I, pp. 152–63. There was also some opposition from the city of Paris (*Registres de Paris*, **1866**, Vol. XI, pp. 210–14).
47. H. Prentout, 1925, Vol. I, pp. 338–9. Valois, Vol. I, Nos 3105, 3130.
48. *Lettres, Henri IV*, Vol. IV, p. 512 (Henri IV – Constable, 4 Mar. 1596).
49. J. Russell Major, 1974, p. 11.
50. *Lettres, Henri IV*, Vol. IV, p. 567.
51. J. Russell Major, 1974, p. 12, a remark quoted from the memoirs of the chancellor, Philippe Hurault, Count of Cheverny (chancellor from 1583 to 1598).
52. *Ibid.*, pp. 10–14. Opening speech reprinted in *Revue Henri IV*, Vol. I, pp. 5–7.
53. Estoile, **1948**, pp. 490–1.
54. J. Russell Major, 1974, p. 15.
55. *BN MS Fr* 3447, fol. 70 (Copy, 10 Jan. 1597, Rouen).
56. R. Ritter, **1955**, p. 109. The deliberations are discussed at length in R. Charlier-Méniolle, *l'Assemblée des Notables de 1596*, 1911.
57. R. J. Bonney, 1981, pp. 50–1. *Revue Henri IV*, Vol. II, pp. 113–25.
58. *Ibid.*, and *Registres de Paris*, **1866**, Vol. XI, pp. 361–72.
59. J. Russell Major, 1974, pp. 24–5. A. Chamberland, 1904.
60. *Lettres, Henri IV*, Vol. IV, p. 764.
61. B. Barbiche, 1978, pp. 23–7. D. J. Buisseret, 1968, Ch. ii.
62. Sully, **1970**.
63. *Ibid.*, pp. 279–80.
64. B. Barbiche, 1978, p. 40.
65. A. Chamberland, 1906.
66. J. Russell Major, 1974.
67. B. Barbiche and D. J. Buisseret, 'Sully et la surindendance des Finances', *Bibliothèque de l'Ecole des Chartes*, Vol. CXXIII, (1965), pp. 538–43.
68. B. Barbiche, 1978, p. 45. Sully, **1881**, Vol. XVI, pp. 362–3.
69. Sully, **1970**, *introduction*. E. H. Dickerman, 1972.
70. Sully, **1970**, p. 170.
71. R-H. Bautier and A. Karcher-Vallée, **1959**.
72. D. J. Buisseret, 1968, p. 59. Sully, **1881**, Vol. XVII, p. 298.
73. For example, *AN* 120, AP 12.
74. For example, *AN* 120, AP 30.
75. Sully, **1881**, Vol. XVI, p. 244.
76. G. Carew, **1749**, pp. 480, 485.
77. L. Romier, **1910**, pp. 93–205; D. J. Buisseret, **1963**, provide the correspondence between Sully and the generality at Caen.
78. G. Carew, **1749**, p. 486.
79. *BN MS Dupuy* 848 fol. 191. *Revue Henri IV*, Vol. III, pp. 200–9.
80. *BN MS Dupuy* 848, fol. 192.
81. *Ibid.*, fols 194–6, 198.
82. *BN MS Fr* 3447, fol. 54; D. J. Buisseret, 1968, ch. viii.
83. *AN* 120, AP 34, fols 79–256. R. J. Bonney, 1981, p. 55.

84. R. J. Bonney, 1981, p. 55. E. Rott, 1882, pp. 181–98.
85. *Revue Henri IV*, Vol. II, pp. 50–60.
86. *Ibid.*
87. R. J. Bonney, 1981, pp. 56–7.
88. *Ibid* and see below, p. 130.
89. R. J. Bonney, 1981, p. 56.
90. L. Anquez, 1887, p. 56.
91. *Ibid.*, p. 58.
92. *Ibid.*, pp. 58–67. Some of the debts were later satisfied, as with the Dutch, in the form of renewed pensions in return for political loyalty (*BN MS Dupuy* 852, fol. 308).
93. Zamet's loans in Valois, Vol. I, Nos 3229, 3428, 3496, 3777–8, 4042, 4254, 4483, 4633, 4990, 5121. Vol. II, No. 7212 for his position in the queen's service. Zamet as gaming partner, Estoile, **1948**, pp. 494, 537, 570, etc.
94. *BN MS Fr* 16626, fol. 21v.
95. Sully, **1881**, Vol. XVI, p. 294.
96. G. Carew, **1749**, pp. 484–6. L. Mouton, 1924, pp. 55–9. Sully, **1881**, Vol. XVI, p. 298.
97. *BN MS Dupuy* 85 (Estat des deniers receus par M. de Guise . . .). Cf. *BN MS Fr* 10839.
98. *BN MS Fr* 10408 (Payment des debtes contractes par feu Monsieur le duc de Mayenne . . .).
99. B. Barbiche, 1978, pp. 83–4.
100. B. Schnapper, 1957, ch. vii. A. Miron de l'Espinay, 1885, pp. 206–37. Cf. Sully, **1881**, Vol. XVII, p. 16. B. Barbiche, 1978, pp. 54–6. *AN* 120, AP 35, fols 68–189.
101. A. Miron de l'Espinay, 1885, pp. 230–1.
102. G. Carew, **1749**, p. 487.
103. B. Barbiche, 1978, pp. 78–9. *AN* 120, AP 36. L. Romier, 1910, p. 235 (15 Dec. 1602).
104. *BN MS Dupuy* 848 fol. 131. Sully claimed in 1610 to have repurchased 80 millions; the reality was much inferior – perhaps 30–35 millions (Sully, **1881** Vol. XVII, pp. 266, 437). For these efforts in Brittany, see R. S. Trullinger, 1972, pp. 389, etc. A. Chamberland, 1903, pp. 243–55 (negotiations to repurchase assigned *rentes* in Champagne). Numerous contracts in Valois, Vol. II, Nos 12922, 12924, 13433, etc.
105. Valois, Vol. I, Nos 2115, 5993, 7150 (imprisonment of the mayor of Troyes, 7 Sept. 1602). Statement of *rentes* issued by the Troyes municipality in *BN MS Fr* 10839, fol. 63.
106. Verification of debts at Troyes Valois, Nos 7825, 9637, Vol. II, Nos 10141, 10187, 14206. At Marseilles. *ibid.*, Vol. I, Nos 5058, 7891. At Clermont-Ferrand. *ibid.*, Vol. I, Nos 7146, 9154, 9389.
107. G. Carew, **1749**, p. 486; 'and where the farms of the whole realm amounted then but to 800,000 pounds sterling, this year, 1609, he had let them out for 1,000,000 pounds and that without exacting any more upon the people than was paid before, but only by reducing that to the king's coffers, which was embezzled by under-officers'.

108. *AN* 90, AP 32, dossier 1. A. Thomas, 1882, p. 2. P. Ducourtieux, 1925, pp. 114–15.
109. B. Barbiche, 1960, pp. 58–96.
110. Isambert, Vol. xv, pp. 226–38.
111. Sully, **1881**, Vol. xvi, pp. 275, 280–3. R. S. Trullinger, 1972, pp. 130 *et seq.*
112. B. Barbiche, 1978, p. 61. D. J. Buisseret, 1968, pp. 61–8. Also, generally, the correspondence with Caen, see above, p. 106.
113. D. Buisseret, **1963**, pp. 298–9.
114. J. F. Bosher, 1973, pp. 19–40. F. Bayard, 1974a, pp. 121–40.
115. B. Barbiche, 1978, pp. 99–101. D. J. Buisseret, 1968, Table iv.
116. F. Bayard, 1974b, pp. 45–80. Cf. *BN MS Dupuy* 848, fol. 52.
117. J. M. Hayden, 1974, p. 21.
118. J. Russell Major, 1966, pp. 363–83; 1974, pp. 3–34.
119. Sully, **1970**, pp. 502–8.
120. G. Carew, **1749**, pp. 481–3. R. Mousnier, 1941, pp. 68–86.
121. D. J. Buisseret, 1966, pp. 27–8. R. J. Bonney, *Political Change in France under Richelieu and Mazarin, 1624–61*, Clarendon, Oxford, 1978.
122. D. J. Buisseret, 1966, pp. 27–8.
123. R. S. Trullinger, 1972, p. 372.
124. P. Gachon, 1887, *Les Etats de Languedoc et l'édit de Béziers*, chs i–iii. J. Russell Major, 1980, pp. 306–18.
125. L. Scott Van Doren, 1975, pp. 35–53. E. Le Roy Ladurie, 1979, chs ii and xiv. The pamphlets produced by the controversy are important and very revealing – mentioned in J. Russell Major, 1980, p. 327 and generally, pp. 324–31, 333.
126. J. Russell Major, 1966; 1980 ch. ix. R. Tait, 1977.
127. C. Laronze, 1890, pp. 34–5.
128. P. Ducourtieux, 1925, pp. 114–15.
129. P. Benedict, 1981, p. 231.
130. *AN* 120, AP 37, fols 120–1 (*c.* 1601). Occasionally, the *chambre des comptes* assisted in these investigations – e.g. *BN MS Dupuy* 854, fol. 102 (memorandum on abuses in the *chambre* at Montpellier).
131. *BN MS Dupuy* 851, fols 41, etc.

Chapter 5

ECONOMIC RECONSTRUCTION

THE TERRIBLE YEARS

In 1582, the Venetian ambassador, Priuli, remarked that it was a tribute to the wealth of the country that warfare had not generated the funereal consequences which would have naturally occurred elsewhere.[1] Regions had, of course, been temporarily ravaged by passing armies. Priuli's predecessor, for instance, was shocked at the consequences of the campaigns of 1577 for the villages on the poor soils of Champagne[2]: 'Everywhere is in ruins; the oxen have, for the most part, been destroyed so that, generally, the land remains fallow. Many inhabitants have abandoned their homes . . . .' But most areas recovered quickly. From such figures as exist for population, yield from tithes, production of cloth in Amiens and other textile centres in northern France, it is reasonably clear that massacres, troops on the march, currency instability, increasing royal taxation and poor trading conditions had been patchy and temporary in their effects before 1585.[3] In some northern regions, there was a continuation of the demographic and economic expansion of the earlier half of the century. In the Midi, where the effects of the wars were more prolonged and intense, some places did not always manage to recover so easily.

The wars of the League from 1585 to 1596 were of a different quality and took place in a different economic environment. Their impact was much more prolonged. The distress they produced was more widely expressed. From 1589 to 1596, warfare took place in the north of France on a scale which had not been witnessed before. The mortality figures in cities like Rouen and regions like the Nantais, the indices of prices for Paris, Toul, Beauvais, Lyons and Toulouse present a grim statistical reality which historians have to translate into human consequences as best they can.[4] The historian of the rural world of the Ile de France, Jean Jacquart, spoke of this period as 'the terrible years'.[5] Burgundy's historian, Henri Drouot, said that the province had not suffered so greatly since the High Middle Ages.[6] Economic historians tend to look beyond the civil wars to explanations for France's problems which include the movements of silver bullion, the patterns of international trade and world meteorological conditions to explain bad harvests and depression. Contemporaries remained more naively convinced that economic miseries and civil wars were intimately and inseparably associated.

It is clear that France's commercial problems began before the wars of the League but were made much worse by them. The two most important arteries for France's international commerce lay through the Atlantic and the Mediterranean. Both were interrupted in the civil wars and completely constricted during the League. Catholic towns on the Atlantic coast were periodically blockaded by Huguenot privateers, and merchants like the Ruiz family had almost ceased to trade by 1589.[7] Only well-fortified Protestant ports like La Rochelle prospered.[8] In the Mediterranean, Spain dominated the trade routes across the Gulf of Lyons so that the shipping through Marseilles and Narbonne was reduced, partly because both ports were isolated from their hinterland by enemy troops. Royal taxation damaged Marseilles' position as a trading port by charging duties on foreign ships and their cargoes which entered the port.[9] The Hermite brothers, important factors in the Marseilles trade to the Levant, gave up business for politics during the League.[10] Between the economies of the Atlantic and the Mediterranean lay the city of Lyons, the pre-eminent trading, banking and printing city of France in the sixteenth century. Lyons' greatness was already threatened in the 1570s when the Huguenots broke the delicate tissue of its merchant commerce and conditions turned unfavourable for the city.[11] The Bonvisi, the greatest merchant bankers in Lyons, managed to survive that onslaught, but the number of letters of exchange that they handled began to decline from 1583 and so did their value from 1585.[12] In the wars of the League, their fortunes and the city's difficulties veered towards a débâcle. Its commercial fortunes seemed beyond repair by 1594.

The traditional staples of much of French commerce were also threatened. The export of canvas and textiles from Brittany and Normandy was, as the Rouen city father said, 'The true gold and silver mines of this kingdom'.[13] Normandy canvas equipped the English navy, Vitry canvas was used as packing in Amsterdam and for doublets throughout western Europe. Buckrams from Brittany provided shirts, pillowcases and lining materials in England and elsewhere. In the wars of the League, French exports collapsed. Production at Amiens began to decline from 1586 and imports to London in 1587–88 were at half the level they had been in 1568.[14] Instead, imports of English woven and finished cloths increased into France, with the dyeing and finishing of the cloths undertaken with French skills and techniques acquired from refugees.[15] The Dutch also broke into the French markets. From 1587, Dutch ships appeared regularly in the ports of Rouen, Bayonne and St Malo, bringing with them grain, salt, fish and cloth. When they left, they swept the bullion from the towns leaving them with a shortage of good coin.[16] One mint in the Netherlands was kept at work during the wars purely by minting silver from the trade with France. The English traders gained bourgeois status in towns like Caen and exemption from port dues in Rouen.

Meanwhile, the production of cloth in the Midi for the Levant market also declined as some of the centres for the industry – Nîmes, Alès and Uzès – went Protestant. At the estates general in 1576, there was a complaint at 'the great number of His Majesty's subjects in Poitou, Languedoc and Dauphiné who, seeing their manufactures cease, have taken up arms'.[17] The estates of Languedoc lamented the decline of their native textile industry and there were increasing calls for protection of French industries, even from traditionally free-trade centres like Lyons. 'Foreigners', it was said, 'had gained little by little over the French.'[18] The other international trade to suffer was that in wine through Bordeaux. The wars of the Midi and a harvest failure in 1572–74 left wine in short and irregular supply. Parts of Gascony suffered as parts of Germany would suffer during the Thirty Years War. Montaigne's description of the civil wars is an accurate representation of the damage that had been done, as it was seen by a judge from Bordeaux.[19] *Daces* or river tolls on the rivers made it expensive to ship wines from 'the high country' while the convoy charges and taxes at Royan and Blaye were bitterly resented by English merchants. Wine shortage worried the English privy council for the amounts shipped through Bordeaux at the end of the civil wars were less than a third the tonnages of thirty years previously.

The vulnerability of French capitalism during the wars of the League is strikingly demonstrated by the monetary instability. France possessed during this period both a money of account (the *livre tournois*) and a circulating coinage in silver (*testons* and, in the 1570s, *francs*), gold (*écus*) and small change (*pinatelles*, *vaches de Béarn*, *sols au fer forgé*, etc, some in copper after 1578).[20] France began to feel the effects of the imported silver from the New World in the appreciation of the price of gold and the depreciation in the price of silver (all relative to the money of account). The crises tended to occur at the same time as grain or raw material shortages so that, in the periods of bad harvest in 1572–74, the official rate for an *écu* rose from 52 *sols* to 58 *sols* and eventually to 65 *sols*.[21] The unofficial rate went, at times, two or three times higher than that. Smaller denominations of coins became so scarce that barter had to take over for smaller transactions. In the face of monetary inflation and a risk of currency collapse, Henri III attempted to produce stability in the coinage by a modest devaluation in the money of account and by harnessing the money of account to the inherently more stable gold currency.[22] After September 1577, all transactions in France over a certain minimum amount were to be expressed in *écus*. The measure was a palliative which worked rather by luck than good management. The rates of exchange were stabilised until the wars of the League when, again, gold began to appreciate rapidly in its value and silver to depreciate in its value in terms of the money of account. Spanish subsidies to the League and their payments of troops on French soil flooded the French market with silver specie causing monetary inflation.[23] In Provence, for example, the *écu*, its official value fixed in 1577 at 60 *sols*, or 3 *livres tournois*, appreciated on the money market at Aix to 66 *sols* in January 1590, 92 *sols* in 1592 and reached a maximum of 240 *sols* for a brief period in March 1593.[24] Monetary inflation excited price rises in basic commodities which were already high because of war. The national grain market fractured into a series of very local, volatile markets in which barter, hoarding and speculation were inevitable.

Currency problems were made more chaotic by the creation of mints. Both sides exploited the minting of substandard coins as a way of paying for their armies. By 1590, the number of mints had risen to over twenty and many produced small denomination silver coins with a silver content as much as three-quarters below that of their face value.[25] Many mint masters themselves made great profits from the speculative enterprise which depreciated the value and inflated the amount of coinage in circulation. Eustache Piémond, a diarist from a small Catholic *bastide* town in Dauphiné, reported that, in March 1593, the *pinatelles* of Valence were only worth 1s. 6d. (instead of 2s. 6d.), those of Nyons, 9d., some from Grenoble only 4d.[26] He recorded the appreciation in prices too, especially from September 1592 to January 1593, when foodstuffs increased by 50 per cent and manufactured products like cloth and silk by 60 and 300 per cent respectively.[27] In landward provinces, copper coins, imported from Germany, made their way into France and began to supplant the French coinage. But they were vulnerable to fraudulent clipping and quickly became a discredited coinage too. Attempts to stabilise the smaller denominations of coins were as painful as the inflation which they had caused. Languedoc merchants anticipated such moves and unloaded their poor quality coins in Dauphiné (where they were still accepted) in exchange for goods. Some coins ceased to be legal tender and this resulted in months when coin disappeared from some villages leaving them, as Piémond said, 'in desolation, without cash, and yet pestered for the payment of *tailles*'. The imminent collapse of the coinage was a presage of the scale of economic damage inflicted by the wars of the League.

Towns felt the impact most severely. They were faced with a multitude of difficulties but the fears of famine, plague and the effects of war overshadowed other problems. 'These are terrible afflictions', wrote Eustache Piémond and added, 'God have mercy on those poor people suffering from them.'[28] His diary chronicles their impact in his region from 1577. Plague assumed a new virulence in French towns during the civil wars and was frequently preceded or accompanied by dearth. In Rouen, Beauvais, Amiens and Paris, outbreaks of plague occurred during the first civil war in 1562–63. Bireben, the historian of bubonic plague in France, attempted to chart its incidence; his results suggest a new breadth and intensity to its manifestation after 1577.[29] There were other infectious diseases too, especially malaria, smallpox, and something called the *grande coqueluche* which afflicted many major towns in 1580 and claimed many victims. In some cities, the plague of 1586–87 was to be the most serious attack during the century. Some of the popular psychology of the League may be ascribed to the return of the plague – processions and confraternities were traditional responses to the scourge of infectious diseases. The mortality figures of the region around Nantes and Rouen and the amounts spent on plague relief in Toulouse reveal the seriousness of the attacks.[30] According to Piémond's own estimates (and they may be exaggerated to gain tax relief for the locality), St Antoine lost half its population in the course of the year 1586–87, something of a blessing in disguise, for if they had all survived they would never have been fed by the meagre harvest of 1586.[31]

Dearth in towns was the result of falling levels of agricultural production but the grain shortages were exacerbated by the political problems of the wars. Catholic cities like Aix, Toulouse, Paris, Chartres, Rouen and Marseilles were, at various times, besieged by armies and cut off from their food supplies. In Rouen, the city fathers brought large amounts of Baltic grain to feed the poor, only to have the ships taken by pirates and the grain sold at Southampton. At the height of the dearth in the early summer of 1586, 14,000 people were in receipt of relief in the city and plague was carrying away a great number each day: 'They dye in evrie streete and at evrie gate, morning and eveninge, by viii or xii in a place, so that the like hath not byne heard of. And the poore doth not onely die so in the streete, but the riche also in their bedde, by 10 or 12 in a daye.'[32]

In the rural world, there was also starvation. In the Lyonnais, the dearth was so great that some communities sold their church bells to raise money to nourish their poor.[33] One diarist reported people dying 'of necessity' in the fields. Lyons itself, a town with an enlightened poor relief tradition, found itself besieged by the migrant poor and did its best to limit the number begging on its streets and entering its workhouse.[34] Overall, it would appear to be a reasonable hypothesis that, in some places, the cumulative effects of famine and infectious diseases temporarily wiped away the population increase during the century. Population decrease on the scale of that which occurred in neighbouring Castile in the 1590s also threatened France.[35]

In the countryside, falling agricultural production can be measured in the returns of tithes to churches and in the leases of lands. In the Parisian region, the product of the tithes began to fall away from its high point on the eve of the civil wars after 1570 and particularly after 1585. In the Normandy Vexin, it declined by about 25 per cent during the wars of the League. In Burgundy, there was a similar decline.[36] This was partly the effect of bad harvests and poor weather conditions. Piémond was an amateur meteorologist and he noted the late frost of the 1580s and 1590s and the accompanying cyclonic conditions which frequently lasted well into July and accompanied the pre-harvest frosts. Piémond speaks of seven sterile years from 1584 to 1591 and only records one harvest from 1580 to 90 as 'reasonably fertile'. The decade 1590–1600 was only a little better with good years in 1593, 1595 and 1599. With the evidence of advancing glaciers around Chamonix destroying villages, late harvests of grapes and other meteorological evidence, some historians have spoken of a 'mini-ice age' during the latter half of the sixteenth century.[37]

There was also the direct impact of military campaigns. Contemporaries talked of two sorts of war. There was the *grande guerre*, the movement of royal armies, the great set sieges. There was every sign of the effect of this on the countryside. The German troops invaded in 1587, pillaging and stealing, cutting a swathe through Lorraine, Burgundy and the Beauce that was observable in tithe accounts ten years later.[38] After 1589, the *grande guerre* moved to the valley of the Seine, out towards Picardy and south towards the Loire at Tours and Orléans. The effects can be seen in the Paris *mercuriale* (the register of grain prices) and many contemporary accounts. Antoine Richart describes the effects of the siege of Laon on the survivors in a dispassionate way.[39] Bread was bought with people's possessions in the town. Peasants either sold up or had left their property and fled. Bodies lay in the fields, unburied. Wolves were a menace because, having fed on human corpses, they became more ready to attack children and unprotected humans. For Piémond, the royal armies were no different from any other soldiery. Their strategy was 'just a mockery', their battles 'a tennis match' which would 'ruin the people'.

Beyond this, there was the *petite guerre*, the war of châteaux, the *guerre guerroyable*, fought by provincial armies, garrisoned soldiers, brigands who had never fought in any army at all, a confusing picture of cattle rustling, skirmish, pillage and raid. Piémond describes the effects on his own small walled town in Dauphiné. *Commissaires des vivres*, army provisioners, arrived without warning and herded up cattle, sheep and farm produce to fulfil their commissions. By March 1590, sowing and tilling had become impossible, since there was no seed corn to sow and the commissioners were besieging the town like an enemy army. Billeted troops pillaged, imprisoned local peasantry, ran protection rackets and seized food supplies without authorisation. It was pointless to appeal to their commanders, for they were frequently responsible for it. Bribery of a regimental sergeant or a captain could be effective, but it could also advertise a town's willingness to be blackmailed.

Compensation for these burdens was theoretically given by 'assigning' the costs on the provincial *taille*, but this handed taxation over to the militia with its inevitable consequences. In any case, more 'assignations' were issued than there was tax to pay for them and, by 1594, there was a distinct possibility that the king would issue an amnesty from all wartime debts. So nobles who still had outstanding 'assignations' began to imprison town deputies, billet companies of soldiers on villages and charge extortionate expenses and rates of interest to constrain them to a quick settlement. As Piémond said, with a private sarcasm, the military captains had 'the mercy of Nero'.[40] The conditions created by the *petite guerre* are revealed in tithe investigations and reports on the *taille*. One from Autun in Burgundy in 1596 presents a tragic picture which could be repeated for many other localities.[41] The reduction in numbers being taxed was over 50 per cent in many villages. Beasts of burden had been seized and could not be replaced. Village communities, having borrowed money to pay for protection against soldiery and ransom, were selling their commons to relieve their debts. Individual peasants with overwhelming debts turned to share-cropping (*métayage*) as the only way of finding working capital for the land; others sold up to local bourgeois, seigneurs, or more prosperous peasants.[42] Here, as in the uplands of the Cévennes in Languedoc and the inland Breton peninsula, the problem with packs of wolves for sheep and travellers was an additional menace.[43] The registers of marriages of the age cohort whose youth was spent during the wars of the League reveal a degree of illiteracy among the rural population which eliminated the increase in rates of literacy which had apparently been achieved in the course of the sixteenth century.[44]

It seems clear that the cumulative effects of plague, dearth and war on rural communities reinforced the pressures for structural change which were already present from a high population and a serious shortage of resources in cultivatable land and new techniques. The indebtedness of villages meant they were less able to resist seigneurial demands in the lawcourts and had to sell communal land on which many members of the village community relied for marginal resources which kept them alive. The resources of individual peasant proprietors could only be recovered by entering into mortgage or rental agreements for their land or their livestock which, ultimately, involved a new dependence on someone else. The civil wars enforced the polarities of rural society between an élite of *laboureurs* and *fermiers* and a mass of cottagers, share-croppers and wage labourers which were typical of the French *ancien régime* in the countryside. One recent historian has used the legal contracts for debts and property transfer registered by notaries to illustrate this process.[45] He found that the number of contracts in which villagers either mortgaged land or borrowed grain to tide themselves over to the next harvest increased in line with grain prices after a bad harvest. The loans for grain, usually for six or seven months, were taken out in April or May and these were followed by a second series of land sales in December or January, as those peasants unable to pay off their loans had to surrender some of their land. The total volume of transactions was particularly high during the years from 1586 to the end of the century. And those who profited from the sales included prosperous peasants (they bought 17.5% of the land sold), nobles and newly ennobled families (35%) and urban merchants, lawyers and artisans acquiring their first parts of the rural world (29%), leaving a small proportion for the clergy (13%) who also had cash to spare to invest in the rural world. This investigation was carried out on the borders of France in the Toulois, where the great engraver Jacques Callot was brought up. His famous series of engravings, the *Miseries of War*, was produced at the time of the Thirty Years War, whose tragedies it is rightly taken to illustrate.[46] But Callot might also have been reflecting the bitter collective memories of the wars of religion, conveyed to him in his youth.

Rural distress could be ignored by neither side. There was a widespread use of 'truces for cultivation' (*trèves de labourage*). These were agreed at provincial or local level – initially for the period covering the sowing and harvesting of grain – at least partly so that the armies could live to fight another year. They began in areas of marginal cultivation like the uplands of the Vivarais and then spread to include the plains of the Ile de France and Picardy. Clauses included freedom of commerce, movement of people who were refugees, medical personnel, clergy returning to their churches, arrangements for garrisoning châteaux, and patrols by both sides.[47] By the end of the League, some of these truces had extended into properly maintained truces lasting a full calendar year, a genuine sign that physical exhaustion played its part in bringing the wars of the League to a close.

Warfare certainly amplified social hatreds in the *plat pays*. Agrippa d'Aubigné's epic poem, *les Tragiques*, first circulated in manuscript in 1593.[48] It included a long passage on the plight of a wounded and starving peasant from the Périgord who had witnessed the slaughter of his wife and children by marauding soldiery.[49] The third estate of the estates general of Blois in 1588 demanded the right of hot pursuit against plundering troops.[50] The Venetian ambassador said that it was the lesser noble captains of the army that were the worst offenders.[51] The *Dialogue between the Noble and the Townsmen* said it had become a war against the inhabitants by the nobility and soldiers.[52] In the *Pleasant Satyre* the Baron de Rieux was the representative of the lesser nobility. His oration to the estates general began[53]:

> Let warre live; there is nothing but to have it, of what part soever it befall. . . . Touching myselfe, I mean nothing of all this, provided that I levie taxes daily, and that they pay my appointments, I care not what betide the Pope, or the pretie wench his wife. I am after my intelligences to take Noyon; if I can bring it about and to effect, I shall be Bishop of the towne and of the fields too. . . . In the meane while I chase the cowe and the inhabitant also, as much as I can, and there shall not be a peasant, husbandman or merchant round about me, and within tenne miles compasse, that shall not pass by my hands, and that shall not paye me custome and ransome

The smaller market towns of the *plat pays* shared the resentments of the surrounding countryside. Some of them had suffered most in the *grande guerre*. La Ferté-Milon was besieged and sacked three times during the wars; Dreux was sacked twice. Châteaudun was besieged and then sacked. Noyon was sacked and two-thirds of its houses burned. Sully described the treatment of Mantes (where his brother was governor) which was sacked and yielded 1,000 *écus* in booty for each of the six captains responsible.[54] To Piémond, the nobility were deeply hated for treating the inhabitants like swine. He reserved his particular venom for the new nobles, the Kentucky colonels of the civil wars, who had become *riches et opulents* through war contracts or captaincies.[55] In the peasant insurrections towards the end of the wars of the League there was a striking unanimity of purpose between the smaller towns and the *plat pays* countryside which gave those revolts a degree of confidence and sense of purpose which rendered them particularly dangerous to established authority.

PEASANT INSURRECTION AND THE END OF THE WARS OF THE LEAGUE

Organised popular unrest against royal taxation and noble brigandage first became a feature of the civil wars in the wake of the edict of pacification in 1577.[56] There were movements in Provence in 1578 (the *Razats*), in the Rhône valley in 1579 (the *ligue des villains*) and in Normandy (the *Gaultiers* around Caen). Peasants of either religion became involved in them. They were led by the smaller towns of the *plat pays* such as Montélimar and Romans. Their aims included the reduction of royal taxation on the countryside, a proper representation in provincial assemblies so that taxes would be more fairly distributed between principal towns and the rest of the province, as well as an end to unjust exemptions to newly ennobled individuals and military captains. They also demanded the right to act against noble brigands. Each movement included manifest expressions of hostility to the local nobility and demands for liberty which were not just rituals in popular revolts and which seriously alarmed contemporaries.

Widespread popular risings also accompanied the end of the wars of the League a decade later. The *Gaultiers* reappeared in 1589, attacking the troops of the Duke of Epernon (already renowned for their disobedience) and those of the Duke of Montpensier who was besieging Falaise for Henri III.[57] The peasant army was repulsed with great violence by Montpensier, but peasant insurrections remained just below the surface in Normandy. Two years later, the *Francs-Museaux* and the *Châteauverts* directed peasant hostilities against plundering League nobles in the province.[58] Their example was followed in other regions. In nearby Brittany, Jean Moreau, priest at Quimper, described the sufferings of the *paysantaille* and their determination to exterminate the brigand nobles.[59] Their targets included the one-armed pirate of the island of Noirmoutiers (Anne de Sanzay, Count of la Magnanne) and a dangerous brigand called Guy Eder de la Fontanelle who withstood an attack from a large peasant force by retreating to an island and he eluded capture until 1602.[60] Further south appeared the *Campanelle* of Comminges who expressed their purpose as '. . . to rally and declare war on the nobility and take possession of the fortified towns of the countryside'.[61] As in Normandy, their enemies were League nobles who were conducting a campaign of terror in the locality. The most serious peasant uprisings occurred at the end of the wars of the League in Burgundy (the *Bonnets Rouges*, 1594, 1597), in the Velay (1595) and, above all, in the south-west (the *Croquants*, 1593–95). The *Croquants* began in the autumn of 1593 in the viscounty of Turenne. By the time that the royal lieutenant in the Limousin had defeated the peasant army in his province in July 1594, the rising had spread throughout Guyenne, creating a movement as serious as the more renowned *Croquants* rising in 1636 and 1637.

In a comprehensive recent study of popular revolts in south-west France, Y-M. Bercé concluded that the *Croquants* of 1593–95 were principally 'a party of the countryside', that they were opposed to the towns, and that they did not consciously break the 'vertical solidarity' – the 'fidelity towards their seigneur'.[62] There was, he said, no 'antagonisme sociale de structure'. Was this, in fact the case? Initially, the peasants called themselves the *Chasse-Voleurs* because their chief purpose (in an area heavily dependent on pastoral agriculture) was to prevent theft of livestock by noble captains. Later, they called themselves the *Tard-Avisés*, the late-comers.[63] They saw favours and privileges being heaped on League nobles and cities and feared that, being the last in the queue for concessions, they would pay for the favours assigned to others. In a sense, they were correct in their fears. In 1594, Henri IV was hoping to raise about 21 million *livres* through the *taille* and a further 8 millions by indirect taxes. Bercé is therefore correct to see the *Croquants* within a tradition of anti-fiscal agitation in Gascony and it is true that the revolt took place in areas which had refused taxation in the past and would continue to do so in the seventeenth century. But the demands to relieve the weight of taxation and the oppressions of the nobility were intertwined one with another. It was impossible for local communities to distinguish between the military *taille*, imposed on them by League nobles as assignations on their revenue, and other royal taxation; brigandage was not just a local difficulty with a few captains for the nobles that the *Croquants* complained about were prominent local figures.[64] Some villages which joined the *Croquant* movement specifically complained of their own seigneur.[65] Initially, it is true, the *Croquants* assembled in April and May 1594 at Abzac wood, Limeul and Montpazier to call on their social superiors to lead and direct their large forces. Their manifesto in June hoped that they would be assisted by 'all seigneurs and gentlemen without reproach'.[66] Such cooperation was not unthinkable, for peasant armies had been raised in Gascony by seigneurs in the course of the League. But even in their initial meetings, enough was said to alarm some nobles and capital cities. One assembly called on peasants 'to take arms and raze to the ground many noble *châteaux* belonging to those who only stole the cattle and beefstock of their neighbours'.[67] At another, they complained about Périgueux, whose inhabitants closed their doors on poor peasants from the countryside in need of shelter, and cooperated in illegal taxation.[68] Among the individuals they mentioned were two receivers of the Périgord and Ogier de Gourgues, a merchant of Bordeaux who had made immense profits from war contracts and tax farming and who died one of the wealthiest men of the province.[69] They also demanded the right to elect their own syndic of the countryside to the local estates. A similar demand had been presented by the smaller towns of the Périgord in 1583 and its reappearance in 1594 suggests that the organisation of the *Croquants* was influenced by the smaller towns and *bastides*.

Bercé writes of 'an imagined subversion' among those in authority in the province. At the time, they thought that the threats were real enough. From Sarlat, the cathedral canon, Jean Tarde, wrote of the anti-noble aspirations of the revolt.[70] The secretary to the town council in Périgueux reported: 'They openly speak of destroying the nobility and being free of everything. The share-croppers (*métayers*) turn against their masters. . . . The brutish people have several times tried to stop grain and other provisions coming to town.'[71] A Limousin observer recalled that: 'They menaced the nobility, held them to ridicule, and did the same to the the towns. . . . In fact, they terrorised and frightened many and it seemed as though the world had turned upside down.'[72] Social antagonisms became more marked still when anti-peasant noble bands (mainly around Sarlat) were formed from League captains and Huguenot nobles who buried their differences to fight against those who 'want to establish a democracy like the Swiss'.[73]

The *Croquants* placed Henri IV in a delicate position. Concessions would easily be misinterpreted as weakness, yet military force would damage his credibility and was not easily spared in the last stages of the wars of the League. The king was personally disposed to leniency. According to Estoile and Agrippa d'Aubigné, he remarked that, if he had not inherited the throne, he would have been a *Croquant* himself.[74] He accepted their demands, presented to the council on 23 May 1594, and sent a commissioner to the Limousin to disperse their armies by persuasion and to spread the news of his 'clemency, goodness and natural justice'.[75] For a time, it looked doubtful whether the king's authority was strong enough to impose the ways of moderation on the provincial nobles. By harvest 1594, all was quiet again. But the harvest was a poor one across France. By the spring of 1595, the poor of the Périgord were dying from starvation and the *Croquants* reassembled. The king once more offered concessions on royal taxation but, this time, a force of gentlemen under the seneschal in the Périgord was allowed to attack and disperse the remnants of the peasant army.[76] Their brutality suggests something of the vengeance to be expected from some of the provincial nobles.

This was the last major popular rebellion under Henri IV. Through its history can be glimpsed the real social hostilities of the wars. It provided a test of fire for Henri IV's government, the memory of which was never forgotten. It advertised the fact that direct taxation had a clear limit beyond which it became unendurable given the limits of production in the peasant economy. It indicated how important genuine peace and recovery were to preserve traditional French society.

REVIVAL AND RECONSTRUCTION

Economic recovery was broadly based after the peace and felt across the whole of France. François de La Noue exaggerated when he said that 'France is so populous and fertile that what war damaged in a year is restored in two' but it is clear that recovery could happen remarkably fast.[77] When Thomas Coryat, an English traveller, went through the country in 1608 he only found one village 'exceedingly ransacked and ruinated by means of the civil wars' still showing the visible scars of its former suffering.[78] Some parts of the countryside reached, although few exceeded, the population densities of 1580.[79] Tithe returns indicate that recuperation had also taken place.[80] The consumption of salt – partly encouraged by forced sales – increased dramatically from 8,000 *muids* to 11,400 *muids* in 1611 in the major salt farms of France.[81] (1 *muid* = a waggon-load of roughly 25 hectolitres). Prices for grain decreased with the coming of peace, helped by a succession of fortunate harvests from 1604 to 1609. There was no dearth and little shortage in the first decade of the seventeenth century. When (as in 1604) the harvest appeared to be mediocre in some regions, royal administration prohibited exports before the crops had been harvested.[82] Low grain prices encouraged a diversification to new cash crops – maize, vegetables, vines and oils – especially in the shadows of main towns. These were the regions where the indebted peasantry had sold up to the new proprietors from the towns who had the cash and incentive to experiment. After 1600, the concurrence of falling grain prices, interest rates and *taille* was unique in the *ancien régime*. It meant that, for the peasant proprietor on 15–20 acres or less, Henri IV's reign brought a welcome respite and was, in reality as well as myth, a golden age.[83]

The atmosphere of rural recuperation and revival is best discovered in the pages of the *Theatre of Agriculture* written by France's most famous agriculturalist, Olivier de Serres, in 1600. He was one of those socially unclassifiable people from the Midi, a seigneur who was not really a nobleman, from a merchant family but without mercantile leanings, a farmer only in retirement from his considerable activity in the Protestant movement.[84] His family came from near Orange. His elder brother, Jean de Serres, became a pastor and Henri IV's official historian, while Olivier de Serres stayed on the family estates. The *Theatre of Agriculture* was not the only work of its kind to be produced during or immediately after the civil wars. But its subtle blend of observed detail, theoretical wisdom and practical advice, and its emendations in successive editions, ensured that it became the textbook for the substantial French farmer in the *ancien régime*. De Serres gives invaluable advice on how to rebuild a seigneurie, on the choice of land, the administration of a farm, the cultivation of an orchard, a vineyard or a meadow. New crops – beetroot, rice, melons and artichokes – do not escape his attention. He comments on new techniques too. From his pages appears a grand barque landscape of staged and ordered nature. The work went through five editions in Henri IV's reign and the king had it read to him in half-hour instalments after dinner.

The towns experienced revival too, but it was far more patchy. Some never recovered their former prosperity. Toulouse, for instance, having lost its woad industry in the civil wars, never recaptured it in the face of competition from indigo.[85] Other towns found some measure of recovery on new foundations. Lyons never regained its banking and trading pre-eminence but it acquired a certain new strength as a manufacturing centre for the silk industry.[86] Marseilles recovered part of its former position in the Levant trade through the import of raw silk from the near East.[87] Henri IV assisted this with the construction of a Mediterranean fleet to combat pirates and the negotiation of a preferential trade treaty with the sultan in May 1604.[88] In the Atlantic, the centres of new prosperity lay in the smaller ports of St Malo, Brest and La Rochelle. Prospering from privateering and blockade, these ports then exploited valuable trade with Spain. This became a principal currency earner for France.[89] The export of grain and cloth to Spain was worth (on one contemporary estimate) 9 million *livres* a year.[90] From these ports were mounted colonial enterprises to the East Indies in 1601 and to Canada from 1598.[91] The government did what it could to assist this commercial sector. A proposed 30 per cent import duty on French goods by Spain in 1604 was removed by retaliatory economic sanctions by France. Privateering was reduced in north-west European waters by a treaty with James I in February 1606. Following the pattern set by the Dutch, the king established trading companies for the East Indies in 1604 and one for 'New France' in 1605. The particular problems with English and Dutch penetration of the French market with their cloth were overshadowed by the growth of the home market in which all, for the moment, could satisfy themselves. In fact, following the seizure of defective English cloth at Rouen in April 1598, the French council prohibited the import of fully finished English textiles.[92] This became part of the dispute over the payments of English debts by the French government. The retaliation by the English government, which prohibited the import of French canvas and linen, temporarily harmed those French industries until, in 1604, an English trade delegation and the English ambassador in Paris succeeded in removing the French prohibition. In fact, the *parlements* of Bordeaux, Rouen and Rennes did not register its removal, so that there was still some import control imposed and English merchants were careful not to export to the French market the kinds of cloth which would bring them into direct competition with the home product.[93]

Sully's most positive contribution to economic revival lay in the creation of a more favourable commercial background. With Sully's assistance, bridges and waterways were improved and the currency stabilised. Commercial rates of interest were reduced in the wake of the reduction in rates of interest on government bonds. He changed the commercial laws of France on bankruptcy, tried to encourage nobles into trade, clarified the jurisprudence of French commercial courts and supported merchant guilds and corporations.[94] He supported protection of native industries and attempted to acquire foreign techniques by attracting to France Dutch drainage engineers like Humphrey Bradley and Italian architects like the Piedmontese Bartholomeo Ricardo.[95]

The creation of the post of *grand voyer* for Sully in 1599 led to an impressive programme of capital investment in roads, bridges and canals. Sully insisted on the strict estimation of costs and supervision of contracts in his regulations of June 1604 and January 1605. The declaration of 1604 gave him powers to create lieutenancies in each generality – an extension of Sully's patronage. He chose pliant treasurers, technocrats and former clients to form an inspectorate of all roads and bridges. These officials met opposition from provincial estates which Sully was able to overcome in Brittany and Burgundy, but which defeated him in Languedoc. The bulk of his work, therefore, came in the *pays d'élections*. In 1608, 8 per cent of the ordinary revenues was spent on carefully conceived bridge and canal schemes with as much finance again probably coming from provincial or municipal sources.[96] At no stage before the eighteenth century was so high a proportion of the national product invested in the 'primary sector' of the economy. By 1610 there were new bridges on the Somme at Ham, Péronne, Corbie, Amiens and Abbeville. The Pont-Neuf in Paris and a new bridge at Châtellerault were completed and many others were begun.[97] At the same time, Henri IV's agents in the *voyerie* investigated river tolls and road charges, cancelling some and reducing others. River improvements and canals were effective in linking land-locked parts of France to the Atlantic economy. By Henri IV's death, Châlons, Reims, Troyes and Dijon were connected to the sea by canal. Ambitious schemes to link the Atlantic with the Mediterranean via the Garonne and also from the Seine (through the Loire, Saône and Rhône) were proposed.[98] In fact, the first stage of the latter project, a scheme to join the Seine and the Loire, was begun in 1604 in the canal at Briare, which, with Sully's protection, was nearly completed in 1610, although the regency stopped further work on it and it was not completed until 1642. These improvements had appreciable regional effects, especially in Sully's governorship in Poitou.[99] In addition, they represented additional employment opportunities and investment in technically advanced areas.[100] Sully's period in office witnessed the establishment of dynasties of technocrats – civil engineers, cartographers, drainage specialists and surveyors – who would serve the French crown.

Some of the currency problems disappeared with the end of the wars; the circulation of defective silver and of debased copper coins was stopped by reform in the mints and the enforcement of an edict of 1596.[101] But the underlying problems of the coinage were still present. A scarcity of gold in 1601 began another round of speculation against the coinage and a marked appreciation in the price of the *écu*, measured against silver. Inevitably, the old parity crumbled and, in an important edict of September 1602, Sully restored the *livre tournois* as the basic accounting unit in France and devalued it against both gold and (slightly less) against silver.[102] The edict met determined opposition from both the sovereign courts and the mint (*cour des monnaies*). The *parlement* of Paris opposed a devaluation as (like the reduction in the rate of interest on the *rentes*) illegal and an attack on individual property rights. The mint in Paris disliked a change in the gold/silver ratio because it marked an interference in their own arcane science. In fact, the devaluation probably did not go far enough to restore the competitive edge to French exports in a period of expansion. Other moneys of account had devalued further than the *livre tournois* and Sully's measure of 1602, while in the right direction, did not prevent currency speculation reappearing at the end of the reign.[103]

The currency problems of 1601 formed a background to the most ambitious programme of industrial stimulation undertaken in France before the ministry of Colbert. Sully argued that only the restoration of French industrial fortunes would solve France's monetary difficulties. He persuaded Henri IV to appoint a controller of mines and one of commerce in 1601–2 and to initiate regular meetings of a council of commerce to investigate and recommend new industrial ventures.[104] The first controller of commerce was Bathélemy de Laffemas (*c.* 1545–1611). Like de Serres, he came from uncertain social origins in Dauphiné. The civil wars ruined his business but released his considerable talents as a publicist.[105] He used his position at court (he was appointed master of the wardrobe) to advance his schemes. In his substantial literary output, de Laffemas argued the case before the assembly of notables in 1596 for a grand, nationally conceived, manufacturing effort.[106]Laffemas was France's equivalent to the *arbitristas* in Spain or the mercantilists in England. The council of commerce was the French equivalent to the junta on reform in Spain and the parliamentary committees on the decay of trade established in England. It was more successful than the English or Spanish counterparts. It held 150 meetings and investigated many industrial ventures, submitting detailed reports on them to the council of state. In one sector, its recommendations produced genuine and striking success. Louis XI and François I had already tried to establish a native silk industry in France. Their methods were employed on a larger scale under Henri IV. With Laffemas' backing and against Sully's scepticism, silk production developed in Lyons, continued at

Tours and spread round Montpellier and Nîmes.[107] Henri IV had mulberry trees (on whose leaves the silkworms were cultivated) planted in his gardens. By 1646, imported silk had declined to one-sixth of its value on the eve of the civil wars. Other textile ventures also took root – fine textiles in Rouen, Flemish tapestry in the *maison* Gobelins in Paris, gold and silver point in the galleries of the Louvre and muslins in Reims.[108] Metallurgy remained the weakest sector of the French economy. The ironmaster, Antoine de Montchrétien, remarked that, if a French peasant wanted to buy a decent spade, he had to buy an imported one.[109]

De Laffemas was only one of the numerous 'projectors' active in France under Henri IV. The atmosphere was alive with economic proposals from Parisian bourgeois, Protestant gentlemen, tax farmers, financiers and court aristocrats. Such schemes included mining (Henri IV ordered an inquiry into mineral wealth in 1600 with the prospect of leasing out concessions for exploration through a controller of mines in 1601), drainage (his council created a master of dykes in 1599, and parts of Poitou, Guyenne and Picardy were drained) and the establishment of a national bank (1608).[110] The king's personal interest in projects of all kinds is evident. He was keenly interested in the *canal des deux mers*, planned a museum of machinery in the Louvre, and established a variety of artisans there.[111] But it would be wrong to suggest that everything went through royal channels. Far more was planned and achieved through individual initiatives than through state intervention. Henri IV's achievement was to give some schemes a sense of direction and to link them to the success of his administration.

Nowhere was this better illustrated than in the reconstruction of Paris. Among the public buildings that were transformed in the reign were the Hôtel-Dieu, the Hôpital de la charité, the Arsenal, the Louvre and the Pont-Neuf. As the newspaper, the *Mercure François*, reported in 1610, '*No sooner was he [Henri IV] master of Paris, than the masons were at work.*'[112] Parts of the city were paved and the sanitation improved. Even the pyramid, erected against the Jesuit Barrière for his attack against the king in 1594, was taken down in 1605 and replaced with a fountain and a Latin inscription which ended: 'To prevent the passions [of civil war] from breaking out and destroying everything, fresh water here will flow for ever.'[113] Aristocrats also returned to the capital and reconstructed their town houses.[114] Henri IV and Sully took part in the speculation. They planned three major squares. Two of them were built at the Place Vendôme and the Place Royale (now the place des Vosges), while some streets of the third, the Place de France, were begun.[115] All three projects were designed as an advertisement for the reign with street names and statues indicating the fact. They involved a new sense of stylistic unity and a degree of cooperation from the office holders and the Parisian magistrature. The Place des Vosges still survives, an ambitious Italian piazza, designed by Androuet du Cerceau and Claude Chastillon with a central market square cut off from through traffic, surrounding which were thirty-six pavilions leased to merchants of the new French enterprises. Above the galleries ran smart town houses which were rented to the office holders 'and courtiers, especially to Sully's clients. Meanwhile Sully was involved in the construction of a completely new town in the principality of Boisbelle in the Nivernais, which he had acquired from Charles de Gonzague, Duke of Nevers.[116] In December 1608, the charter for the new town of 'Henrichemont' was unveiled. Its subscribers included Sully's financiers and colleagues in the Arsenal. When Sully fell from power, the clients backed away from the project, leaving Sully with a half-finished enterprise. The Place des Vosges was more fortunate and was completed in April 1612, a good example of the union of privilege, wealth and productive enterprise which was at the heart of France's new-found and delicate equipoise.

REFERENCES AND NOTES

1. *BN MS It* 1732, fols 261–2. The problems of Champagne are touched on in J-M. Pesez and E. Le Roy Ladurie, 1977, pp. 96–9.
2. G. Fagniez, 1897, p. 7.
3. A. Croix, 1974, chs iv and v, esp. pp. 116–26. P. Benedict, 1975, pp. 232–3. J. Jacquart, 1974, pt ii, ch. v, esp. pp. 171–89. P. Goubert, 1976, pp. 171–94. F. Lebrun, 1965, pp. 49–50 P Deyon, 1963 pp. 948–9. R. Gascon, 1971, Vol. II, pt ii. G. Cabourdin, 1977, esp. Vol. I, pt ii, and pt iv, chs ii and iv. J. Goy and E. Le Roy Ladurie, 1972, pp. 21, 44–57 (Paris region); pp. 146–7 (Burgundy); pp. 176–7 (Lyonnais); pp. 198–9 (Auvergne); pp. 236–9 (Toulousain), E. Le Roy Ladurie, 1966, Vol. I, pts ii and iii. P. Leclercq, 1979. No attempt has been made to analyse in detail the economic data included in these works which, for the period of the wars of religion, must be regarded as providing only provisional conclusions. The detailed and illuminating regional studies on the seventeenth century in France have not yet been matched by research of comparable quality for the period before 1598.
4. M. Baulant and J. Meuvret, 1960 (Pais). P. Goubert, 1960, p. 77 (*graphiques*) (Beauvais). P. Benedict, 1975, pp. 232–3 (Rouen). A. Croix, 1974, pp. 80–4, 126–38 (Nantes). A. Latreille, *Histoire de Lyon*, Privat, Toulouse, 1975, p. 167. G. and G. Frêche, 1967 (Toulouse). R. Baehrel, 1961, pp. 534–5, 554 and *graphiques* (Grenoble, Arles and Aix). E. Le Roy Ladurie, 1966, Vol. II (*Annexes*) (Montpellier, Béziers and Narbonne).
5. J. Jacquart, 1974, pt ii, ch. v. Cf. F. Braudel's remarks about 'cette

étonnante montée de misère du XVIe siècle finissante' quoted in P. Leclercq, 1979, p. 33.

6. H. Drouot, 1911, p. 361.
7. H. Lapeyre, 1955, p. 251–3
8. E. Trocmé and M. Delafosse, 1952, ch. vi, esp. p. 145.
9. J. Billioud, 1951, pp. 186–202.
10. M. Baulant, pp. XXV–XXVII.
11. R. Gason, 1971, Vol. ii, pt ii.
12. F. Bayard, 1971, pp. 1234–60.
13. *Rouen, Inventaire sommaire des délibérations* (Series B – 10 May 1601).
14. P. Deyon, 1963, pp. 948–9; H. A. Nicholle, 1976, p. 89, appendices vii–ix.
15. *Ibid.*, pp. 154–69.
16. F. C. Spooner, 1958, pp. 203–5, 218–19. R. Boutruche, 1966, p. 124 (for their appearance in Bordeaux). E. Trocmé and M. Delafosse, 1952, p. 104 (La Rochelle).
17. R. Gascon, 1971, Vol. ii, p. 614.
18. *AN*, H 748[17] fol. 46. The trend towards protectionism in the traditionally free-trade city of Lyons is documented in R. Gascon, 1971, Vol. ii, pp. 675–731. The distinction between duties on imported primary products and manufactured products appeared in an edict on tariffs in 1570.
19. T. Malvezin, 1883, Vol. ii, pp. 224–6. R. Boutruche, 1966, pp. 91–138. C. Higounet, 1971, p. 277. As Montaigne said, the wine trade was 'un moyen des guerres religieuses'. The complaints of London merchants appear in *BL Harleian MS* 288.
20. F. C. Spooner, 1972. A. Blanchet, 1930, pp. 235–7.
21. R. Gascon, 1971, Vol. ii, pp. 549–72. Coligny (Actes du colloque, 1972), 1974, pp. 672–701. F. C. Spooner, 1972 pp. 157–97.
22. R. Gascon, 1971, Vol. ii, pp. 576–7; F. C. Spooner, 1972, p. 163. LN, No. 921. The edict was only enforced with difficulty in the Midi.
23. F. C. Spooner, 1972, pp. 164–7, 212–47. Money minted at Paris from Spanish sources enumerated in *BN MS Fr* 4019, fol. 206v.
24. F. C. Spooner, 1972, pp. 582–93.
25. *Ibid.*, pp. 105–15.
26. J. Brun-Durand, **1885**, p. 310. Cf. the works of J. Bailhache on the various small mints in French provinces during the League in *Revue numismatique* (1928–32).
27. J. Brun-Durand, **1885**, p.311.
28. *Ibid.*, p. 77.
29. J-N. Bireben, 1975, Vol. i, pp. 377–88.
30. A. Croix, 1974, pp. 126–39 (Nantes region). P. Benedict, 1975, pp. 214–22. M.Greengrass, 1979, p. 263. F.Rolle, 1865 (deliberations of the town of Lyons – analysis of registers BB104–117).
31. J. Brun-Durand, **1885**, p. 199.
32. P. Benedict, 1981, p. 173.
33. A. Latreille, *op. cit.*, p. 167 (cited in n. 4).
34. J-P. Gutton, 1970, esp. pp. 298–300. For the effects on Marseilles, see J. Billioud, 1951, p. 183.

35. B. Bennassar, 1969.
36. J. Goy and E. Le Roy Ladurie, 1972, pp. 50–7, 140–1, 146–7, 151–2.
37. E. Le Roy Ladurie, 1971, ch. iv.
38. P. de Saint-Jacob, 1961, pp. 34–49. A. Tuetey, 1883. The methods of fighting the *grande guerre* are amply referred to in the memoirs of François de la Noue, Jean de Saulx-Travannes and Blaise de Monluc.
39. J. Jacquart, 1974, pp. 179–88. A. Richart, **1869**, pp. 480–90. Cf. the remissions for *tailles* and *décimes* in Valois, Nos 1790, 1873, 1914, etc. Henri IV fought in the Beauce, Paris' main source of provisions and permanently changed the pattern of Paris' provisioning. See P. Goubert, 1961, pp. 797–801.
40. J. Brun-Durand, **1885**, p. 187.
41. P. de Saint-Jacob, 1961, pp. 34–49. Other similar evidence from commissioners investigating the non-payment of *décimes* around Toulouse (AD Haute-Garonne 1G 187). Cf. records of tithes around Rouen in P. Benedict, 1981, pp. 224–5.
42. L. Merle, 1958, pp. 179–80. J. Jacquart, 1974, pp. 200–53. E. Le Roy Ladurie, 1966, Vol. I, pp. 33–53.
43. H. Wacquet, **1960**, p. 275 – this evocation of the deprivations of Breton peasants at the time of the League ends by saying that, if he attempted to describe them all, his diary would be accounted a fairy story.
44. E. Le Roy Ladurie, 1966, Vol. I, pp. 333–56 and accompanying tables.
45. G. Cabourdin, 1977, pp. 377–424. A similar process is revealed in P. Leclercq, 1979, pp. 58–67.
46. *DBF*, Vol. VII, cols 707–9.
47. G. Fagniez, 1897, pp. 14–15. Examples from the *Midi* to be found in L. Ménard, 1750–68, Vol. IV, pp. 187, 239, 246. For the north of France, examples in *BN MS Fr* 3646, fol. 82, 3982, fol. 137; (Ile de France, 1 Sept. 1592); 3983, fol. 4 (Orléanais, 10 Jan. 1593).
48. A. d'Aubigné, *les Tragiques* (ed. Bailbé, J.), Garnier-Flammarion, 1968, p. 17.
49. *Ibid.*, pp. 68–9.
50. G. Picot, 1888, Vol. II, p. 214.
51. G. Fagniez, 1897, p. 7 (Priuli, 1582).
52. Cromé, **1977**, p. 75. Cf. the comments in G. Fagniez, 1897, p. 9 on the *casaniers*, gentlemen who remained neutral during the wars and protected their estates. The same problem would occur during the English Civil War.
53. *A Pleasant Satyre or Poesie; wherein is discovered the Catholicon of the League* (London, 1595, *BL* 1080, f 20).
54. G. Fagniez, 1897, p. 79; Sully, **1970**, p. 87.
55. Piémond's hostility towards the nobility was typical of the small town officials of the *plat pays*. It would also be present in the leadership of the *Croquant* rebellion. J. Brun-Durand, **1885**, pp. 235–6, 252, 295, etc. Cf. D. Hickey, 1978, pp. 25–49 for an interesting analysis of the newer nobility which claimed exemption from taxation in the province.
56. E. Le Roy Ladurie, *Le Carnaval de Romans*, Gallimard, 1979; J. H. M. Salmon, 1979, pp. 25–40.

57. J. H. M. Salmon, 1975, pp. 278–9 and refs. The papers of La Pope-linière (*BN MS Fr* 20782, fols 573–6) give an account of the beginnings of the *Gaultiers*.

58. R. d'Estaintot, 1862, pp. 95–8, 109–13, 124–7 describes the problems around Falaise through the surviving letters of a tax collector.

59. H. Waquet, **1960**, pp. 80–3.

60. J. Baudry, 1920, unravels the mythology connected with Fontanelle. He was executed in Paris in September 1602 with some popular satis-faction (Estoile, **1958**, p. 80).

61. This revolt was partially encouraged by the League lieutenant for the region (J. Lestrade, *Les Huguenots de Comminges*, 2 vols, 1900–1, p. 239). Cf. H. Drouot, 1937a, Vol. II, pp. 272–93 for the *Bonnets Rouges*.

62. Y-M. Bercé, 1974, Vol. I, pp. 291–2.

63. Y-M. Bercé, 1974, Vol. I, p. 258 presents the explanation for their name rather differently. His bibliography of sources is the fullest, but the account of J. H. M. Salmon, 1975, pp. 282–91 is also inter-esting. J. Nouaillac, 1912, should be added to the accounts mentioned in Y-M Bercé, 1974, pp. 258–9. I have drawn on some documents mentioned in R. G. Tait, 1977, ch. vii. His analysis of the *Croquants* modifies that of Bercé in important respects.

64. Already in the *cahier* of the third estate of Périgord to the estates of Blois in 1588, there were complaints that the nobility had appropriated royal taxes and forced an 'infinite' number of *corvées* from peasants, interfering with their rights to commons and demanding huge rents from peasants in places where their rent rolls had been destroyed in the civil wars. The Périgord *Croquants* complained that their nobility had taken over royal taxes and imprisoned more than 200 peasants 'for their *tailles*'. The community of La Linde, which played a promi-nent part in the Périgord rising, complained in 1594 that their own seigneur oppressed them and sold them to the enemy side, leaving them to pay their ransoms. There were similar complaints from the villagers surrounding the fortified site of Penne in the Agenais.

65. *BN MS Dupuy* 744, fol 147. Cf. Y-M. Bercé, 1974, Vol. I, pp. 272–7.

66. Cayet, Vol. XII, pp. 574–5.

67. *BN MS Fr* 23914, fol. 373v.

68. Deputies sent from the peasant assembly at Abzac wood in April 1594 to the king asked for royal permission to deal with 'the king's enemies' at Périgueux, Bergerac and Sarlat. They also demanded the right to appoint a syndic to represent the *Plat pays* at the local estates. This demand had been previously expressed in 1583, at the time of the provincial commissioners for reform, despatched by Henri III (*supra*, p. 17).

69. For Ogier de Gourgues, see Y-M. Bercé, 1974, Vol. I, pp. 274–5, 281–2.

70. Jean Dupont, sieur de Tarde, canon at Sarlat cathedral. His diary was edited in 1885. This passage appears in C. Higounet, 1971, pp. 212–15.

71. Y-M. Bercé, 1974, Vol. I, p. 285. There were other alarmed reports from the *parlement* of Bordeaux and the seneschals of Périgord and the Agenais (Bourdeille and Monluc) in *BN MS Fr* 23194.

72. Y-M. Bercé, 1974, Vol. I, p. 286.
73. *Ibid.*, pp. 287–8.
74. Estoile, **1948**, p. 420 (June 1594). d'Aubigné, Vol. IX, p. 121. Cf. *Henri IV, lettres*, Vol. IV, pp. 112–13, 154–6.
75. J. Nouaillac, 1912, pp. 321–50.
76. Y-M. Bercé, 1974, Vol. I, p. 281. R. G. Tait, 1977, ch. vii. The king eventually granted amnesties to the *Croquants* in 1596 on the insistence of the syndic of Périgord to prevent a group of nobles ruining villages in legal suits for damages to their property.
77. F. de La Noue, **1967**, p. 190.
78. T. Coryat, *Coryat's Crudities*, Glasgow, 1905, Vol. I, p. 167.
79. The evidence is summarised in E. Le Roy Ladurie and M. Morineau, 1977, pp. 727–9.
80. J. Goy and E. Le Roy Ladurie, 1972, pp. 22, 145–7, 210.
81. E. Le Roy Ladurie and M. Morineau, 1977, pp. 750–1.
82. D. Buisseret, 1968, p. 172.
83. E. Le Roy Ladurie and M. Morineau, 1977, p. 762.
84. G. Fagniez, 1897, pp. 36–8. *Les Travaux et les jours dans L'ancienne France*, 1939. E. Le Roy Ladurie, 1966, Vol. I, pp. 64–7, 353–5. F. Lequenne, 1942. A. Jouanna, 1976, pp. 1050–4. O. de Serres, *le Théâtre de l'Agriculture et Mesnage des Champs* (Paris, 1600, *BL* 441, i. 1).
85. Suggestive pages in P. Chaunu and R. Gascon, 1977, pp. 326–333. For Toulouse, P. Wolff, *Histoire de Toulouse*, Privat, Toulouse, 1974, pp. 309–14. *AD Haute-Garonne* C 2285, fol. 36 (Catholic estates of Languedoc estimated in October 1587 that the amount of woad exported from Toulouse had declined from 100,000 bales to 6,000 per year 'since foreigners invented a way to increase their production and export it to France without paying any duty'. Toulouse, like Lyons, demanded the protection of native manufacture.)
86. G. Fagniez, 1897, pp. 126–30. But Lyons was not the only city to develop a silk-weaving industry and there were problems with internal competition (*ibid.*, pp. 121–6).
87. G. Fagniez, 1897, pp. 317–22. M. Baulant, 1953, pp. XXVII–XXIX.
88. G. Fagniez, 1897, pp. 260–5. D. J. Buisseret, 1964a, pp. 297–306.
89. G. Fagniez, 1897, pp. 260–5. A. Girard, 1932, pp. 50–1, 54–7.
90. G. Fagniez, 1897, p. 260. G. Carew, **1749**, pp. 430–1.
91. G. Fagniez, 1897, pp. 278–88. M. Trudel, 1973, pp. 62–106.
92. H. A. Nicholle, 1976, pp. 178–80. English merchants said that the actions the French 'showeth evidentlie that the Edict was procured by them of Roan for their privat good ther to restraine draperie or to gain the cullouringe of our English draperie to themselves . . .'. Henri IV was more concerned at the loss of the English alliance than the loss of English trade as his letters to his English envoy make clear. For Benedict Webb, see J. Thirsk and J. P. Cooper, 1972, pp. 206–8.
93. H. A. Nicholle 1976, pp. 182–3.
94. G. Fagniez, 1897, pp. 170–285. There is a discussion of Sully's attitude towards trade protection in D. J. Buisseret, 1968, ch. ix.
95. G. Fagniez, 1897, pp. 84–6, 102, 269. J. Nouaillac, **1908**, p. 133. D. J.

Buisseret, 1964b, on the *ingénieurs du roi*, some of whom were foreigners employed in royal service too.

96.   D. J. Buisseret, 1968, ch. vi.   B. Barbiche, 1978, ch. vi.
97.   G. Fagniez, 1897, pp. 174–87.
98.   *Ibid.*, pp. 188–208. D. J. Buisseret, 1968, pp. 107–8, 117–8, 117–19.   G. Carew, **1749**, pp. 431–2, 470–1.
99.   D. J. Buisseret, 1965, pp. 43–53.
100. G. Carew, **1749**, pp. 461–2.
101. F. C. Spooner, 1972, pp. 167, 170.
102. *Ibid.*, pp. 168–9.   Fontanon, Vol. II, p. 227.
103. B. Barbiche, 1963, pp. 3–17.   F. C. Spooner, 1972, pp. 172–5.
104. G. Fagniez, 1897, pp. 31–4, 100, 353–5.   Sully, **1881**, Vol. XVII, p. 404 for the search for precious metals behind the interest in mining.
105. G. Fagniez, 1897, pp. 88–91. Estoile is suitably sceptical of de Laffemas' position and influence (**1958**, pp. 61, 221).
106. G. Fagniez, 1897, pp. 109–12. *Règlement général pour dresser les manufactures en ce royaume* (Paris, 1597, *BN*, L 38090).   Cf. H. Champollion-Figeac (**1841–74**), Vol. IV, pt 2.   *Arch. cur. de l'hist. de France*, Vol. XIV, pp. 221–45 (*Recueil présenté au Roy de ce qui se passe en l'assemblée du commerce au palais à Paris*, 1604).
107. Sully, **1881**, Vol. XVI, pp. 514–16.   More generally, Sully and de Laffemas were both flexibly protectionist and Sully supported Laffemas' schemes (D. J. Buisseret, 1968, pp. 174–5).
108. G. Fagniez, 1897, pp. 83–4, 147, 151, 160, 237–8. Also pp. 101–2.   Cf. P. Benedict, 1981, pp. 229–30.
109. A. Lublinskaya, 1968, pp. 112–3.
110. G. Fagniez, 1897, p. 234.   The dramatic increase in the number of patents issued by the king is noted in J. U. Nef, *Industry and Government in France and England*, Cornell UP, 1957, p. 84.
111. *Ibid.*, pp. 102–3.
112. J-P. Babelon, 1965, p. 13.   Cf. *Henri IV, lettres*, Vol. VII, pp. 219–20 (Henri IV–Cardinal of Joyeuse, Fontainebleau, 3 May 1607) – '. . . at Paris, you will see my large gallery, which runs to the *Tuileries*, now finished . . . the *Place Royale* near the *Porte Saint-Antoine* and its factories is three quarters completed and will be finished next year; at the end of the *Pont-Neuf* a beautiful new street runs to the *Porte de Bussy* and the houses along both sides of it will be finished by the end of next year; more than two or three thousand workshops are employed here and there for the embellishment of the city so it is impossible that you will not notice a change'.
113. A. Miron de l'Espinay, 1885, p. 106.
114. R. R. Harding, 1978, pp. 172–3. Cf. H. Sauval, 1724, Vol. II, pp. 67–8, 120, 122, 123, 127, etc. for the speculative development of town houses by aristocrats in Paris. Henri IV joked that the rebuilding of the *hôtel* de Nevers would take so long that no one alive would ever see its completion.
115. J-P. Babelon, 1965, pp. 16–25.
116. B. Barbiche, 1978, pp. 121–5.   Charles de Gonzague, Duke of Nevers, also constructed a new town (Charleville), beginning in 1606

France in the age of Henri IV

with the architect Clément Métezeau (who had designed royal buildings in Paris). The Duke of Montmorency planned a grand new port on the Languedoc coast (Montmorencette – now Sètte), while Henri IV was enthusiastic for a new planned addition to the city of Rouen (P. Benedict, 1981, p. 230).

Chapter 6
THE LONG ROBE

THE PROFESSIONS

There was a traditionally close association between the professions of the law and the Catholic Church. Judges and clerics shared a common educational background, a similar official dress (the long black or red robes being the familiar public physiognomy of the professional classes) and a series of shared assumptions about professional conduct. As the chancellor Bellièvre remarked, justice was a 'Holy thing'.[1] To François Le Breton, the lawyer and League martyr: 'Religion and Justice are bound up so closely with each other that they are inseparable; the same zeal guides and inspires us and strengthens our courage. . . .'[2] In courtrooms, large missels or paintings of the Crucifixion were used as objects of veneration on which witnesses swore to speak the truth.[3] Some clerics were members of the *parlements* and some magistrates were canons of cathedral chapters. Some lawyers trained to become clerics (*faire la profession* as the taking of Holy Orders was commonly called) before turning to the study of civil law. Many of the qualities commonly regarded as most edifying in a cleric were, with the exception of chastity, also taken to be most becoming a judge. Modesty in dress, gravity of gesture, propriety in conduct and association were qualities regularly alluded to in the speeches to the assembled barristers at the beginning of each new legal session by the royal attorney. Eulogies and biographies turned judges like Achille de Harlay (the first president of the *parlement* of Paris) into something approaching counter-reformed saints.[4] La Roche Flavin, the lawyer from Toulouse, wrote an extensive account of the sovereign lawcourts of France in which he devoted a chapter to the question of judicial proprieties and included a number of malicious stories of judges who had failed to live up to their calling. This resulted in an effort to have the book suppressed.[5]

Professions have conservative tendencies, and the legal and clerical world of sixteenth-century France rested heavily on history and precedent to prove the importance of tradition as the basis for legitimacy and consent to the law and the Catholic Church.[6] Lawyers used 'the old authors' and studied ancient chronicles in order to cite them in courtrooms in the same way as theologians and clerics consulted the biblical canon and church fathers. To contemporaries, the conservatism of the Latin language used by clerics and the fossilised legal jargon of the courtrooms was very striking. The professions shared a number of common interests and concerns where their conservative instincts were noticeable. The judges, for instance, punished offences against the moral order most severely. These included homicide, perjury, blasphemy, brigandage, infanticide (which Jean Bodin thought was a crime resulting from a pact with the devil) and parricide.[7] The law and the church were inevitably drawn closely together in certain other public affairs. Cases of sorcery and witchcraft were judged by royal courts but frequently required clerical testimony. To judge from the numbers of cases being presented on appeal to the *parlement* of Paris and the contemporary alarm, the fear of witchcraft had grown considerably during the civil wars. Both clerics and lawyers were perturbed that: 'the practices of sorcerers are in such profusion that a majority of people and families are in continual peril and apprehension, both on their own account and also on account of the fruits of the earth and their cattle'.[8] Jean Bodin, among others, urged judges to relax their standards of evidence and testimony in order to close the legal loopholes through which, he claimed, many sorcerers escaped conviction.[9] Administration of poor relief and the operation of hospitals as well as the problems of education were also matters of mutual concern. The church had responsibilities towards the poor and sick and the judges wanted to prevent civil disobedience. In the civil wars, charitable institutions and hospitals did little to alleviate poverty and private charity was often uncoordinated. Royal legislation demanded that both *parlements* and clerical administrators cooperated in the management of what resources there were.[10] The universities were in a somewhat analogous position.[11]

There were also common differences of opinion within the professions. One debate concerned the position of the Jesuit colleges in France, which had been established especially in the first decade of the civil wars.[12] On the one hand, these appeared to challenge the rights of established universities to issue degrees and to expropriate the education of youth frequently to foreign-born teachers. On the other hand, some prelates were anxious to encourage the new Order in their dioceses and some judges wanted a cheaper education for their sons. The Jesuit issue was but one part of a wider debate about the Gallican rights of the French church. These rights had been articulated from the early fifteenth century when the schism in the

Papacy permitted the French church to express certain aspirations to independence from both the Papacy and from French kings. The Pragmatic Sanction of 1438 represented clerical aspirations at their fullest but this was revoked by François I in all but its purely internal disciplinary decrees by a Concordat reached with the Papacy in 1516. The Concordat removed the French churches' claims to elect its senior clergy, denied it the right to hold councils of the church without royal permission and restored papal taxation. The Concordat was bitterly disliked by the judges of the *parlement* of Paris and by the theologians of the Sorbonne.[13] In 1560, there was an attempt to re-establish the Pragmatic Sanction through the estates general and in 1579 the clergy asked for internal elections of senior clergy to be instituted, but all without success. In 1586, an assembly of the French church vigorously resisted a further alienation of church wealth which had been proposed by the king and supported by the Papacy, and appealed to the Gallican rights of the French church. Although judges were naturally prudent in their treatment of the Gallican question, barristers and lawyers were more straightforward in their support for the clergy's rights to a freedom from interference from royal or papal power – a freedom which was as essential a professional requirement in the *ecclesia* as in the *parlementum*.

THE SALE OF OFFICES

Contemporaries frequently remarked on the corruption within the French church and alluded to the widespread non-residence, nepotism, pluralism and simony among the senior clergy as one of the principal causes of the French reformation.[14] But, in the case of simony, or the sale of offices, royal service was far more afflicted than the church. This 'vile commerce' (as Estoile described it) was widely regarded as an evil in the state for the same reasons as it was in the church, namely, that it promoted unsuitable individuals to a sacred task and involved the possibility that they would attempt to profit from the procedures of punishing sins and enforcing justice.[15] In theory, the money paid into the bureau of casual revenues (the *bureau des parties casuelles*) for the right to hold a royal office was a loan to the king and reimbursable.[16] Royal office holders had to swear an oath on taking up their posts that they had paid nothing for the privilege of exercising royal authority, an oath which survived until 1598, by which time theory and practice were too far apart to be sustained.[17] The market in royal offices was already widely known in the reign of Henri II and the prices for various posts were openly discussed. The numbers of offices for sale began to increase as the king attempted to finance his wars on resources beyond the revenues of the *taille*. The *parlement* of Bordeaux doubled its size in the first half of the sixteenth century; its twin at Toulouse tripled.[18] The formation of the lesser legal tribunals known as *présidiaux* in 1555 created 550 new offices at once. In Paris, the practice of having more than one officer to a post (and a rotation between them) began in the 1550s. The civil wars turned a stream of new offices into a flood. In 1573, there were about 146 senior magistrates and 741 lesser office holders in 502 posts in the city of Rouen. By 1604, there were 162 senior magistrates with, 1932 lesser officials in 922 posts.[19] As the lawyer, Charles Loyseau, commented: 'in every town, the honnêtes hommes have offices'. With the increase in royal offices went an increase in lawyers, clerks and notaries to service the professions. The numbers of solicitors in the *parlement* of Dijon increased fivefold between 1550 and 1580, and La Roche Flavin commented on the 'many regiments, even a small army' of attorneys in Toulouse by the beginning of the seventeenth century.[20]

The sale of new offices went on at all levels of royal administration and the prices of offices also began to increase rapidly, particularly after the revenue of the *parties casuelles* was put out to farm in 1575.[21] The tax farmers sold offices more aggressively to the highest bidder and dropped the pretence of the purchase price being a loan. In Rouen, the price of a councillorship in the *parlement* doubled between 1575 and 1588.[22] It was probable that royal office-holding may have become more attractive as an alternative to mercantile or even landed investments in the unstable conditions of the civil wars. There was certainly no shortage of lawyers wanting to move into a royal office. It was also relatively easy to obtain the reversion, or inheritance, of an office for a son, heir or family relative. The pattern was rather similar to the *resignatio in favorem* procedure which the church allowed for cathedral prebendaries and other clerical posts.[23] Individuals could purchase the right to hand on their post for what was called the third or fourth penny, or a third or fourth of the value of their office, paid to the king in return for letters of resignation. As in the church, these letters had to be granted at least thirty-nine days before the death of the incumbent in the office in order to prevent fraudulent resignations. Estoile recorded the competition for offices and resignations in Paris in the civil wars[24]:

> As soon as His Majesty has thought of creating an office, no matter how small, there are disputes about who shall have it, and he [the king] is importuned about the reversion of it; for there is no officer so poor that he does not wish to secure his estates and cannot find the ready money to buy the rights of reversion, and yet who does not criticise the king and blame him for the multiplication and sale of offices of which he is the first and prime mover.

Others recorded how the increase in the number of judges also encouraged a recourse to the law so that, as one contemporary put it, 'never was a kingdom, province, country, estate or manor, so occupied in litigation as France'. The chancellor remarked on this 'great deluge' of lawsuits which he blamed on 'the multiplication of offices in all the nooks and crannies of the kingdom'.[25] By the end of the wars of religion, therefore, office-holding represented a significant social fact in France. Some commentators like La Roche Flavin spoke of the office holders as a kind of 'people of the middling sort'. He regarded them as Aristotle had done, as 'the steadiest element, the least eager for change' in society.[26] In doing so, La Roche Flavin chose to ignore the widening gap between senior officers and those in posts of little value and to overlook the distinction between judicial and other posts in royal service, both of which made it difficult to regard the office holders as a coherent group in society. When it came to the holding of the estates general in 1576, the second estate rejected any notion of a 'fourth estate' of office holders and reminded the deputies of the third estate (the majority of whom were royal officials) that they belonged to the bourgeoisie.

The lesser nobility was particularly alarmed at the rapid spread of venality and its effects on the price of offices. They quoted, almost as a proverb, that those who bought offices of justice 'sold retail what they bought wholesale'.[27] At the estates general, they said that noblemen from old noble families were being squeezed from royal office by the rise in prices. There is considerable evidence to suggest that this was, in fact, the case. In the early sixteenth century, there had been a significant number of old nobles serving among the magistrature.[28] In the civil wars, this ceased to happen. This was partly because of the military demands of the civil wars which emphasised the demeaning character of professional duties. Monluc, for instance, could not understand why 'so many of our fine youth live uselessly' among the lawcourts when they could be discovering honour and valour on the battlefield.[29] Even judges like Michel de Montaigne or lawyers like Etienne Pasquier admitted that nobility in France was, in practice, to be associated with the military.[30] But it was also because the costs of entering the magistrature increased beyond the pockets of many lesser nobles. Legal education almost certainly became more expensive in the sixteenth century, as the cost of books, travel and the length of time required to acquire a qualification rivalled the costs of purchasing military livery and becoming a lackey in a military company. The rising costs of purchasing an office made it more difficult to raise the necessary money without resorting to borrowing or to selling the patrimony. At the same time, observers like La Noue expressed the resentments of lesser nobles, who felt that judges were becoming more wealthy and more established as a provincial nobility in certain regions around the cities where the sovereign courts resided.[31]

In fact, the return on an investment in a royal office probably changed its character in the wars of religion. The salaries of royal officials failed to keep in line, either with inflation or with the price of offices, and especially so after the 1570s.[32] The rising costs of wages to the new officers explained why the monarchy could not contemplate raising its servants' salaries. As it was, expenditure on official salaries rose from 2.3 million *livres* in 1576 to 5 million *livres* in 1585.[33] For those senior judges and financial officials who were wealthy enough for their investment in office not to make a complete inroad into their capital, or for those who had invested in offices where the salaries were very substantial, this did not greatly signify. For those ordinary judges in provincial *parlements* or lesser judicial officials in courts of first instance where salaries were only a few hundred *livres*, it was an important matter.[34] In addition, they were less able to make up the difference by legal fees, commissions and retaining fees for advising aristocrats on their legal affairs. They were unlikely to be offered the royal pensions available to presidents of *parlements* and other senior officials who were regarded as particularly important for monarchical authority. As one councillor in the *parlement* of Rouen said in 1570: 'The president wants to rule the councillors by tyranny and fear; he gets the honours and the large salary, while the councillor receives nothing and is ill-treated.'[35] La Roche Flavin compared the investment in an office with the investment of a similar sum in *rentes* and concluded that *rentes* represented, in purely monetary terms, a much better return and 'with no effort at all . . .'.[36]

As a result of these trends, office-holding became less attractive in monetary terms and more attractive in terms of status and social pretensions. Charles Loyseau, a distinguished lawyer at the Paris bar, defined an office as a 'dignity with a public function' and, by 'dignity', he meant the corpus of privileges attached to the office and its tribunal.[37] Among the individual privileges for judges in sovereign courts were an exemption from the billeting of troops on their town houses and, for all office holders, an exemption from payment of *taille*. First presidents of the courts were treated as the equivalent of princes of the blood in that it was regarded as a treasonable act to plot against their lives.[38] Many magistrates purchased letters of nobility and others married into the high magistrature to create a series of cohesive groups of families in each tribunal.[39] In some *parlements*, there were efforts by some judges to prevent those who were not from good families gaining offices.[40] One Protestant pamphleteer sneered at these pretensions and called the *parlement* of Toulouse a 'consistory of princes'.[41] The corporate privileges of the tribunals of judges were also to become more important. The most notable of these was the right to refuse to register royal edicts in the sovereign courts. This was, in essence, a right to review all royal legislation and, in order to overcome it, the legislation had either to be modified, or the king had to present himself before the sovereign court in person and demand its registration in a *lit de justice*, a ceremony which had only been used twice in the period from 1515 to 1559, but which was used five times between 1550 and 1598. Constitutional lawyers of the period of the civil wars invested the ceremony with a great mystique, emphasising the necessity of a monarch to act according to the law, and making it a moment of accountability for French kings.[42] Some judges spoke as though they saw themselves as Roman senators, self-appointed guardians of the *res publica*. Others wrote extensively on the origins, the privileges and importance of the French sovereign courts.[43] It is not surprising that some lawyers disputed the pre-eminence of military virtues as the prerequisite for noble status and suggested that the dignity of a judge was, in some ways, more secure than that of a military nobleman. Jacques de La Guesle, the *procureur général* to the *parlement* of Paris, told the assembled judges in 1594 that the nobility of the law was above the caprices of princes: 'It enlarges itself ceaselessly and, with the king's authority, it extends to all Frenchmen, embracing their lives, wealth and honour.'[44] Even lesser tribunals had rights of precedence over municipal corporations which they enforced in public processions and official occasions. They thus displayed their growing eminence in French society.

Personal and corporate ambitions became so enmeshed that history can only be written at this stage by resorting to example. Thanks to the intimate diary of his son (a record, as he said, of 'the means to success'), the apparently irresistible rise of a senior office holder at the end of the sixteenth century can be documented.[45] Born in November 1525, Olivier Lefèvre d'Ormesson was the son of a legal clerk, whose mother was the daughter of a solicitor. His son candidly admitted that his family was 'mediocre in extraction and property'. After attending the college of Navarre (a nursery of many sixteenth-century legal talents), he was apprenticed to an attorney to learn 'to write and earn a living'. Good fortune attended him, and Olivier was attached to the service of André Blondel, sieur de Roquancour, treasurer to the future Henri II. Attached to the coat-tails of this up-and-coming man, Olivier prepared to better himself. He became first clerk to Roquancour and helped his brother to buy the post of treasurer of special war expenditure (*trésorier de l'extraordinaire des guerres*). The investment was repaid in the first year of office, and when his brother died, Olivier became heir to an estate worth over 25,000 *écus* and an office which he was able to transfer to his own name. Henri II was a good patron and Olivier subsequently never spoke of 'the king who loved him well' without emotion.

Wealth, once achieved, needed to be protected. Olivier bought the respectable seigneurie of Ormesson, near Nemours, and, henceforth, always called himself 'M. d'Ormesson . . . for the name of Lefèvre was too common'. This proved inadequate to screen him from the charge of embezzling public funds and he was forced to surrender his office (although he was compensated for his losses). Thereafter, 'realising how difficult it was to survive for any length of time . . . without support and assistance, he resolved to marry and thus to ally himself with some well chosen family . . .'. He chose Anne du Morvilliers, daughter of the bishop of Orleans. It was a shrewd choice and the bishop protected him during the civil wars. Olivier became a treasurer in Picardy and then an *intendant des finances* and a *conseiller d'état* in 1573. When the bishop died in 1577, Ormesson hastily retreated from public life. He sold his offices and retired to Ormesson near St Denis to live the life of a country gentleman. But the life bored him, not being (his son tells us) a 'cultivated man'. Although over fifty years old, he deployed every vestige of his influence to obtain a respectable, secure judicial office. Eventually, he persuaded the chamber of accounts in Paris to overlook his embezzlements and, with 40,000 *écus*, bought the office of president there. His dress, manner of life and investments, all became more conservative to match his new-found dignity. At last, the *nouveau-riche* financier could feel secure in the knowledge that, at least for his children, his family was among the great notables of France. He sent his three surviving sons to the best schools, bestowed seigneuries on them, married them into the best legal families of Paris. But, even then, Ormesson was vigilant, aware that security was never complete and that ambition bred resentments. In his last years, he shored up the family's defences by offering lavish entertainments to Henri IV at his smart town house in the rue Beaubourg. Even the king warmed to his hospitality and remarked that 'without the *président* d'Ormesson, there would be no fun at Paris. He is the father of youth . . . .' But on 29 May 1600, riding back from Ormesson to Paris, he fell from his horse and died. To those in the council of state who tried to prevent the inheritance of the office passing to Olivier's eldest son, Henri IV is supposed to have replied 'I was fond of *le bonhomme*' and the reversion was granted. Olivier's prudence had not been in vain. He had risen to nobility in one generation and his family had 'arrived'.

Other families – the Séguier, Harlay, Camus, Bellièvre or Groulart – might have been chosen to illustrate the aspirations of what one contemporary described as 'the demi-Gods of our age'.[46] There is no doubt that their success caused resentment among those judges who were either not so lucky or not so enterprising. Among the lawyers without offices, there was a pronounced feeling of being excluded from any chance of fame and fortune. The dislike for the *politiques* in Paris and other provincial cities at the time of the League was, in some senses, a resentment directed by lawyers and lesser office holders against those who had been more successful than themselves. Some historians have even spoken of a *société bloquée* where increased heredity in offices caused promotion blockages in the legal professions.[47] This may have been true of older and smaller tribunals, but was not the case in Rouen or Paris. The fact that the younger and more recently appointed judges tended to side with the League suggests that it was an accumulation of resentments (the costs of office, a dislike for venality, a jealousy of those notables as successful as d'Ormesson) rather than a simple division between 'ins' (those in senior office) and 'outs' (those without an office, or without hope of promotion). In any case, the antagonism of the League preachers and pamphlets was frequently directed against all the senior judges. As one of the League orators said[48]:

> You, Lords of justice, with palms lined with gold, purses full of coins and houses full of money, whence comes your luxury, your shining success? How did you come by your tunics, red as the blood of Christ? By stealing from the poor! I tell you that the blood of Christ cries out for mercy on behalf of those so unjustly and unfairly treated and your robes call for vengeance against you because they represent the blood of so many poor people.

THE ALIENATION OF ECCLESIASTICAL WEALTH

The forced sale of ecclesiastical wealth, demanded of the Catholic Church by the last Valois kings as a way of financing royal debts, had as disruptive an effect on the church as the sale of offices had on the legal profession. It was widely condemned among Catholics; and Papire Masson, a hard-line defender of the massacre of Saint Bartholomew, could not decide who had damaged the church more, Charles IX or the Huguenots. The *parlement* of Paris repeatedly condemned the alienations of church rights and property as the sale of the Lord's domain, an infringement of the church's independence, as well as an illegal attack on property rights. The senior clergy reluctantly accepted papal bulls and royal authorisations to alienate wealth in order to assist the king at critical moments and protect the kingdom from heresy. They were mostly appointed by the king and they risked (as in 1586) being criticised in the assemblies of clergy unless there was papal authorisation for the alienation. This sale of church wealth was in addition to the *décimes*, a regular contribution from all the benefices of the realm, organised on the basis of a contract drawn up at Poissy in 1561, and renewed and renegotiated (always to royal advantage) roughly every five years by the assemblies of clergy.[49] The amounts that were alienated were considerable, although not as large as the sale of royal domain which also took place in the wars of religion.[50] The operation was a complicated one, partly because of the need to equalise the quota for alienation between wealthy and poor dioceses. In the first alienation, Charles IX used royal officials to undertake the task, but the results were unsatisfactory to all parties. Greedy royal officers in Protestant areas sold more church property than was necessary to meet the diocesan quota and were reluctant to organise its repurchase in 1564, when the king agreed that churches could recover their wealth and rights if they could reimburse the new owners to whom it had been sold.

Aware of ecclesiastical sensibilities on the issue of church freedom, Charles IX and Henri III left all other alienations in the hands of the church itself. As a result, some alienations were imposed as subventions and involved no sale of property or rights. When they did sell something, minor rights and outlying properties were surrendered first, especially those which had proved difficult to collect in the civil wars.[51] In some dioceses, bishops and prominent lay Catholics bought the alienated property to prevent it falling into Protestant hands. Some of the large northern dioceses avoided having to sell much before the alienation of 1574–75.[52] The dioceses of the Paris basin and central France were obliged to sell something to meet their quotas from 1563 onwards.[53] In a band of southern dioceses, the region was in Protestant hands and no sales of ecclesiastical wealth could be undertaken in wartime. The tithes were already expropriated to Huguenots' coffers and the properties leased to Protestant farmers.[54] Some farms and properties were inevitably despoiled in the process and the revenues from bequests and church courts declined. In some dioceses, there were intermittent tithe strikes by both Catholic and Protestant inhabitants.[55] Where the farmers of ecclesiastical properties were Protestants, the cathedral chapters or episcopal officials were forced to negotiate in order to obtain a proportion of the revenues. Some tithes and rents remained completely unpaid for twenty-five or thirty years. The extent of the problem by the middle of the civil war period appears in the remissions granted by the king on the alienation of church wealth in 1576. A decade later, in the alienation of 1586, fifteen dioceses defaulted on at least half their quota and a further seven still owed at least a quarter of the amount in the years 1599–1600.[56]

The conditions in the worst affected dioceses can be substantiated by visitation records and investigations for the non-payment of tithe. In the diocese of Toulouse, for instance, the damage done to churches alone was enormous; 138 churches or 41 per cent of the total in the diocese were damaged, of which 45 had been set on fire,

37 destroyed and 23 badly affected. A further 19 had no roofs and 14 had been pillaged. A much larger proportion lacked essential fabric to celebrate Catholic rituals – fonts, altars, holy ointment and sacramental vessels.[57] At the same date, the visitations conducted in the nearby diocese of Agen by the bishop, Nicolas de Villars, revealed a still more sombre picture.[58] Only 24 churches in the main towns of the diocese were in an acceptable state. The majority of the 427 parishes had churches with no roofs, no glass in the windows, cemeteries appropriated by local landowners and ruined presbyteries.

Alienations and *décimes* generated an enormous paperwork and many disputes. Some of the latter occurred between the assemblies of clergy and the general receiver for clerical revenues. There were also acrimonious exchanges and altercations between the provost of the city of Paris and the receiver, for these revenues went to pay the *rentes* on the *hôtel de ville* in Paris. Philippe de Castille, the receiver for much of the later period of the civil wars, was imprisoned once and threatened with imprisonment several times over. The political consequences of the alienations and taxes on the church are visible in the clerical support given to the Catholic League.

Those who profited from the alienations can be analysed from the registers of sale preserved by the general receivers. They included notable Protestant leaders like the Prince of Condé who purchased a substantial amount of wealth in 1563.[59] But Catholics like the royal secretary Jacques Gassot also invested in the spoils of their church.[60] Merchants prudently took up some of the wealth, and peasant proprietors who had the means to, bought out the obligations they owed to the church or extended their patrimony. As the civil wars progressed, the proportions of nobles and military captains participating in the purchases increased – a way to invest the profits of war. According to the third estate in Dauphiné, some captains gained nobility on the basis of the seigneuries they bought.[61] Taken with the alienation of the royal domain in the civil wars, this considerable speculative opportunity offered a significant shift in landed fortunes in the French *ancien régime*.

DIVIDED LOYALTIES IN THE LEAGUE

For the senior clergy and magistrates, the League presented invidious choices. There is a tendency to suggest that the prelates were *predominantly* supporters of the League while the senior magistrates assisted Henri IV by their *fundamental* royalism. In fact, their reactions were both more complex and alike in their response to the difficult decisions which faced them after the assassinations at Blois in 1588. At the estates of Blois, it is true that a majority of prelates were supporters of the League. The most prominent among them was the Archbishop of Lyons, Pierre d'Epinac, the so-called *courrier* of the League in 1588.[62] Others present included Arnaud Sorbin of Rennes and Aymar Hennequin of Nevers, both of whom had defended the massacre of St Bartholomew and whose ardent Catholicism drove them to the League.[63] But there were also some royalist bishops who were articulate and influential supporters of the king. These included Claude d'Angennes, Bishop of Le Mans, Renaud de Beaune, Archbishop of Bourges and (although he was in Rome at the time of the estates) the Cardinal de Joyeuse, Archbishop of Toulouse.[64] After the assassinations, some royalist prelates such as Joyeuse joined the League under the influence of the decrees of the Sorbonne. Nevertheless, despite the excommunication of Henri of Navarre by the Pope, about 35 bishops became royalist, with nearly 50 declaring for the League and a further 15 remaining neutral, abandoning their dioceses, retiring to monasteries or returning to Italy.[65] Some of the fifty League bishops declared their support under duress, and Nicolas Fumée of Beauvais was taken prisoner by League forces and then ransomed in 1590 for 900 *écus*.[66] The royalists retaliated with the capture of the League incumbents of Embrun, Riez and Evreux. Claude de Sainctes, Bishop of Evreux, was even put on trial for his treasonable pamphlet praising the assassination of Henri III. While the support of the League bishops to the Catholic cause as diplomatic and military agents was occasionally significant, it was not as important as the royalist bishops would become to Henri IV's propaganda. By the end of 1589, Henri IV could depend on the loyalty of two archbishops and cardinals (Lenoncourt and Vendôme). Vendôme's allegiance in October 1589 was very valuable because, as Henri IV's cousin, he had as good a claim to the throne as a Catholic Bourbon. When Charles, Cardinal de Bourbon, died in May 1590, Vendôme might have been an alternative League king had he not already recognised Henri IV.

For these royalist bishops, Gallican aspirations suddenly acquired a new significance. In September 1591, at Chartres, nine royalist prelates issued a declaration against the papal bull threatening the clerical supporters of Henri of Navarre with excommunication.[67] Their statement declared that the papal bull was against the privileges of the French church and would create a schism. One royalist prelate, Renaud de Beaune, Archbishop of Bourges, campaigned to become patriarch of France in order to set up an independent French church discipline in the spirit of the Pragmatic Sanction. The importance of de Beaune to the royalists became clearer in 1593. He was the only royalist prelate among the royal negotiators at Suresnes for the conference with the League.[68] He played a conspicuous part in the discussions with the Archbishop of Lyons there. Scripture, canon law, French customs were cited by the two prelates in defence of their position, but de Beaune was able to secure from d'Epinac a declaration that the League's only objection to Henri of Navarre's kingship was his religion. The scene was set for de Beaune's announcement in May that Henri IV intended to call on the bishops of France to instruct him in Catholic doctrine. Two months later, the Archbishop of Bourges lifted the excommunication of the king in the name of the French church. Once Henri had attended his first Mass, numerous League prelates rallied to his cause, leaving only a minority of Catholic diehards. Some of these did not accept him as king, despite the papal absolution in 1595. The Bishop of Vannes in Brittany continued to use the clause 'until there is a Catholic king in France' in episcopal documents until the Pope, Clement VIII, reminded him in September 1596 that this was an offensive anachronism.[69]

The senior magistrates proclaimed their royalism more frequently than the prelates but it was, in some respects, less evident during the League. After the Day of Barricades in May 1588, the first president in Paris firmly reminded the Duke of Guise: 'My company is founded on the *fleur de lys* and, since it has been established by the king, it can only function in his service. We would all rather sacrifice our lives than consent to act differently.'[70] A year later, all but about 10 judges of the *parlement* were in revolt against the king and 41 had been led to the Bastille by the *Sixteen*.[71] On 26 January 1589, 108 *conseillers*, 2 presidents and a royal attorney had sworn allegiance to the League.[72] In May 1589, 11 judges were among 44 principal felons condemned for rebellion against the king by Henri III.[73] Of the eight *parlements* of the realm, 6 went over to the League and only one *parlement*, that of Bordeaux, remained royalist and continued to support Henri III and Henri IV. Many judges later claimed that they were terrified into supporting the League and there was some veracity to their claims.[74] Estoile recalls the famous incident when the first president was placed in a difficult position by a League preacher in Paris when he was asked to demonstrate his support for the *Sixteen* or risk being declared a heretic from the pulpit as well as being publicly humiliated: 'Raise your hand *Monsieur le Président*, raise it high, still higher', cried the preacher, 'so that the people can see it.'[75] Other judges said that they stayed at their posts to protect their property or to spy for the king. But by November 1589, only twenty-one magistrates from the *parlement* of Paris had assembled at Tours and there were only nine judges in the royalist *parlement* at Caen.[76] A majority of magistrates in Paris supported the claim to the throne of the Cardinal de Bourbon. By implication, they lent support to the fundamental law that only a Catholic could inherit the throne and they also denied the legality of the case for the Gallican liberties of the French church, partly by putting a cardinal on the throne, and partly by legalising the excommunication of Henri III and Henri IV. Letters patent from the *parlement* of Paris in March 1591 even began their preamble: 'Our Holy Father, in accordance with the jurisdiction which should be his in matters relating to the preservation of the crown of France . . ..'[77] This submission to the papacy increasingly worried many fundamentally Gallican councillors and was responsible, with the fears for the *Sixteen* in the capital, for causing a drift of magistrates towards the royalist *parlements* and away from the League *parlements*. By 1592, there were seventy-six League judges in Paris as compared to eighty-nine royalist judges at Tours and Châlons.

The failure of the estates general of the League in 1593 to agree on a candidate to elect as king was followed by an edict from the League *parlement* on 28 June 1593. The chief spokesman in the debate was Guillaume du Vair (1556–1621), the master of reasoned eloquence, later Henri IV's keeper of the seals.[78] He had attacked the League before, but in a speech of great fervour, he reminded magistrates of their obligation to defend the rights of the crown and the laws of the kingdom (including Gallican rights): 'Therefore arouse yourselves, sirs, and display today the authority of the laws which are entrusted to you. For, if their evil admits of any remedy, you alone can provide it.'[79] The court resolved by a majority on a decree outlawing any *elected* king as against the Salic (and fundamental) law. This step has been called a courageous act of political conviction by fundamentally royalist magistrates.[80] It certainly brought the recognition of Henri IV one stage nearer and annoyed the Duke of Mayenne who demanded its revocation. But it was as much an act of realism as of courage, a response to de Beaune's declaration that Henri IV was preparing to convert to Catholicism. There was an air of desperation in their relieved discovery of the Salic law. In fact, another six months had to pass before the magistrates of Paris, warmed by the king's generous pardon for all rebellion in October 1593, could welcome him to their city. Provincial magistrates supporting the League waited still longer before they followed the capital's example. In Rouen, Sully arrived in March 1594 to negotiate for peace and was welcomed by the judges, especially by the president of the court, who had initially been appointed by the Duke of Mayenne.[81] In Dijon, the officers of the *parlement* were tactfully addressed by Henri IV as 'my good friends' and they helped to popularise the king's image to an initially sullen League populace. In Toulouse, the attempts of some judges to negotiate with royal agents were frustrated by their own divisions and by continuing League sentiment. They had to wait until January 1596 before they could light the *feux de joie* to signal their allegiance to the new king. This was one of the last major office-holding strongholds to accept Henri IV's authority. By the edict of Folembray on

31 January 1596, every office holder who had supported (or been appointed by) the Duke of Mayenne was guaranteed his office and his rebellion was pardoned.[82]

In the course of these years, the magistrates found themselves required to take political decisions. They did so unwillingly, their procrastination displaying the scruples of their consciences as well as their aversion to becoming too closely connected with the world of politics. The prelates, on the other hand, were not so reticent, for most of them had been appointed because of their political usefulness or as a result of their political skills. The magistrates acted on stimuli from their most conservative instincts. They were aware that their property, wealth, privileges and laws were vulnerable to the pressures of war, the fates of military commanders, the wiles of popular movements outside their control, and their own divisions. The prospect of a state of federated communes run by an independent, zealot clergy had been a frightening one, even for those like Brisson who were supposedly in a position to influence it. No judge could fail to be aware of how fragile the rule of law had proved to be. As a result, there emerged a magistrature somewhat humbled and chastened, and willing to pay some price for the existence of a strong monarchy.

THE PAULETTE

Like most contemporaries, Henri IV believed that many superfluous offices would be discontinued once hostilities had ended. As early as 1593, a familiar proposal was resurrected to prune the excess number of royal posts. From 1594, Henri IV granted few reversions of office and enforced the forty-day rule with rigidity.[83] More proposals were laid before the assembly of notables in 1596, involving a reduction in the number of offices to cut the costs of salaries from 2.5 million *livres* per year to 1.5 million.[84] But these well-rehearsed schemes evaporated during the expensive campaign to recapture Amiens in 1597 and then again during the Savoyard War (1600–1). But there were also deeper reasons why reform was stillborn. The fundamental pressures towards venality and inheritance were too great to be resisted. Lesser tribunals fought tooth and claw to maintain themselves against extinction through any reduction in the numbers of officers.[85] The *partisans* – tax farmers and jobbers for office creation and sale – also exercised influence on the council of state. Sully recorded the example in his *Economies Royales* (for which there is independent corroboration) of one financier who offered diamonds worth 2,000 *écus* to two mistresses of councillors (besides other payments to Sully's wife) if, between them, they secured approval for a set of newly proposed offices.[86] Against this corruption, Henri IV's reliance on Sully's vigilance to check each creation as it was proposed was insufficient.

The pressures on magistrates to secure the inheritance of their posts, having spent so much to acquire them, were great. Among lesser office holders, the edict on the *tailles* in March 1600 ruled that, for the purposes of tax, an office which had passed from father to son in three generations granted the third-generation official and his successors the right to hereditary nobility.[87] Three generations – or 100 years – also became the recognised period over which old nobles had to prove their family nobility to commissioners for tax purposes.[88] This edict created many problems in French jurisprudence, as Loyseau admitted in 1610, but it also increased the pressures for a formal system of reversion of offices.[89] By enforcing the forty-day rule strictly, Henri IV encountered fraud at a local level. An unsavoury case came to light in 1600 in the *parlement* of Toulouse of a president paying for a *survivance* to an office twelve days *after* the death of the incumbent, and arranging with a doctor to keep the body of his predecessor on his death-bed for forty-five days, as though alive, in order to circumvent the forty-day clause.[90] One enterprising jobber offered – for a fee – to create an office to investigate such scandals. Other tribunals, it was also discovered, ignored the king completely, and did not bother to secure proper inheritances to their offices at all.

There was also the problem of the king's revenue. Fewer offices created, fewer reversions sold, meant a decrease in the revenue of the *bureau des parties casuelles*. The civil wars had left a legacy of royal debts and, if offices were a curious form of royal debt, it could not be denied that they were more solidly funded and on a longer-term basis than other parts of the royal debt. It was more important to clear the short-term debts rather than to try and tackle a fundamental reform which would require time, patience and political strength. This is the background in which to approach the criticism of Henri IV's failure to tackle the fundamental problems of office-holding. Reform is notoriously difficult from within, and it is clear that he did attempt some changes. It is also clear that his failure was because a change of any dimension would require a shift in attitudes and mentalities among a group whose support was very important for both political and financial stability. His task was to provide a basic stability for the magistrature as a necessary pre-condition for the administration of law and for consent to the monarchy. He did not wish to undertake a reform, the implications of which would shake the pillars of his scarcely secure state. Venality and heredity were not abandoned for any length of time in the later history of the *ancien régime* and this is perhaps a sign that the task of reform had gone beyond the reach of anyone working within the regime itself.

This is a necessary prelude to a discussion of Henri IV's most notorious measure, the institution of the *paulette* in 1604. In essence, the *paulette* was a tax on heredity. The proposal arose – at least superficially – from among the speculators in the royal administration, the *partisans*. It was presented to the council of state with the approval of Sully in 1602 by a consortium of financiers and administrators headed by Charles Paulet, sieur de Corbéron, a Languedocian from a family of financiers and a secretary of the king's chamber.[91] The idea was to invite a cash payment (called the *droit annuel*) each year of one-sixtieth of the assessed price of each office from every magistrate in return for a grant to them of the inheritance of their office and the waiving of the forty-day clause. The strength of the *paulette* proposal lay in its equal appeal to all parties. To the office holders it made financial and social sense. The annual rate was a reasonable insurance proposition, universally available in return for the guarantee of heredity and the continued enjoyment of their investment by their heirs. To the king, it was administratively easy and politically sound. Collecting the money each year was farmed out to the company of financiers (initially to Paulet). It ensured a steady annual revenue to the *bureau des parties casuelles* at a time when the revocation of the *pancarte* tax had created a shortfall in the royal budget.[92] It also controlled the political pressures on the council and discouraged fraud. Richelieu later recorded in his *Testament Politique* that he 'learnt from the late duke of Sully that this consideration was the most pressing on the late king [Henri IV] for the institution of the *droit annuel*; he was less concerned about the revenue it would raise than about the political embarrassments it would avoid in the future . . .'.[93] Henceforth, every office holder who paid the *droit annuel* would be reminded each year that he owed his loyalty to the king, rather than to any intermediary through whose favour he might (otherwise) have gained the office or its reversion.[94]

When the *droit annuel* was first proposed in council, Sully supported it, but was opposed by the chancellor, Pomponne de Bellièvre. The objections were long, detailed and shrewd ones.[95] The measure would provide ammunition to the king's critics who would claim that 'peace is harsher than war'. It abandoned 'holy and necessary promises' undertaken by monarchs before numerous estates general to reduce office-holding. It was offensive to the professional dignity of magistrates and 'all the discipline of the *parlements* will be dissipated'. Since it was proposed that tax farmers would take over all vacant offices and all those offices without a reversion to them, kings would no longer control their servants and 'dangerous monopolies' would occur. When offices became private property the king would no longer be able to reward his faithful servants. The price of offices would be bound to increase still further as 'the boldest and most corrupt speculators' acquired royal posts. The magistrature would be despised by the rest of society and industry would be starved of investment capital which would be siphoned off into royal administration.

Bellièvre only succeeded in postponing the measure for two years and the contract was passed with Paulet on 6 December 1604, part of it being published a week later.[96] A large register of assessed prices of the major offices of the kingdom was drawn up for use by the tax farmers.[97] Paulet did not remain the farmer of the tax for long, but his name became the term for the popular new 'insurance' of heredity offered to royal servants. Some of Bellièvre's financial predictions proved correct. His prophecy of a continued rise in the price of offices proved to be an accurate one for senior legal positions (see Fig. 3). Loyseau claimed that, on average, prices had doubled in the period from 1594 to 1609. In his book on the jurisprudence of office-holding, he described how, during the frosts of January 1608, he went to spend an evening with the tax farmer of the *paulette*, only to find his office besieged by anxious customers[98]:

I found him still busy with a host of them pushing and jostling one another to be the first to pay their money. Some of them still had their boots on, having not bothered to take them off when coming in. I noticed that, after they were dealt with, they went straight to a notary to register their letter of resignation, and it seemed to me that they walked as though trying to avoid any patches of ice for fear of losing their footing and dying in the street. Then, when it was quite dark, the tax farmer closed his register and I heard a great clamour from those who were still in the queue demanding that their cash be taken from them because (they said) they knew not whether they would still be alive the following day. Thinking this over, I began to reflect to myself: Lord, if only we were as concerned to save our souls as we are to save our offices! . . . Both are imperilled by dying but what a difference lies between them. For, once dead, what is the use of an office, and (on the other hand) how important it is to save our souls for eternity . . . .

Estoile, less philosophically, despised[99]:

the miserable conception of the century, the vain and scandalous ambition of men of the age, which makes the prices of offices rise so high and so fast that you can see them go up, not year by year, nor month by month, but day by day and week by week, a despicable and infamous prostitution . . . . Councillors of the court go for 46,000 francs; masters of requests at 70,000 francs . . . that is 46,000 follies and 70,000 stupidities . . . .

In other respects, Bellièvre was proven wrong. The *paulette* may not always have automatically increased the trends to heredity and endogamy beyond the pressures which were already there. In Paris, for example, it has been proved that more new officers entered the *parlement* of Paris in the twenty years after 1604 than in the twenty years before that date.[100] Turnover in offices was brisk, encouraged by rising prices, and this attracted new families – generally from lesser offices – to broaden their investment. The *paulette* did not immediately create a caste of office holders in the French administration at the expense of ability or loyal service. It is also unlikely that the *paulette* diverted wealth from trade to royal posts. The revenue that it created was useful and, if it had not been generated from the office holders, it would have come from other sources – perhaps from indirect taxes – which would have affected commerce more seriously.

Bellièvre's arguments were repeated in a continuing debate about the merits of the *paulette* which lasted beyond 1610.[101] For brief periods the *paulette* was even suspended (as in 1617 and 1648), but political crisis ensued. Although many judges were convinced that behind the *paulette* lay a monstrous engine for corporate corruption, yet they loved it dearly. By 1604, a major reform which challenged the existence and privileges of the robe was impossible. What was possible, and what the *paulette* did, was to strike a bargain between the monarchy and its officials in which corruption was open, institutionalised and to the monarch's advantage.

PERCEPTIONS OF REFORM IN THE CATHOLIC CHURCH

In a carefully prepared speech before the assembly of clergy in 1605, Henri IV flattered his audience and congratulated himself: 'As to elections [of prelates] you see how I go about it. I am proud to find that I have installed prelates that are different from those of the past'.[102] The assembly in fact contained examples of both a reforming and a complacent prelacy. Among the latter were bishops who had never been ordained, a cavalry captain who only visited his diocese once a year for its festival, and the blind bishop of Clermont who showed an immodest eagerness to identify his female visitors by using his hands.[103] Among the former were bishops who attempted to reform their dioceses by holding synods, developing clerical education and persuading the religious orders to undertake their own reform.[104] The path to reform was clear, although the practical obstacles from the large and intricate Gallican church establishment were considerable. Some of the most distinguished prelates of the period, such as Cardinal Du Perron, appear, in retrospect, bland and lacking in zeal. Even the energetic François de Sales (1567–1622) was almost overwhelmed by the problems in his diocese at Annecy.[105]

Many reforming bishops were appointed by Henri III, a result of his misunderstood Catholic concern. Nicolas Villars, a *conseiller* at the *parlement* of Paris, was appointed to the diocese of Agen in 1587 and proved to be a vigorous reformer.[106] Even his predecessor, Janus Frégoso, the last Italian bishop in the see, attended a regional council at Bordeaux to introduce Tridentine decrees into the archdiocese.[107] In Provence, the Italian bishops in the diocese of Aix and Arles were responsible for the first steps towards Tridentine reforms.[108] During the wars of the League, Henri IV was less concerned about the quality of his bishops and more interested in their loyalty and the revenues of their sees. He used the dioceses as a source of patronage and posts were sold for money.[109] By 1594, about six archdioceses and thirty dioceses were vacant either because no appointment had been made or because the bishops had not been confirmed at Rome.[110] By 1596, the number of vacancies had risen to about forty.[111] It took many years for the political pressures surrounding League and royalist candidates to vacant sees to be resolved. Some royal nominees were ill regarded at Rome and had to wait for their confirmations. Arnaud de Beaune was kept waiting for eight years until he was transferred from Bourges to the see of Sens, metropolitan to Paris and therefore one of the most prestigious posts in the French church. At Grasse, the League nominee was eventually accepted in place of the royalist whose marriage and four children embarrassed his candidature. At Nîmes, the bishopric became the object of rival aristocrats' clients in 1597. On the one hand, there was the Dominican Louis de Vervins (later, Archbishop of Narbonne), a client of the Cardinal of Joyeuse. On the other, there was Jean Valernod, brother of the secretary to the constable, Henri de Montmorency-Damville. Valernod was eventually victorious, thanks to the support of his patron both at the royal court and in Rome.[112] The results, politically speaking, of the disposal of many bishoprics to royalists was a compliant prelacy which put up little resistance to the edict of Nantes in 1598. If it was also a reforming prelacy, this was perhaps more by luck than good management. It is nevertheless an interesting reflection of the close identity between long robe and clergy that the most determined and successful reformers were originally members of the magistrature, particularly from the *parlement* of Paris.[113]

Some clerical requests for reform in the French church were satisfied by royal edict. Henri IV restored the Catholic Church to its property in an edict of May 1596, repeated in the edict of Nantes in 1598.[114] In 1606, he gave the church rights to reacquire any alienated property for which it could provide compensation for the original purchase price.[115] In 1606, another edict confirmed the ordinances of Blois in 1579 and agreements reached at Melun in 1580 to exclude laymen from abbeys and priories and forbid gentlemen from farming tithes and other ecclesiastical revenues without special clerical consent.[116] More often, the king invited the church to reform itself and amalgamate benefices to attract well-trained, literate clergy to its ranks. What could be achieved by a vigorous bishop in an unpromising diocese can be demonstrated by the achievement of Nicolas Villars at Agen.[117] When he arrived in his diocese, his initial visitations revealed that he was satisfied only with 18 of the 307 *curés* and 146 *vicaires* in his see. He deposed 7 *curés* and 36 *vicaires* immediately for irregularities and ignorance. One was a collector of *taille* who had suborned the parish chest; several others were renowned vagabonds and pickpockets according to village testimony (although village testimony should not be taken too uncritically, for it was an amalgam of spite and petty quarrels). Forty-eight priests were disciplined and many vicars did not know the name of the rector of the parish. By 1608, the efforts of the seminary established at Agen were beginning to have an effect on clerical standards in the diocese, although more in urban than in rural parishes. The evolution towards a Tridentine Catholic Church in France was bound to be a long and uneven process. Henri IV did not encourage it to the extent of accepting the decrees of the Council of Trent in their entirety in his realm and by royal edict. As the papal nuncio wrote in 1608, 'This is a lost cause, at least for the present.'[118] Henri IV also refused categorically to have anything to do with a revived Inquisition in France, aware that Gallican sentiments would be aroused against such a proposal from all quarters.[119] He did accept that the clergy should set aside some funds to persuade heretic ministers to return to the Roman faith; however, the assembly of clergy in 1605 was unwilling to accept an additional burden of 10–15,000 *écus* on the *décimes*.[120]

The spirit of evangelical Catholicism was more alive among the regular religious orders and, by 1610, the Capuchins, Feuillants and Récollets, as well as reformed houses of cloistered monks, had active groups in Paris. More surprisingly, the Jesuits were allowed back to France after long and complicated negotiations in 1603.[121] They had been expelled by the *parlement* of Paris in 1594, anxious to demonstrate its royalism and eager to exercise its new unity against what senior and effective lawyers like Pasquier argued was an ultramontane, papal and Spanish fifth column in France. Henri IV allowed them back under strict conditions which made them more responsive to royal influence than any other religious order in the kingdom. In the debate over the registration of the edict for their reinstatment, the king let it be known that he wanted the Jesuits to return because of their skills as teachers. More privately, he may have wanted to prevent the Jesuit order becoming too dependent on Spanish Habsburg influence. Once reinstated, the king patronised the Jesuits with zeal. Through the influence of his favourite, Guillaume Fouquet they established a new college at La Flèche in the *ressort* of the *parlement* of Paris with royal pensions.[122] Later, the king's heart would be buried at La Flèche. He gave another pension to the Jesuits to found a house in Canada and introduced the order to Béarn. In 1608, he took the able and seductive preacher, Pierre Coton, as his confessor and sponsored the 'commemoration' of Loyola and Xavier at Rome as the first step towards their canonisation by the Vatican. In October 1609, they obtained the necessary royal permission to teach theology at their college in Paris, and thus directly challenged the Sorbonne, the theological faculty of the university of Paris. Gallican theologians and lawyers attempted to discredit the Jesuits by refuting at length the theoretical arguments advanced by some members of the order for the superiority of papal over royal jurisdiction. Edmund Richer, the austere principal of the Collège Cardinal Le Moine and one of the reformers of the university of Paris in 1600, edited the works of Jean Gerson in 1606. Gerson was the leading Gallican theorist of the early fifteenth century, and the papal nuncio in Paris immediately asked a Jesuit, André Du Val, to answer the edition when it appeared in Venice.[123] Henri IV largely stood aside from the debate, not wishing either to alienate the Papacy or outrage the Gallicans. But the Roman Inquisition banned several Gallican works in 1609, including the royal edict against Jean Chastel for his attempted assassination of the king in 1594. Also banned were the published volumes of Jacques-Auguste de Thou's history of the civil wars which had reached the year 1584. Henri IV then diplomatically asked the Papacy to remove the Inquisition's ban on the royal edict against regicide but did not press for the ban to be released on de Thou's history. When the first volume had appeared in 1603, it had been warmly received by the king who ordered the laudatory preface to him to be translated and reproduced as a separate work (it went into six editions by 1617). But the first volume had treated the period to 1560 and, as the history proceeded to the more uncomfortably recent times, the king was less keen to encourage its publication.[124] He preferred his subjects to forget more recent events and remember that regicide was never justified under any circumstances.

THE NEW ORDER

Politically chastened by the events of the League, the long robe lost none of their privileges or social position. Peace enabled them to consolidate their corporate strength within society. Economically, too, it provided the climate for a good return on their investments. With the coming of peace, house prices in Paris rose dramatically and the senior magistrates who had prudently invested in real estate there found it paying handsome dividends. Those who had not done so, hastened to construct elegant town houses on the reclaimed marshlands in an area to the north-east of the city known as the Marais.[125] They made it as exclusive a residential suburb for Bourbon Paris as Harley St, Wimpole St or Portland Place would be to Hanoverian London. Henri IV participated in the speculation himself by organising the construction of his new squares. In the countryside, the seigneurial investments of the *robe* benefited from the favourable economic climate at the end of hostilities. Rentals began to rise and some prudent *robins* were encouraged to farm their estates directly. Those who wanted to consolidate their estates did so by acquiring (at low prices) parcels of land from ruined peasants or desperate villages selling their commons to pay off debts. Henri IV ensured that the interest on investments in government securities (*rentes*) were paid, albeit at a lower rate of interest than during the civil wars. Wages were also paid on time. The numbers of cases before tribunals increased as the litigation resulting from the civil wars passed through the courts, so that there were large fees still to be gained.

The social tensions which had scandalised the *robins* were also reduced with the coming of peace. Peasant rebellions and popular risings were much less likely to occur after 1600. The army was garrisoned or disbanded so that the possibility of undisciplined soldiers roaming the roads and countryside receded. Judges in the *parlements* were employed to survey town constitutions, limiting town franchises where possible to prevent 'factions and monopolies' in municipal government. A commission from the *parlement* of Paris reformed the university of Paris in 1600.[126] The judges were used to censor libellous and blasphemous publications and to oversee cases of demonic possession. The sovereign courts were entrusted with the enforcement of order in the provinces. They were given general powers to deal with seditious preaching and treasonable plots to assassinate the king. They took their duties seriously and investigated rumours of plots with considerable vigour. They also enforced the laws against duelling, and themselves passed new edicts against the crenellation of castles, the carrying of firearms and the illegal manufacture of offensive weaponry. Since the provincial governors became largely absentee during the reign, the *parlements* became the policemen of the provinces.

Between the magistrates and Henri IV there developed a consensus, based on a shared view of society, which was more important than the differences of opinion which occurred between the king and his magistrates over individual issues. This can be glimpsed through the extensive writings of one of the lawyers of the period, Charles Loyseau. Loyseau began his career as a *lieutenant particulier* (a minor royal officer) in Sens and ended it as a barrister, having retired to a prudent seclusion in the period of the League.[127] He was a direct heir to the flourishing tradition of legal philosophy in sixteenth-century France and his family was related to that of Guy Joly as well as to François Hotman. He was well read and in all his works he successfully orchestrated legal theory and jurisprudence, never becoming too abstruse or overburdened with citations, nor ever losing sight of his (considerable) legal and classical knowledge. He wrote in French, and this ensured him a wide audience, and almost everything that he published was of direct. practical and immediate importance. His treatises on mortgages, bankruptcies and seigneuries explained in clear language the detailed complexities of the law on debt, real estate and liability, concentrating on the common problems which were occurring at the end of a long period of civil wars.

One of his most popular works was his treatise on offices (*Des Offices*, 1608). It would not be an overstatement to say that, single-handed, Loyseau codified the practices and precedents behind venality and heredity of royal and seigneurial offices. He put to one side most of the moralising criticism of office-holding and systematically analysed it as a new branch of the law with its own rules, precedents, actions and damages. It is impossible to imagine the work being written a decade earlier, given the confusions that prevailed in the law on office-holding, and the opposition felt towards the magistrature. Its appearance in 1609 is a witness to the importance of the officers as a legal and social fact in seventeenth-century France.

His most ambitious work was undoubtedly his last, the treatise on orders (*Traité des Ordres et simples dignitéz*, 1610). In it, French society is stratified and arranged into a neat hierarchy. An order, he explains, is a 'rank with a particular fitness for public authority . . . and, in France, it has the special name of 'estate' . . .'.[128] Each of the main estates, however, is then subdivided into ranks. The ecclesiastical order, Loyseau describes as a hierarchy running from the cardinals, primates and patriarchs down to those 'who have just taken the tonsure', since that is 'what makes a man a cleric and distinguishes [him] from the people'. Likewise, the order of nobility is divided into princes of the blood, princes, the chivalric orders of the higher nobility, down to the ordinary gentlemen who enjoyed the profession of arms. The third estate was the most intricate in its gradations. At the top of the order came the 'men of letters' – doctors, licentiates and bachelors of arts. Then came the barristers. Lower down the scale were the financiers, next the 'practitioners or men of affairs'. Below the merchants in their various 'honest professions' (all of which are graded) appeared those 'who depend more on manual labour than on trade or on the sharpness of their wits and whose occupations are therefore the most base'. These too are graded from the top (the *laboureur*) to the very bottom (vagabonds and tramps) who live in 'idleness and without care and at the expense of others'. Loyseau explained at length how the various orders of society were maintained in their position. Each order had 'its special mark or outward ornament' – robes, hats, gloves, rings, etc, for public appearances. Each possessed its own titles and forms of address; 'Sire' for kings, 'Monseigneur' for princes, 'Messieurs' for knights, 'Monsieur' for ordinary nobles and 'Maistre' for men of letters. He outlined the principles behind common rules for precedence, such as who should give way to whom in the street, in the pews of a church or at a municipal ceremonial. Each different rank, he noted, had its own corporation or fraternity which dedicated itself towards maintaining its status. This was a picture of a stable, hierarchical society. But it was not entirely static. Individuals could acquire new ranks in society through good fortune, wealth, education or the king's favour. They could also lose them through failing to live up to their rank (*dérogéance*), through treason or criminal activity. Nevertheless, the ranks of society themselves remained clearly delineated and did not change.

Loyseau's picture was based on Aristotelian premises.[129] It was immensely popular and his complete works went into six editions in the seventeenth century. His theoretical picture of a hierarchical society was not new, but it had never been presented so coherently or with such observant attention to the detail of day-to-day social customs. Its date too – coming at the end of a reign devoted to the re-creation of a stable society – is immensely significant. The legal and financial professions had, in their corporate ambitions in the sixteenth century, disproved the existence of the static hierarchical society by becoming a new *couche sociale* (the term is more appropriate than the formal 'order' or the anachronistic 'class'). Having glimpsed the consequences of such mobility at the end of the sixteenth century. they espoused the most traditional view of French society and worked hard to see it enforced in laws, ordinances and their own social customs. In the process of assimilating them to the world of traditional French society, Henri IV's regime played a significant role.

The king was the guarantor of the stable, organic society of Loyseau, for every organ required a governing principle, a *pars principans*. The king could govern only when there was a commonly accepted harmony between himself and the polity. This harmony came from the divine basis of the social and political bonds of the community. Loyseau's Catholicism was essential to his conception of a hierarchical society in harmony with itself. Other lawyers and theologians of the period drew on the writings of Neoplatonists – Christian, Gnostic and Jewish – to explain this harmony. They strongly influenced Jean Bodin when he came to write the *Six Books of a Commonweal* in 1576. Replying to the *Francogallia* of François Hotman and the Aristotelian political thought of Louis Le Roy, Bodin explained his theory of monarchical sovereignty in terms of mystical oneness. Society itself required geometric (or harmonic) proportions, as in music, to keep the various orders in tune with each other and in harmony with their sovereign king.[130] Bodin's theories of sovereignty would become important among seventeenth-century French judges, but this was partly because they were reinforced by other theological contributions. The divine right theories of the absolute monarch (as preached, for instance, on the death of Henri IV) and the theory of celestial hierarchies expounded by Pierre de Bérulle from the writings of the Neoplatonist Denis the Areopagite reinforced the picture or ideal of the society of orders which became so prominent in the aftermath of the civil wars.

REFERENCES AND NOTES

1. *Revue Henri IV*, Vol. I, p. 187.
2. F. Le Breton, *Remonstrances aux Trois Estats de la France* . . . (n.p. 1586, *BL* 901, a 10, 5, 6) p. 72.
3. M. Rousselet, 1957, 2 vols. J. Dewald, 1980, p. 21.
4. C. Kaiser, 1982.
5. B. de La Roche Flavin, **1617**. Biography in P. Boyer, 1921.
6. J. Dewald, 1980, pp. 31–41.
7. J. Dewald, 1976.
8. A. Soman, 1978.
9. J. Bodin, *De la démonomanie des sorciers* (2nd edn, Paris, 1581, *BL* 719, i 17).
10. R. Doucet, 1948, Vol. II, pp. 802–12. The edict of 1561 was confirmed in 1566 and 1579, giving the laity a major power over hospital and Poor Law management. For charity in Paris, see C. Paultre, 1906, p. ii. Cf. J. Dewald, 1980, p. 98.
11. R. Doucet, 1948, Vol. II, pp. 791–802. For the *parlement* of Paris and the university of the capital, see E. Maugis, 1914, Vol. II, app. ii.
12. R. Chartier, *l'Education en France* SEDES, 1976, p. 187.
13. A. Thomas, 1910, Vol. III.
14. For example, Guy Coquille: 'Que les maux de la France pendant la Ligue venoient faute de réformation principalement de l'estat ecclésiastique . . .' (*Oeuvres* (Paris, 1666), Vol. I, pp. 310–11).
15. Estoile, **1958**, p. 234 (Mar. 1611). The dislike of venality is widely expressed towards the end of the sixteenth century. R. Mousnier, 1971, p. 76 (for the views of Montaigne). F. Hotman, **1972**, pp. 519–21.
16. M. Rousselet, 1957, Vol. I, p. 97. J. Dewald, 1980, p. 136. C. Stocker, 1978, p. 25.
17. *Revue Henri IV*, Vol. I, p. 265.
18. R. E. Mousnier, 1971, pp. 41–3.

19. J. Dewald, 1980, p. 69.
20. B. de La Roche Flavin, **1617**, p. 238. The number of solicitors at the *parlement* of Rennes increased from 60 to 80 in the period from 1555 to 1572 and there were 110 in 1600. For the numbers of attorneys in Paris, see M. Yardeni, 1966, pp. 483–6.
21. Estoile, **1943**, p. 115 (Mar. 1575).
22. J. Dewald, 1980, pp. 138–40.
23. G. de Maynard, *Notables et Singuliers Questions du droit écrit* (Toulouse, 1751), p. 43. R. Doucet, 1948, Vol. I, ch. xviii.
24. Estoile, **1943**, p. 115 (May 1576).
25. P. Bugnyon, *Traité des loix abrégées et inusitées . . .* (Paris, 1605, *BL* 707, b 2), p. 12. According to Chancellor de l'Hôpital: 'the great deluge of lawsuits began under the reign of Henri II with the establishment of the *présidiaux* and the multiplication of offices in all the nooks and crannies of the kingdom'.
26. B. de La Roche Flavin, **1617**, p. 350. Quoted in J. Dewald, 1980, p. 70. This lack of 'people of the middling sort' was much lamented by the *arbitristas* in Castile during this period (J. H. Elliott, *Imperial Spain*, Arnold, 1963, p. 305).
27. F. de La Noue, **1967**, pp. 126–7; Bugnyon, *op. cit.*, p. 15 (cited in n.25).
28. J. Dewald, 1980 pp. 70–80. Cf. J. Powiss, 1973, pp. 27–36.
29. B. de Monluc, **1964**, p. 345.
30. M. de Montaigne: 'La forme propre et la seule et essentielle de noblesse en France, c'est la vocation militaire' (**1962**, Vol. II, p. 165). Etienne Pasquier: 'Tant est demeurée recommandée entre nous cette vieille impression des armes sur laquelle nos premiers Français establirent le fondement de leur noblesse' (*Recherches* (1621 edn) p. 128). See A. Jouanna, 1976, pp. 241–452.
31. F. de La Noue, **1967**, pp. 126–7. Cf. R. E. Mousnier, 1971, pp. 74–7, 462–9. Also J. Dewald, 1980, ch. iii. G. Snyders, 1965, pp. 36–7.
32. R. E. Mousnier, 1971, pp. 74–5. J. Dewald, 1980, pp. 148–50.
33. R. E. Mousnier, 1971, p. 74.
34. *Ibid.*, p. 148.
35. Examples of the pensions to *présidents* are to be found in the lists of royal pensions in *BN MS Dupuy* 852 (for 1576, 1578, 1603, 1605, etc). The average pension was about 2,800 *livres* in Henri IV's reign. Remark from the councillor in Rouen quoted in J. Dewald, 1980, p. 149.
36. B. de La Roche Flavin, **1617**, p. 350.
37. C. Loyseau, **1611**, p. 7.
38. Isambert, Vol. XIV, p. 245 (Jan. 1572).
39. The *parlement* of Rennes granted itself noble status in 1544, 1545, 1562. The *parlement* of Grenoble confirmed its noble status in 1573. In 1546, the *parlement* of Paris was the first to authorise the nobility of its judges and this edict was the subject for Tiraqueau's notable treatise *De Nobilitate* in 1549 and the debate about nobility which began with it. The king attempted to limit the claims to exemption from taxation by all office holders in royal edicts (Isambert,

Vol. XIV, pp. 540–8, Mar. 1583). The growth of endogamy in the senior tribunals can be measured at Rouen (J. Dewald, 1980, p. 76) and Toulouse (M. Greengrass, 1979, p. 72).

40. J. Dewald, pp. 100–1.
41. N. Froumenteau (pseud. N. Barnaud?), *Le secret des finances* (n.p. 1581, *BL* 283, c.14).
42. S. H. Madden, 1982. The *parlement* also increased their jurisdiction in the church and, in 1560, the *parlement* of Paris registered the recommendations of the estates general.
43. There was a flood of literature on individual styles and judgements of the various courts of France as well as discussions of judicial authority.
44. J. de La Guesle, *Les Remonstrances* (Paris, 1611, *BL* c. 78.b.11) p. 281. Cf. A. Jouanna, 1976. pp. 945–51.
45. A. Chéruel, **1860**, pp. ii–viii. The diary was used by G. Huppert, 1977. pp. 50–7, whose account is closely followed here.
46. Pierre de Saint-Julien de Balleure, *Meslanges Historiques . . .* (Lyons, 1588, *BN* 8'L[46] 3) p. 600. The author was a canon at Chalon cathedral and his biography is in L. Raffin, 1926. Cf. A. Jouanna, 1976, pp. 658–63; D. Richet, 1976, pp. 54–61.
47. J. Dewald, 1980, p. 97 and P. Benedict, 1981, pp. 182–3.
48. B. d'Estang, *Les Parlements de France* (Paris, 1857), p. 173.
49. R. Doucet, 1948, Vol. II, pp. 831–45. J. Viguier, 1906. L. Serbat, 1906. The alienations of church wealth were as follows:

Date	Rente	Interest	Notes
Feb. 1563	100,000 *écus*	denier 12	—
Aug. 1568	150,000 *livres*	denier 12	Converted to an *octroi*
1568–69	50,000 *écus*	denier 24	
1574–75	Alienation to million *livres*	raise 1	Additional subvention of 500,000 *livres*
July 1576	50,000 *écus*	dernier 24	
1586	50,000 *écus*	?	
1587–88	50,000 *écus*	?	

(*Sources:* I. Cloulas, 1958 and C. Michaud, 1981).

50. I. Cloulas, 1958, pp. 6–19. In Languedoc, for example, provincial institutions resisted the sales very vigorously (*AD Haute-Garonne* B56, fols 395–6; *AD Hérault* G316, etc). The diocese of Nimes alienated more than it needed to, in order to reach its quota by over 300 per cent, the diocese of Montpellier by 400 per cent. In Béziers, one of the royal commissioners sold himself some of the best church properties (J. Hilaire, 1952, pp. 146–58).
51. This appears from case studies of individual dioceses – L. Welter, 1946; N. Becquart, 1974; I. Cloulas, 1964.
52. I. Cloulas, 1958, pp. 17, 47–8.
53. *Ibid.*, p. 18.

54. The process of farming ecclesiastical properties was governed by regulations laid down by Protestant-political assemblies. For the operation and accounts of Languedoc's Protestants during the civil wars, see M. Dainville, *Inventaire sommaire des archives départementales de l'Hérault* – Series B(VI) (Montpellier, 1951), cols 381–462.
55. E. Le Roy Ladurie, 1966, Vol. I, pp. 375–89. Cf. *AD Haute-Garonne* B57 (21 Jan. 1564). In 1569, a deputy of the clergy of Béziers claimed that forty benefices there were occupied and in sixty-nine others there was a tithe strike (J. Bellaud-Dessalles, 1902, pp. 106–7). There were regular complaints over tithe impropriation by gentlemen of both religious persuasions.
56. I. Cloulas, 1958, pp. 52–3.
57. G. Baccrabère, 1956.
58. L. Bourrachot, 1963, pp. 129–43.
59. I. Cloulas, 1958, p. 14.
60. I. Cloulas, 1964, pp. 95–6.
61. D. Hickey, 1978.
62. P. Richard, 1901, pp. 272, etc.
63. C. Labitte, 1849, pp. 7–8, 28.
64. F. J. Baumgartner, 1978, pp. 102–4. F. J. Baumgartner, 1979.
65. *Ibid.*, p. 285.
66. *Ibid.*
67. *Ibid.*, pp. 289–90.
68. *Ibid.* Cf. the classic account in A. Poirson, 1862–65, Vol. I, pp. 396–408.
69. F. J. Baumgartner, 1979, p. 292.
70. E. Maugis, 1914, Vol. II, p. 53 questions whether the speech was ever made in the form that has now been preserved.
71. F. J. Baumgartner, 1979, p. 36.
72. Estoile, **1875–96**, Vol. III, pp. 235–6.
73. E. Maugis, 1914, Vol. II, p. 127.
74. *Supra*, p. 52.
75. Estoile, **1943**, p. 604.
76. F. J. Baumgartner, 1979, p. 37. A. Desjardins, 1879, p. 482. E. Maugis, 1914, Vol. III, pp. 282–5.
77. *Ibid.*, Vol. II, p. 76.
78. *DBF*, Vol. V, cols 905–1.
79. R. Radouant, *G. Du Vair. L'homme et l'orateur jusqu'à la fin des troubles de la Ligue*, 1907.
80. For example, J. H. Shennan, *The Parlement of Paris*, 1968, pp. 230–1.
81. Sully, **1881**, Vol. XVI, pp. 141–5.
82. Isambert, Vol. XV, p. 111.
83. R. E. Mousnier, 1971, pp. 134–5.
84. *Ibid.*, p. 136. *Revue Henri IV*, Vol. I, p. 18.
85. For example, the provincial treasurers, whose *bureaux* were abolished in 1598, following the advice of the assembly of notables, but were re-established in 1608, on payment of 600,000 *livres* (R. E. Mousnier, 1971, pp. 139–40).
86. Sully, **1881**, Vol. XVI, p. 250.
87. Isambert, Vol. XV, p. 234.
88. J-M. Constant, 1977.

89. *Ibid.*, p. 83.
90. R. E. Mousnier, 1971, pp. 226–32.
91. *Ibid.*, pp. 234, 242–3.
92. B. Barbiche, 1978, p. 98. R. E. Mousnier, 1971, p. 234. R. J. Bonney, 1981, pp. 61–2. *Revue Henri IV*, Vol. I, p. 184.
93. R. E. Mousnier, 1941, pp. 68–86.
94. G. Carew, **1749**, p. 474 – 'so many tenures which draw necessary dependence on the king'.
95. *Revue Henri IV*, Vol. I, pp. 182–96.
96. Fontanon, Vol. II, pp. 576–8.
97. *BN MS Fr* 3435 (Estat de la Valleur et estimation faicte au Conseil du Roy de tous les offices de judicature . . .).
98. C. Loyseau, **1611**, p. 143.
99. Estoile, **1958**, p. 498–9 (Aug. 1609).
100. M. C. Cummings, 1974, pp. 139, etc.
101. *Ibid*. Cf. D. Bitton, 1969b.
102. Quoted in F-T. Perrens, 1872, Vol. I, pp. 249–50.
103. Examples in J. M. Hayden, 1977, pp. 28–9.
104. *Ibid.*, pp. 30–1.
105. R. Kleinman, 1962. For a less than flattering portrait of Du Perron, see F-T. Perrens, 1872, Vol. I, pp. 237–8.
106. L. Bourrachot, 1963, p. 129.
107. *Ibid.*, p. 136. R. Boutruche, 1966, pp. 369–83.
108. J-R. Palanque, 1975, ch. v.
109. F. J. Baumgartner, 1979, pp. 293–4.
110. *Ibid.*, p. 292.
111. R. Ritter, **1955**, p. 69.
112. R. Sauzet, 1979, pp. 54–6.
113. J. M. Hayden, 1977, p. 38. Examples can be found among the families of the Potier, Miron, Hennequin, Hurault and Zamet.
114. Clause three of the edict of Nantes, Isambert, Vol. XV, p. 173.
115. *Ibid.*, p. 313 (Dec. 1606).
116. *Ibid.*, pp. 303–13. Poirson, 1862–67 Vol. I, pp. 743–9 overestimates the importance of the edict.
117. L. Bourrachot, 1963, pp. 142–3. R. Doucet, 1948, Vol. II, pp. 799–801 is unenthusiastic about the achievements of the seminaries. But see J. Lestrade, *Revue des Pyrénées*, Vol. XVIII (1906) pp. 551–69 for the pioneering efforts in Toulouse. Cathedral accounts reveal more being spent on preaching and fabric in the period 1598–1610.
118. F-T. Perrens, 1872, Vol. I, p. 299 (19 Aug. 1608).
119. *Ibid.*
120. *Ibid.*, p. 301.
121. *Revue Henri IV*, Vol. II, pp. 94–110 for the negotiations leading to the edict of 1603. For the Jesuits in France, the fundamental work is H. Fouqueray, *Histoire de la Compagnie de Jésus en France*, 5 vols, 1910–25 (esp. Vol. II). For anti-Jesuit pamphlets in this period, see C. Sutto, 1977.
122. *Revue Henri IV*, Vol. I, pp. 8–14, 97–9.
123. The debates surrounding Richer are usefully summarised in F-T.

Perrens, 1872, Vol. I, ch. v.   The fundamental (but prejudiced) work on Richer is E. Pujol, 1876.   Cf. E. Préclin, 1930, pp. 241–69.
124. F-T. Perrens, 1872, Vol. I, pp. 341–5.   Cf. S. Kinser, 1966, ch. ii.
125. B. Veyrassat-Herrem and E. Le Roy Ladurie, 1968, pp. 541–55. Also E. Le Roy Ladurie and P. Couperie, 1970, pp. 1014–15.
126. C. Jourdain, *l'Université de Paris*, 1862, 2 vols, Vol. I, pp. 18 *et seq.*
127. J. Lelong, 1909.
128. R. E. Mousnier, 1979, pp. 4–16.
129. H. Lloyd, 1981, pp. 53–82.
130. D. Parker, 1981, pp. 277–82.

Chapter 7

THE OLD NOBILITY

THE TITLED NOBILITY AND ITS CLIENTS

Among the buildings which house the National Archives in Paris are the remains of the *hôtel* Clisson, the Paris residence of the Dukes of Guise. To its rear, the severe, military aspect of the edifice reflects something of its sixteenth-century past when, in the civil wars, it had served as a citadel in the capital. The hotel had seen more glorious moments, especially in 1559–60 when the Guise family was at the height of its prestige. The wealth and interests of its owners were best depicted in the fine chapel, built in the 1550s. The décor included a painting by Primaticcio of the *Adoration of the Magi* in which François, Duke of Guise appeared as a Magi king proudly standing (rather than kneeling!) before the Almighty.[1] A few hundred yards away stood the most elaborate of the four houses owned by the Duke of Montmorency in Paris. Although now destroyed, its magnificence can be reconstructed from contemporary inventories which described the forty splendidly furnished apartments, the sumptuous library and the marvellous collections of linen and glass, a testimony to the wealth and interests of the Montmorency family.[2]

These two powerful families characterised the closely Knit French titled nobility of the sixteenth century. Both were recently created dukedoms, dating from the first half of the sixteenth century when a significant number of laymen, both foreigners (Guise came from the House of Lorraine) and natives (Montmorency stressed his French background) were raised to the peerage.[3] Both possessed substantial landed inheritances spread through many provinces. Properties of the Dukes of Guise were to be found mainly in Champagne while those of the Dukes of Montmorency were concentrated in the Ile de France. Marriages increased their wealth and influence. The House of Montmorency was related to foreign nobles (the Horn and Montigny in Flanders), French courtiers (Coligny) and influential provincial nobles (the Montmorency had married the richest and most powerful families of the Midi – the Turenne, the La Trémouille, the Ventadour and the Candalle). The Guise family was closely related to the House of Stuart as well as to the Dukes of Montpensier and Nevers.[4] Through this network of kinship, these two 'potent Houses' exercised political influence.

The power of the peerage had traditionally been exercised through membership of the royal council which enabled them to obtain favours and privileges for their followers.[5] This was still the case during the reigns of François II and Charles IX and the registers of the royal council record at whose request pensions and other favours had been granted. Then, in 1574, Henri III limited his council to the princes of the blood and eight trusted *fidèles*, removing from it other princes and titled aristocrats.[6] At the same time, he merged this small 'privy' council with his council of finance and made it more difficult for Montmorency or Guise to obtain patronage. This explains some of the difficulties the last Valois experienced in obtaining the confidence of his aristocrats. In any case, during the civil wars, the peerage was also able to exercise its powers through the post of provincial governor.[7] The most important governments lay on the borders of France in Guyenne, Languedoc, Provence, Dauphiné, Burgundy and Champagne. In theory, these were not permanent posts but temporary commissions granted to 'great and notable persons' to exercise during the King's good pleasure. In practice, there was a strong trend towards heredity, especially during the reign of Charles IX.[8] By that time, the House of Montmorency regarded itself as hereditary governors of Languedoc, having controlled the province since 1526, and hoped to gain control of the government of the Ile de France which it had held in the family since 1538. The House of Guise installed itself in the province of Champagne in 1524 and extended its influence over neighbouring Burgundy in 1543 so that, by the wars of religion, the family was secure in both localities. An increasing number of cash transactions accompanied the growth of heredity so that governorships threatened to become as venal as judicial posts.[9]

Letters of commission to governors gave them wide and unspecified powers to oversee every aspect of provincial affairs including imports and exports, the summoning of provincial estates, the investigation of royal officials and, if they were charged with a part of the royal army during wartime, authority to exercise justice and levy money too.[10] In some provinces like Dauphiné and the Nivernais, governors had certain prerogative powers as a matter of custom.[11] But their principal function involved the military disposition of the province, its security, and the payment and upkeep of its garrisons. During the civil wars, therefore, it was natural that the governors would become both more numerous and more important in French politics. In some provinces, they appeared to act like viceroys, and cities anxious to acquire their protection offered them lavish entry ceremonials with royal canopies. The mayor at Dijon during the League told the Duke of Mayenne, its governor, that he was 'the image of God'.[12] Pasquier said that fidelity to a provincial governor could be used to hide treason in the civil wars.[13] Loyseau recorded: 'Of all the dangers that menace France, there is not one greater than the tyranny of the governors . . . who, by means of their governments in provinces and towns, have made themselves lords, practically sovereigns, over their localities . . .'[14] The estates of Blois in 1576 petitioned the king to reduce the powers of military governors, compel them to run well-ordered households and undertake their military duties conscientiously.[15] In practice, the authority the king possessed in provinces where there was a powerful governor was to appoint a loyal lieutenant. Lieutenants were generally not peers but chosen from well-established noble families and sometimes kinsmen of the governor himself.[16]

Governors possessed substantial, armed, noble retinues. In 1556, for instance, the governor of the Ile de France, François de Mont-morency, arrived in Paris accompanied by 200 noblemen.[17] In 1561, his father, the constable, entered Fontainebleau with 800 noblemen in his train. Companies of cavalry (*gens d'armes*) formed the most important part of these retinues. The gendarmerie was a unique force in western Europe – a paid, standing army reserved exclusively for the nobility. the *gens d'armes* were organised into companies under captains who controlled their recruitment and promotion.[18] They wore the captain's livery on their cassocks (*hocquetons*) and it was illegal to remove the livery or enlist in another company without his consent. The captain's name, reputation and colours were the focus of their pride and morale. Theoretically, each company consisted of 100 men-at-arms with a further 150 archers to assist them. Many were relatives of the captain and all were theoretically required to be nobles. By 1560, there were about 6,500 serving in the gendarmerie and on it came to rest much of the theory and practice of 'clientage' among the French nobility.[19] The Italian wars popularised the 'pastime' and 'game' of war among the nobility. Writing in the civil wars, Blaise de Monluc, a Catholic gendarme captain, lieutenant of Gascony and, eventually, Marshal of France, described the great battles of the Italian wars and also revealed the ethos of the rela-tionship between noble and captain, between lieutenant and governor, and between captain and gendarme, that of honour, service and protection.[20] Jean de Saulx-Tavannes (*c.* 1533–*c.* 1629), the lieutenant in Burgundy for much of the later part of the sixteenth century, looked back in his memoirs to his father's great exploits in those wars and stressed his family's 'fidelity' – that powerfully diffused sense of honour, duty and service, developed from military origins to form a code of behaviour which permeated the French nobility.[21] Andrè de Bourdeille, sieur de Brantôme, wrote in his retirement in the last stages of the League, his memoirs of *Famous Men and Great French Captains*, a kind of Valhalla in which various sixteenth-century nobles were immortalised for their chivalry, fidelity, Catholicism and military prowess.[22] He reserved his highest praise for 'Monsieur de Guise le Grand' (François de Guise, 1519–63) and Anne de Montmorency (whose shield, he remarked, carried the legend 'sans fraude et très-fidelle').[23] These were all works by authors who were, in some measure, discontented by the civil wars. Monluc and Saulx-Tavannes felt their prowess was not rewarded by their king; Brantôme's writings were curiously old-fashioned. For a number of reasons, the bonds of fidelity had become strained during the wars of religion.

Firstly, the civil wars divided the aristocratic families in France both within and among each other. Attempts to appeal to a family loyalty fell on deaf ears. Nobles found it difficult to exploit the loyalties of religious parties to extend their own support because Huguenot political assemblies or League councils were more responsive to religious faith than to aristocratic fidelities.[24] Prominent members of the nobility were either killed in battle or assassinated during the civil wars. Secondly, the aristocracy was affected by a progressive decline in the number and value of aristocratic royal pensions. The swiftest contraction of patronage occurred during 1559–61, but the whole period of the civil wars remained one of austerity. Payments of pensions, gifts and wages were periodically postponed, curtailed or diverted. In the reign of Henri III, the problems were exacerbated by the *mignons* so that, as Villeroy (one of the royal secretaries) remarked: 'It was no longer possible for princes and seigneurs of quality to intercede with the king on behalf of others, as they did in the past, which greatly angers them. . . .'[25]

Among the problems of the higher nobility generally, the greatest during this period was their indebtedness on the king's behalf. Provincial governors and lieutenants raised armies and provided loans to the king but they were not repaid. Other members of the aristocracy became heavily indebted by their revolts against royal authority. In 1586, the Savoyard ambassador recorded that the poverty of the Duke of Guise was well known and was forcing him to sell some of his best estates.[26] In November, the duke begged the royal secretary Brûlart to ask Henri III for assistance: 'You know my funds and my credit and I do what I can. All that I can mortgage has been mortgaged. I beg you to solicit the king for me as there is nothing else to be found.'[27] It is not surprising that several friends counselled him to be cautious in 1588 to save the family fortunes. In 1594–96, 300,000 *écus* of debts were accepted by Henri IV on behalf of Charles de Guise and his father, and 600,000 *écus* on behalf of the

Duke of Mayenne.[28] Other examples of indebtedness are more astonishing. Louis, Duke of Nevers, died in 1588 leaving a debt of over 1 million *livres*, having spent the civil wars trying to keep his estates intact.[29] The debts of the Prince of Condé were disavowed after his death in 1588 because they were so substantial.[30] Henri de Montmorency-Damville's family wealth was already mortgaged when, in 1586, his estates were confiscated by the king. In 1597, the income from his devastated lands was so low that his banker, Sébastien Zamet, threatened to withdraw further credit.[31] In the same year, Montmorency-Damville was informed by the son of the lieutenant of Guyenne, Charles de Matignon, that his father (who had gained a reputation for rapacity in office) had died 'with a world of debts on his shoulders'[32] His colleague, the lieutenant in Lyons François de Mandelot, had died in 1588 in similar circumstances.[33] The growth in size of aristocratic dowries did not help aristocratic fortunes, but the opportunities for making a wealthy marriage were still present for individual hard-pressed aristocrats. Some nobles were more able to press their 'assignations' on royal revenues and obtain cash from provincial treasuries or grants of profitable alienated royal domain. François de Bonne, seigneur de Lesdiguières (1543–1626) was widely believed to have profited from the wars in Dauphiné both before and after he became lieutenant in the province in 1597.[34] But it is not difficult to understand why some aristocrats – Guise, Montmorency-Damville, Mercoeur, Joyeuse and Epernon – should seek pensions from Spain or Savoy to maintain their political influence and protect them from bankruptcy.

Decline in royal favours, the growth of aristocratic indebtedness, the rival attractions of new religious beliefs and the bitterness of civil war eroded the fabric of fidelity elsewhere in society, especially among the gendarmes. As a result, the standards of discipline declined. One captain reported from Brittany that his troops, their wages unpaid, had deserted him to pillage the surrounding region: 'There is so much due to the men of my company . . . that I am neither feared nor obeyed. I was never a happier man than when it pleased His Majesty . . . to give me an ordnance company but it seems now that I have only a company of 100 horses.'[35] He was luckier than Captain Jarnac who, in the same year, reported that his company, unpaid for a year, had eaten its horses and retired home. At least ten edicts of considerable ferocity in the course of the civil wars attempted to assert royal authority over the gendarmes.[36] Their reputation grew more tarnished as complaints of their pillage spread. One edict in February 1574 bluntly said: 'The *gendarmerie*, which ought to contain gentlemen respecting their honour, has committed (to our grave regret) as much pillage of our subjects as foreigners and vagabonds.'[37] The offences of stealing, pillaging, and the various abuses in their muster and payment were to be heavily punished, some by martial hanging and strangling. But, a decade later, Henri III lamented in another edict that the civil wars had 'corrupted the police and discipline' of the gendarmerie, and proposed to assign a priest to each company to restrain its lawless elements. . . .[38]

The most evident sign of indiscipline was the growth of duelling and feuding. The cavalry returned from the Italian wars carrying the contagion of the private duel to the French provinces. The Protestant captain, François de La Noue, recorded in his *Discourses* (1586) that more noblemen died in France from 'private discords' than from the civil wars.[39] Jean de Saulx-Tavannes estimated that 6,000 noblemen of his generation had died in duels.[40] Both authors thought that duels led to feuds and vendettas which encouraged civil wars. In the army, duels were controlled by the marshals; both the Catholic Church and the Protestant synods outlawed the practice. But in the provinces, it went on largely unchecked and even involved provincial lieutenants.

In another respect, the gendarmerie was but a tattered remnant of its former noble glories. Although officially still reserved for nobles, there were increasing numbers of non-nobles appearing in its ranks. Foreign-born gendarmes had always been exempt from proving their noble status. To those native-born cavalrymen who were not noble, the king resorted to the distribution of nobility and knighthood instead of payment of salary. The abuse was at its worst in the reign of Charles IX, and the royal edict of February 1574 which lamented the 'disdained, despised and devalued' quality of noble service was somewhat hypocritical.[41] The changing nature of warfare also stimulated this unease. Infantry and artillery were becoming more important, especially in sieges. As Montaigne said; 'Valour has become popular in our civil wars.'[42] The third estate in Dauphiné claimed in 1596 that the 'common people' had done as much fighting as the nobility and should thus share some tax exemption.[43] The unease among the nobility remained widespread and emerged in complaints from the second estate at the estates of Blois in 1576 and 1588.[44]

For the fact was that the civil wars represented a challenge to the inherited ideal of nobility. This ideal was an amalgam of traditional medieval social theorising and some Renaissance popular philosophising. In essence, the basis of nobility lay in virtue. As one (thoroughly typical) treatise on noble virtue explained in 1567[45]:

> To fight to maintain the honour of God and a peaceful kingdom, to spread more widely the king's authority against his enemies, and, on such occasions, not to be afraid of cold or heat, but to offer one's life courageously, these are the proper qualities of virtue. And that is how Nobility originated and why it is worthy of its privileges.

But wherein lay the 'honour of God' in a religious war, and how did 'gent-pille-hommes' maintain the king's authority? Some noble commentators were compelled to condemn noble violence, ignorance and inability to prevent usurpation by commoners, especially during the League. The greater the gap between the ideal and the reality of nobility, the more they relied on a more stark justification for nobility in terms of birth, blood and lineage.

HENRI IV AND THE TITLED NOBILITY

Henri IV attempted to rebuild the bonds of fidelity with his aristocracy by generous pensions, careful management of the provincial governorships and sensitive creations of new peers and by a (sometimes contrived) cultivation of the old-fashioned virtues of 'loyalty to a prince'. He was most successful in winning over the League nobles and most ruthless towards those who had, or who sustained those who possessed, a claim to his throne.

The treaties with League nobles recognised the importance of fidelity and did not try to obtain loyalty on any other terms. The treaty with Charles de Guise, for example, involved Guise giving the king a solemn oath in writing of his fidelity and that of his followers 'such as good and faithful servants and subjects ought and are by nature obliged to render to their legitimate and natural king'.[46] In return, Henri IV accepted 'these good subjects into his obedience and especially because he holds them dear to him . . .'. Even the corpulent Mayenne bent the knee in formal submission before the king while the avaricious Duke of Villars in Rouen expressed his new loyalty to Henri IV in the rich, emotive imagery of fidelity which had so often eluded Henri III.[47] They were given lavish pensions, matching, in some cases, those of the princes of the blood, and they raised no further problems during the reign. Mayenne retired to Soissons, an ill man, dying in seclusion in 1611. Mercoeur went on crusade to Hungary, and died in Nuremberg in 1602. Henri de Bouchage-Joyeuse, the last of the Joyeuse brothers, retreated from his lieutenancy of the province of Languedoc to the world of mental purgation and severe seclusion in a monastery in Paris in 1599 which he had left in 1592 to take on his family duties and head the Toulouse League. Henri IV was delighted and remarked that 'peace will be here to stay for a long time since our captains are turning into Capuchins'.[48] At *frère* Ange's (Joyeuse) funeral in 1609, a procession of monks and gendarmes formed a cortège through the streets of Paris both incongruous and pathetic after a decade of peace.[49]

Towards others in revolt, Henri IV was less disposed to be generous. The Duke of Epernon, for instance, had supported the king in the early years of his reign but he then joined the League in Provence. In his final treaty with the king, he failed to acquire any satisfaction to his demands for the government of Provence and only a portion of his war debts was underwritten. His compensation lay in the less significant government of Poitou, Angoumois, Aunis and Saintonge which lured him away from his landed influence in Guyenne. The king encouraged him to spend his time (and considerable fortune) in building a vast palace for himself on the Garonne at Cadillac.[50] He retained the important frontier government of Metz, but a royalist lieutenant reduced his influence there.[51] Epernon continued to cause periodic tension both at court and at Guyenne, being suspected of fomenting revolt in 1602, but Henri IV's delicate combination of firmness and tact reduced his power for mischief.[52]

Some royalist aristocrats felt that Henri IV had rewarded League nobles at their expense, and that they were excluded from the new regime. Their continued exclusion from the king's council was particularly disliked. The constable's brother, at the time of the revolt of Biron, expressed the resentments of many royalist aristocrats when he told Villeroy[53]:

Why are these factions in the state? Does the king think that he can govern this huge kingdom through Rosny [Sully] and Villeroy, that God has given these two prudence enough to manage it on their own? The remedy lies in establishing a good council [*bon conseil*] with governors in their dignity, for, otherwise, these upheavals will never end. Who would put up with it? We are deprived of all our dignity and only the title is left for us.

The complaint was comprehensible but the remedy was unacceptable to the king. He could not restore power to royalist governors and loyal aristocrats without also giving it to League princes. But loyal aristocrats were also rewarded by the increasing value of royal pensions to governors, so the reign was not without some dividends for them. Montmorency-Damville was made constable and the king became the protector of his infant son and heir.[54] Hunting expeditions, in which the king took enormous pleasure (unlike his predecessor), gave the aristocracy an illusion of being involved with royal affairs even if they had no longer an open access to obtain the favours and privileges that they had gained in the past. The king ensured that provincial governors no longer exercised powers of justice or finance. He did his best to see that provincial government rested in the hands of those he could trust. Governors were encouraged to reside at court, rather than in the provinces.[55] In their place, the king utilised loyal provincial lieutenants, where venality and heredity was not yet a major problem, and chose them from the provincial families rather than from the peerage. These lieutenants – Alphonse d'Ornano in Guyenne after 1597, Anne de Lévis-Ventadour in Languedoc from 1594, François de Bonne-Lesdiguières in Dauphiné from 1597 – were significant figures in limiting the extent and seriousness of those provincial noble revolts which did occur in the realm.

Towards those who had a claim to his throne, Henri IV was more ruthless than tactful. Although he had legitimacy on his side, he was still weak in his fundamental dynastic right. If he could gain the throne, then it was open to almost any prince of the blood to claim the succession too in the event of the lack of direct heirs. In addition, the validity of the king's divorce from Marguerite of Valois and, therefore, of the claims of Marie de Médicis' children to the throne, was still questioned in some quarters. Hence, in December 1602, it was reliably reported that the king's avarice and ingratitude had ensured that, if he died, many aristocrats would proclaim the Prince of Condé, rather than the dauphin, as king; shades of the Old Adam, returning 'vel canis ad vomitum', commented the Dutch envoy d'Aerssen on similar rumours in 1601.[56] As a result, the king treated the young Prince of Condé with little respect, casting doubts on his legitimacy, providing his household with inadequate pensions, encouraging his disordered education and ensuring that he was brought up a Catholic, as opposed to his family's Protestantism.

Condé's nephew, the Count of Soissons, also possessed a claim to the throne and was financially well endowed, not having ruined his fortune in the civil wars. Henri IV deliberately excluded his councils, favoured Sully at his expense and, as with Condé, interfered with the upbringing of his son.[57] Charles d'Auvergne, the illegitimate son of Charles IX, who had been encouraged by Henri III to think that he had a claim to the throne, plotted against the king in 1597 and again in 1602 and spent a period of time in prison before being released on good behaviour. The pleas of the royal mistress, the Marquise de Verneuil, saved him from the scaffold, but the extent of his betrayal of other noble conspirators to the king meant that he was never trusted again in noble conspiracies against Henri IV.[58] The king's rigour ensured that there was no uprising from the princes of the blood for most of the reign, but it was short-sighted and his success was short-lived. In 1609, the Prince of Condé, suspecting the king of wishing to make his fiancée, and then, bride – Charlotte de Montmorency – a royal mistress, fled across the frontier to Brussels. Attempts to repatriate him and Charlotte de Montmorency caused a major diplomatic incident which was worsened by Condé's journey from the Low Countries to the Spanish fortress at Milan.[59] There, Condé learnt of the death of Henri IV and quickly made peace with Marie de Médicis, lest he become accused of having plotted to assassinate the king.[60] Whether, had the king lived, the exile of Condé would have been a serious threat to the regime is difficult to assess. It is clear that, in the conditions of a minority, princes of the blood had a different constitutional position, so little can be inferred from Condé's later rebellions. The history of seventeenth-century France suggests that, although there was no permanent solution to the ability of princes of the blood to break any political consensus, there were limitations on their success in raising rebellion and putting anything constructive in the place of royal government.

'Discontented persons of greatness and reputation' (to use Francis Bacon's phrase) still raised revolts. The two most serious ones centred round nobles from the province of Gascony. The first concerned Charles, Duke of Biron (1562–1602), whose château in the Périgord is a massive feudal bastion from which (on a clear day) one can see the Pyrenees. The other involved the Duke of Bouillon from the neighbouring viscounty of Turenne, with extensive patrimonies in the Périgord and the Limousin. Both were close personal friends or protégés of Henri IV and had benefited from royal favour. Biron had been made an admiral in 1592, a marshal in 1594 and a provincial governor in Burgundy in 1596.[61] His disillusionment with the king arose after the siege of Amiens and was fostered by agents from Brussels and Turin.[62] It intensified and, during the war with Savoy, he negotiated with the enemy and planned to assassinate the king.[63] The peace with Savoy at the end of the war discontented him still further and, despite his having confessed to some of his treason to the king, he continued to negotiate with Savoy and Spain and may even have reached some kind of treaty of association with them. By May 1602, there were reports of meetings of disaffected nobles in the Auvergne, Quercy and the Périgord who were planning to capture major strongholds in France.[64] Henri IV acted quickly, despatching troops to all the affected areas and arresting both Biron and Charles de Valois. Gascony remained calm while Biron was found guilty of treason in a show trial, stage-managed by Sully. Sully may have manufactured some of the damaging testimony against him, but much of the important evidence came from Biron's duplicitous secretary, Jacques de La Fin. His supporters and relatives met the king on their knees 'bearing the supplications of more than a hundred thousand men' begging him to commute the sentence to life imprisonment. Biron was executed a fortnight later, but the king did not confiscate the family estates, resting (he said) 'content that he has been punished as he merited'.[65] The king's tactics worked and, although there was a 'large assembly' of nobles at the funeral service to the duke in the ample chapel of the château Biron in the Périgord, there was 'more rumour than malevolence' towards the king among those who attended it.[66] In Paris, Catholics thronged to the lying in state of the body at St Paul's Church (the king had arranged for the execution to take place at the Arsenal to avoid a public riot) but, as the Dutch envoy noted, 'the more intelligent' realised that the king had acted justly.[67]

The execution of Biron was rightly regarded as 'one of the great coups of the century', and the implications of the revolt were far-reaching.[68] D'Auvergne implicated many other aristocrats in the rebellion. The Constable Montmorency, his father-in-law, was suspected and briefly feared that he would be disgraced.[69] The Duke of Montpensier had to go down on his knees and beg for forgiveness.[70] La Trémouille was told he had been suspected and he also sued for a royal pardon. The Duke of Bouillon, also d'Auvergne's relative, was clearly involved too.[71] He held hastily arranged conferences with his advisors and then left the court, first going to the Protestant Midi where he hoped to find friends and where he intended to present his case before one of the courts of the edict (*chambres de l'edit*).[72] The case was dismissed by the chamber at Castres and, a pathetic figure, Bouillon fled the country to Geneva and his sovereign territory at Sedan. Two years later, rumours of renewed conspiracy in Guyenne became strong and, by October it was clear that Bouillon was behind a renewed series of noble assemblies in Quercy and Périgord.[73] These involved former League nobles as well as Protestants. Premature discovery by the king ruined the revolt and Henri IV was quickly inundated by confessions.[74] One noble went to court to confess and submit on behalf of 120 gentlemen who had plotted to take the town of Villefranche-en-Rouergue.[75] By the time Henri IV reached Limoges on his way to Gascony with an army, almost all Bouillon's houses had surrendered. Over 1,000 nobles came from the province to visit the king there to demonstrate their loyalty, and, although the king established a special tribunal to sentence the ringleaders to death, only a handful were finally executed in December 1604.[76] Bouillon, in exile in Sedan, held out for a few more months with a few hundred troops hoping for reinforcements from German princes; but, in April 1606, he also submitted before a powerful siege train in return for a pardon and a confirmation of all his offices.[77] Henri IV was exultant about his victory, vaunting that, like Caesar, he could say 'I came, I saw, I conquered.'[78] The Bouillon revolt was the most ambitious aristocratic revolt against Henri IV. Its failure was partly a measure of the inherent weakness of purely factional aristocratic conspiracy, but it was also a demonstration of stability from a province which had been among the most disaffected in France during the civil war.

THE LESSER NOBILITY

The end of the wars of the League saw a determined effort to reduce the numbers of gendarmes in the standing army Many companies had been, or were, transformed into units of *chevau-légers* which were cheaper and which had fewer, or no mounted archers to accompany the cavalry officer.[79] Those gendarme companies which remained were retrenched to 30 *lances* by the constable who also attempted to reduce the number of garrisoned and fortified strong-holds in the country.[80] He met with considerable opposition from those with substantial arrears of pay or with expectations of captain-cies and, in the short term, retrenchment was probably a contribution to the support of some nobles for the revolts of Biron and Bouillon. In the long term, Henri IV mitigated its effects by increasing the number of pensions in church and state for the lesser nobility, on which the English ambassador remarked[81]:

> Touching the inferior nobility in general, consisting of Gentlemen of private families, or of great families who have but small means; he hath them much more obsequious to him than to any of his predecessors; and thereof his Majesty hath to myself both vaunted often, and shewed me the effects and tokens of it. The course, which he taketh therein is this; that those, who are anywise eminent for military or civil ableness, he bindeth them to this obsequiousness, by giving them pensions, (of which there are a great number, and well paid), so long as they continue in their dutifulness. But upon the least disobedience, they are sure to have their pensions stopt; which maketh them very careful, not to do anything against his will, neither in great matters nor in small.

But old mentalities died hard and noble feuds reached unprecedented heights of violence in this period. When the new president of the *parlement* of Toulouse arrived in the province from Paris in 1600, he was horrified to find up to forty nobles at a time settling their quarrels by force 'with an excess, licence and brutality which made them seem more like wild beasts than men . . .'.[82] Henri IV had already been compelled to prevent noblemen from carrying offensive weapons and, in April 1602, following reports of several duels involving his provincial lieutenants, he published a controversial edict against duelling.[83] Henri IV had originally taken the view (like Jean Bodin) that duelling was a kind of safety valve, purging the nobility of its evil humours and reducing the likelihood of civil wars.[84] Others, with a direct experience of government, viewed duelling as an encourage-ment to noble disputes and insurrection. The Act of 1602 made it treasonable, punishable by death, to conduct a duel, and encouraged nobles to seek the mediation of the lieutenant of their province or the marshals and Constable of France.[85] The edict was enforced, where possible, by the *parlements*. The first president of Toulouse reported that, in the first six months of its operation in Languedoc, he had ordered the edict to be printed and distributed as widely as possible and he had composed over 200 quarrels saving over 300 gentlemen's lives.[86] The Constable de Montmorency was also kept very busy mediating between nobles who were engaged in feuding.[87] But it was impossible to impose a change of attitude overnight. The edict had only a temporary effect and required reissuing in 1609. In some parts of France, notably in Brittany and the Auvergne, noble violence re-mained endemic (it is significant that Ravaillac, Henri IV's assassin, came from the Auvergne) and only began to wane after 1660.[88]

It was also widely believed that the best way to tame the lesser nobility and render them useful was to establish academies to educate them to the ways of civil society. The theoretical concern in the treatises on nobility at the lack of education among the old nobles (especially noticeable in those treatises written by those whose nobility was recently acquired) gave way to practical schemes to form gentlemen's academies.[89] The treatise by Pierre de La Primaudaye called *The French Academy*, written in 1577 by a Protestant gentleman in Anjou's service (whose father had served in the royal mint in Paris), was particularly popular and influential.[90] The most famous academy was established in Paris by Antoine de Pluvinel to provide a noble-orientated education which included formal dressage, fencing, deportment, mathematics and modern languages. Other academies emulated Pluvinel's in the provinces, and the example spread to England.[91] Some of them were run by mountebanks and they did not affect a large proportion of the lesser nobility, but they did represent a more settled view of the status of nobility in society.[92] The most popular treatises on nobility in Henri IV's reign (among which were Salomon de la Brou's *French Cavalier* and Jean Pelletier's *Nourishment of Nobility*) were less confused about the origins and nature of nobility. Nobility rested on birth; this explained both its pre-eminence and its continued existence. Further speculation was irrelevant. The writers of treatises on nobility reflect, as did Charles Loyseau's writings, a renewed realism about, and confidence in, the stratified society.

REFERENCES AND NOTES

1. J-P. Babelon, 1958.
2. L. Mirot, 1918–19.
3. J-P. Labatut, 1972, ch. ii.
4. H. Forneron, 1893. F. Decrue de Stoutz, 1889, pp. 377–420.
5. R. R. Harding, 1978, pp. 34–5.
6. Villeroy, **1881**, Vol. XI, p. 108. I. Cloulas, 1979, p. 276–7. For a contemporary view of the privy council, Claude Figon, *Discours des Estats et Offices tant du gouvernement que de la justice et des finances de France* ... (Paris, 1580, *BL* 795, d 3/1) fols 2–3.
7. R. R. Harding, 1978, pp. 88–107.
8. *Ibid.*, p. 121.
9. *Ibid.*, pp. 125–6. M. Greengrass, 1979, pp. 22–5.
10. *Ibid.*, ch. i. G. Zeller, 1964, pp. 207–39. R. Doucet, 1948, Vol. I, ch. ix.
11. Rights of governors in Dauphiné noted in M. Greengrass, 1979,

p. 16.   Cf. Isambert, Vol. xiv, p. 484 for the edict of 4 July 1580 against these prerogatives. It seemed that they may have survived until the time of Richelieu (R. R. Harding, 1978, p. 29).   For the Nivernais, see L. Despois, *Histoire de l'authorité royale dans le comté de Nivernais*, 1912, p. 482.

12.   'The image of God and one of his ministers on earth' quoted in R. R. Harding, 1978, p. 13.

13.   E. Pasquier, 1723, Vol. ii, cols 447–8.

14.   C. Loyseau, **1611**, p. 348.

15.   R. R. Harding, 1978, p. 70.

16.   *Ibid.*, pp. 9–10, 132–4. Professor Harding's study does not include the *lieutenants* and this weakens some of his conclusions.   H. Drouot, 1937a, Vol. i, pp. 77–9 suggests that *lieutenants du roi* were frequently regarded with suspicion by provincial governors.   This has been questioned in M. Greengrass, 1979, pp. 12–13 and P. Benedict, 1981, pp. 32–3.

17.   R. R. Harding, 1978, p. 21.

18.   *Ibid.*, pp. 22–6.   R. Doucet, 1948, Vol. ii, ch. vi.   Fontanon, Vol. iii, p. 62, etc. contains numerous edicts on the *gens d'ordonnance* or *gendarmerie*.

19.   R. R. Harding, 1978, p. 23.

20.   A. Jouanna, 1976, pp. 638–50.   Cf. P. Courteault, 1909.

21.   G. de Saulx-Tavannes, **1881**, Vol. viii, pp. 3–21, 68, etc.

22.   Brantôme, **1864–82**, Vols. iii and iv.   Cf. A. Jouanna, 1976, pp. 696–703.

23.   Brantôme, **1864–82**, Vol. iii, pp. 294–350; Vol. iv, pp. 187–279.

24.   R. R. Harding, 1978, chs iii–iv.

25.   Villeroy, **1881**, Vol. xi, p. 108.

26.   R. de Lucinge, **1954–55**, pp. 118–19; **1966**, p. 106 (14 Mar. 1586); p. 160 (1 May 1586).   Cf. J. Russell Major, 1981.

27.   de Croze, 1866, Vol. ii, No. 40 (Guise-Brûlart, 24 Nov. 1586).

28.   *BN MS Fr* 3646, fol. 77 (Charles de Guise); 4019, fol. 360 (Mayenne).

29.   R. R. Harding, 1978, pp. 143–9.   Amplified and corrected in D. Crouzet, 'Recherches sur la crise de l'aristocratie en France au XVIe siècle; les dettes de la maison de Nevers, *Histoire économie et société*, Vol. i (1982), pp. 5–50.

30.   Carew, **1749**, p. 447.

31.   Towards the end of 1597, Zamet, who was contracted to provide 5,000 *écus* per month to the constable for his household, threatened to default for lack of funds from the constable's estates (*Archives du château de Chantilly* A, carton 3 and L, Vol. xl, fol. 394). In May 1598, the constable's steward urged the immediate sale of forest land 'aultrement sans doubte vos debtes absorberont votre maison' (*ibid.*, L. Vol. xli, fol. 131). A summary of the constable's unsecured debts totalling 40,000 *écus* is to be found in *ibid.*, L. Vol. xliv, fol. 115 (undated – *c*. Oct. 1598).

32.   *BN MS Fr* 3549, fol. 20 (24 Aug. 1597, Charles de Matignon–constable).

33.   R. R. Harding, 1978, p. 127.

34.   C. Dufayard, 1892, ch. xiii.   Cf. the example of Blaise de Monluc in

R. R. Harding, 1978, pp. 149–54. Cf. also the optimistic assessment of J. Russell Major, 1981.

35. Morice, 1742–46, Vol. III, cols 1295–7.

36. R. R. Harding, 1978, pp. 74–6.

37. Fontanon, Vol. III, p. 111 (1 Feb. 1574).

38. *Ibid.*, p. 129 (9 Feb. 1584).

39. F. de La Noue, **1967**, p. 281.

40. G. de Saulx-Tavannes, **1881**, Vol. VIII, p. 154.

41. R. R. Harding, 1978, pp. 80–4 and refs. Cf. D. Bitton, 1969a, ch. ii.

42. *Ibid.*, p. 76. Changes summarised in R. R. Harding, 1978, p. 75. Montaigne, **1962**, Vol. II, p. 661.

43. Cf. memorandum quoted in A. Jouanna, 1976, pp. 656–8.

44. D. Bitton, 1969a, pp. 18–26.

45. P d'Origny, *Le Hérault de la noblesse de France* (Reims, 1578, *BN*⁺E 4982) p. 31. Cf. E. Schalk, 1976, pp. 20–1.

46. *BN MS Fr* 3646, fols 77, etc. Sully, **1970**, pp. 455–6. Sully, **1881**, Vol. XVI, p. 226.

47. R. E. Mousnier emphasises the importance of fidelity in 1979, pp. 99–111.

48. Estoile, **1948**, p. 565. P. de La Guesle, *Lettres et ambassades de Messire Philippe de Canaye* (1635), p. 532.

49. Estoile, **1954**, pp. 463–4. A certain religious austerity overcame several of Henri IV's aristocrats. The constable seems to have been influenced by it and was eventually buried in the habit of a Capuchin at Notre Dame de Grau, in Agde (P. Apollinaire, 1892, p. 192). His son-in-law, the Duke of Ventadour became very pious through the influence of his wife. The Duke of Nevers became involved in an elaborate project for a Crusade against the Infidel and went to fight the Turk at Buda in 1603 (E. Baudson, 1947, pp. 44–84).

50. J. d'Welles, 1960.

51. C. Derblay, 1927, pp. 135–50. L. Mouton, 1924, pp. 72–4.

52. *Ibid.*, ch. v.

53. J. Nouaillac, **1908**, p. 147 (reported in 19 Apr. 1602). Cf. A. Desjardins, **1859**, Vol. V, p. 496.

54. R. R. Harding, 1978, p. 139. M. Greengrass, 1979, pp. 283–7.

55. R. R. Harding, 1978, ch. xii.

56. J. Nouaillac, **1908**, p. 112 (15 June 1601).

57. G. Carew, **1749**, pp. 447–50.

58. B. Zeller, 1879, pp. 146–50, 158. J. Nouaillac, **1908**, pp. 159, 182. Cf. M. Greengrass, 1981, pp. 336–7 for d'Auvergne's part in 1597.

59. P. Henrard, 1870, presents the best case for the obsession of the king with the Princess of Condé and the distress it caused royal ministers (pp. 96 and 115–16). The affair was clearly a potential danger to Franco-Spanish relations at the delicate period of the Jülich–Clèves dispute (*infra*, pp. 195–7).

60. *Ibid.*, pp. 148–9.

61. B. Zeller, 1879, p. 132.

62. *Ibid.*, pp. 133–5. Cf. LN, No. 2313.

63. B. Zeller, 1879, p. 136. Also A. Dufour, 1965, pp. 434–5, which

assesses Savoyard Policy in the light of Biron's proposed coup; the case for Biron's treachery is reinforced.

64. B. Zeller, 1879, p. 143. J. Nouaillac, **1908**, p. 141. References to meetings in G. Lacoste, 1883, Vol. I, p. 285.
65. R. G. Tait, 1977, ch. viii. M. Dumoulin, 1895, pp. 170–286.
66. *Henri IV, Lettres*, Vol. V, p. 648. Also *BN MS Fr* 23197, fol. 54 (Ornano – Henri IV, 26 Aug. 1602).
67. J. Nouaillac, **1908**, p. 172 (6 Aug. 1602).
68. *Ibid.*, p. 184.
69. *Ibid.*, p. 182 (4 Oct. 1602). Cf. A. Desjardins, **1859**, Vol. VI, pp. 499–501.
70. B. Zeller, 1879, p. 142. J. Nouaillac, **1908**, p. 184.
71. *Ibid.*, pp. 186, 198.
72. *BN MS Fr* 15598, fol. 235; 23197, fol. 562; 3589, fol. 104 and v.
73. *Henri IV, Lettres*, Vol. VI, p. 234 (Henri IV – La Force, 23 Apr. 1604). *Ibid.*, pp. 305–6, 330.
74. G. de Gérard, **1887**, p. 403.
75. For example, *AD Dordogne* 2E, 599/15 piece 15. *Henri IV, Lettres*, Vol. VI, p. 526.
76. *Ibid.*, pp. 514, 552–3.
77. D. J. Buisseret, 1968, pp. 158–9.
78. *Henri IV, Lettres*, Vol. VI, pp. 601–2 (5 Apr. 1606).
79. R. R. Harding, 1978, p. 74. Cf. de Montmort, 1953.
80. J. Russell Major, 1974, p. 20. There was considerable opposition from the constable's own province. M. Greengrass 1979, pp. 296–7.
81. G. Carew, **1749**, pp. 459–60.
82. *BN MS Fr* 15598, fol. 102.
83. Fontanon, Vol. I, pp. 665–6. L. Mouton, 1924, pp. 62–4. J. Nouaillac, **1908**, p. 117 on the case of Louis de Cambonasier, sieur du Térail (who had been implicated in the 1597 Auvergne rising). He fled the court for the service of the archdukes in 1601 after having killed a gentleman at the royal court.
84. J. Bodin, *Six Bookes of a Commonweale* (ed. A. D. McRae) 1962, pp. 527–9.
85. Fontanon, Vol. I, p. 666.
86. *BN MS Fr* 15598, fol. 490 (13 Oct. 1603).
87. *BN MS Fr* 3461 (Accordes des querelles faictes par monseigneur le connestable de Montmorency . . .). His most notable reconciliation in his own province was between the House of Apchier and that of Polignac in the Velay.
88. A. Lebigre, *Les Grands Jours d'Auvergne, désordres et répression au XVIIe siécle*, 1976.
89. E. Schalk, 1976, pp. 21–2.
90. P. de La Primaudaye, *Académie Françoise*, 1577, *BL* 526, n. 7.
91. F. Yates, 1947, pp. 276–84.
92. Sully, **1970**, pp. 64–5 describes his disappointing experiences at a fencing academy.

Chapter 8

PAX GALLICANA

The unchallenged assumption of French foreign policy in the sixteenth century was the threat to France from Habsburg power, possessions and influence. Habsburg interests were global and encircled France. The Spanish Habsburgs possessed the territories of Franche-Comté, the Netherlands and Naples and Milan in Italy as well as numerous claims to territory in England and the Pyrenees. The Austrian Habsburgs enjoyed extensive hereditary possessions in Austria, Bohemia and Hungary. The head of the Austrian branch was invariably elected Holy Roman Emperor through which he could claim direct power from the Almighty and some influence over the German empire's princes and territories. The sense of encirclement increased after the revolt of the Dutch in 1566. The Spanish gained the consent of a string of states in Italy, the Alps and Germany to despatch and reinforce its troops through their lands. There were several alternative routes to this 'Spanish Road' (*chemin des Espagnols*) as the French christened it.[1] Having crossed the gulf of Lyons, the route passed from Genoa through the Spanish fortress city of Milan. From this point, the shortest route to the Netherlands lay through the Little Saint Bernard pass, Savoy, Franche-Comté, the duchy of Lorraine and Luxembourg. A longer route ran from Milan to the Tyrol via the shores of Lake Como and through the Engadine or Valtellina passes to southern Germany and then down to Rhine, avoiding the hostile Rhine Palatinate and three bishoprics of Metz, Toul and Verdun, which had been ceded to the protection of France in 1559.

Henri IV took Habsburg imperialism seriously. Parts of his hereditary sovereign territory of Navarre were in Habsburg hands. Philip II had supported the Catholic League through subsidies to the Duke of Guise from 1585. In 1590, he had sent a contingent of troops to fight at Ivry and a Spanish army under the Duke of Parma had raised Henri IV's sieges on Paris and Rouen in 1590 and 1592.[2] Spain assisted Marseilles until 1596.[3] The Spanish ambassador in Paris had advanced Spanish interests there while Spanish agents offered provincial governors like Mercoeur in Brittany and Joyeuse in Languedoc some subsidies and troops.[4] Spanish allies also advanced their own interests at France's expense. On 30 November 1588, Charles Emmanuel, Duke of Savoy, invaded the marquisate of Saluzzo, a French territory since 1548 in the western Alps, and took the important fortress which overlooked Savoy at Carmagnola.[5] Although this was accomplished without Spain's prior knowledge, the invasions of Provence and Dauphiné in 1589 and 1593 and the establishement of his son as governor in Lyons (Charles de Nemours), were doubtless undertaken with Spanish consent.[6] Charles III, Duke of Lorraine, also overran the bishopric of Toul in August 1589, again with Spanish approval.[7] Therefore Philip II's intentions were clearly displayed, even though he did not officially declare war on Henri IV before 1595.

THE DEFENCE OF THE FRONTIERS

As the League crumbled, Henri IV felt more acutely the threat posed by Spain to France's security. By the end of 1594, Spain maintained an army of 60,000 men in Flanders, Charles Emmanuel was still on a war footing at the main approaches to Lyons and the Duke of Lorraine was still the 'protector' of Toul. Spanish forces still assisted the League in Languedoc and Brittany. Henri IV did not need much persuading to fan a popular, anti-Spanish sentiment in France and declare war on Philip II on 17 January 1595.[8] His declaration was supported from many quarters including England and Holland. Turenne saw it as an important moment to put together a grand pan-European Protestant alliance against Spain and was very influential in persuading Henri IV of the merits of such a war. Other Protestant leaders like Sully believed (as Coligny had in a previous generation) that: 'The true means of setting the realm at rest is by keeping up a foreign war, towards which one can direct, like water in a gutter, all the turbulent humours of the kingdom.'[9] Du Plessis-Mornay also advised the king that the Spanish Road was vulnerable to an attack from France in several places. The Protestant leader in Dauphiné, Lesdiguières, proved him correct when, in 1597, he occupied the Maurienne and Tarantaise valleys in Savoy, two crucial arteries which connected Genoa with Habsburg Franche-Comté.[10] Spain countered by occupying the city fortress of Amiens in Picardy. This was a vital point of defence on the Somme for the whole of Picardy and its recovery became a focus of tremendous effort. As the Cardinal of Florence wrote to the Pope in March 1597[11];

> I recognise that the loss of Amiens is a great blow which gives heart to (Henri IV's) adversaries and that there may be worse to follow. However, I do not despair because the Spanish are so hated in this kingdom that if any individual appeals to them in dire necessity, the broad mass will not let the appeal succeed. Already, all the grandees can be seen flocking to the king . . . and there is no distinction of party (League or otherwise) between them because all are for the king who is a great and courageous soldier.

In fact, Amiens was only recaptured in the teeth of bitter fighting; the *parlement* of Paris opposed the financial sacrifices which the campaign entailed while the Protestants used it as a lever to gain greater concessions. But the campaign convinced an exhausted Spain of the need to concentrate her forces on a victory in the Netherlands and demonstrate to France's new rulers how vulnerable her frontiers were to attack. Hostilities were eventually concluded by the treaty of Vervins, negotiated with papal mediation on 2 May 1598.[12] The treaty returned Calais, Toul, Metz, Verdun and Amiens to France, thus maintaining France's north-eastern frontier. In return, France agreed to papal arbitration over all France's claims to Saluzzo.

Pope Clement VIII's envoys found negotiations over Saluzzo particularly intractable. Spanish and imperial pressures prevented their making any headway and the Pope acknowledged his defeat eighteen months later. The Duke of Savoy then came to Paris in December 1599 and Henri IV modified French demands, offering to accept the duchy of Bresse instead of Saluzzo as an attempt to gain a lasting solution to this important frontier question. It was during this meeting that Henri tried to convince Charles Emmanuel of France's resolve to defend its frontiers as well as of his own popularity. Hardouin de Péréfixe's later description of the occasion may have been a product of his own imagination, but it was to provide the king with the most enduring of his legendary *bons mots*[13]:

> When the Duke of Savoy came to France, the king invited him to play tennis at the *faubourg* Saint Gemain (in Paris). After the game, the duke looked out of a window towards a street and, seeing a large crowd, told the king that he could never sufficiently wonder at the beauty and wealth of France and asked him what the royal revenues were worth. This generous prince, deft at handling such questions, replied, 'It is worth what I want.' The duke, finding this reply too vague, asked him to be more specific. The king replied, 'Yes, what I want, for I have the confidence of my people and I can take what I like for, if God grants me life, I will ensure that there is not a peasant in the kingdom without a chicken in the stewpot' and added 'yet I will not neglect to maintain enough soldiers to bring to reason those who challenge my authority.'

A draft treaty was agreed and Savoy was given three months to make its final decisions. But Charles Emmanuel was encouraged to prevaricate by Spain because it did not wish to see Bresse in French hands and lose the ability to send troops through the *Val de Chézery*. Eventually, in August 1600, Henri IV was persuaded to declare war on Savoy by Lesdiguières and Sully. It was, as the Dutch envoy d'Aerssen remarked, a 'timid' declaration so as not to alarm other Italian princes.[14] But the military invasion by 50,000 French troops was decisive and, by the end of 1600, France held all the territory west of the Alps. Spain provided over 2 million ducats to assist its Savoyard ally and, as Spanish military forces congregated at Milan, Henri IV hastily accepted a papal offer of mediation in January 1601. By the treaty of 17 January 1601 at Lyons, France ceded the marquisate of Saluzzo in return for the territories of Bresse, Bugey, Gex and Valromey and 800,000 *écus* in compensation for the war effort. By a further clause, the Duke of Savoy was permitted to retain the use of the Val de Chézery and the Grésin bridge over the Rhône connecting Savoy and Franche-Comté in return for 100,000 *écus*.[15]

Lesdiguières was disappointed at the terms of the peace of Lyons. He remarked that Henri IV had bargained like a trader and Charles Emmanuel had negotiated like a prince. The shrewd Savoyard ambassador René de Lucinge, also thought that the treaty was more favourable to Savoy's interests than could possibly have been expected.[16] Other contemporary diplomats like d'Aerssen and Sir Ralph Winwood regarded it as shameful, while the distinguished French diplomatic historian, Edouard Rott, called the peace 'one of the great errors' of diplomacy.[17] Not only was Saluzzo more profitable a principality than Bugey, Bresse and Gex, but it also presented France's Italian allies with a guarantee of French protection in the region. The peace was even more favourable to the Spanish for, although Henri IV could cut the *chemin des Espagnols* at the Pont de Grésin (and was to do so at the time of the Biron rising), the route would remain open in time of peace. During a war, it would probably have been unusable, even if France did not possess its new territories in Bresse. France's diplomats would probably have replied to these criticisms that Saluzzo did not dominate the *only* pass from France to the Italian peninsula. If French troops were needed to assist any Italian ally, they could still use the Col de Tende, the Mont Cénis route, the Val d'Aoste or, if the Valais allowed, the Simplon pass. They would also have pointed out that the existence of 10,000 troops in Lombardy rendered the small French garrison at Carmagnola in Saluzzo strategically less valuable. But, that having been said, the peace of Lyons made the task of France's diplomats harder when it came to sustaining French allies menaced by the power of Milan, particularly in the central Alps.

For the rest of the reign, Henri IV, impressed by the barrier fortresses which Maurice of Nassau was constructing to protect the frontiers of the Netherlands, invested in a similar defensive network.

Jean Errard, his military engineer, was commissioned to produce new citadels in Amiens and Calais.[18] Defensive works were improved in Champagne by new bastion walls at Metz and Rocroi and reconstruction at Langres and Châlons in Burgundy. French frontier provinces were surveyed and mapped; arsenals and granaries were kept to a full complement.[19] In Dauphiné, Fort Barraux became a good example of the latest military architecture, while the new bastions round Grenoble turned the regional capital into one of the strongest defensive positions in France.[20]

PAX GALLICANA

From 1601 to 1610, there was a delicate peace on France's borders but it was a wary, cautious affair, unsustained by common interests of a long-term nature. Savoy, having been militarily defeated, encouraged discontented nobles to rise in revolt against the French monarchy; only in 1609 was there a real *rapprochement* with the mercurial Savoyard leadership.[21] In Brussels, the Infanta (Clara Isabella Eugenia) and her husband (Archduke Albert), governors in the Spanish Netherlands, despatched refugee leaders of the League to contact disaffected elements in France until the truce of Antwerp in April 1609 made it imprudent to disturb French internal security. In Madrid, the French ambassador was imprisoned and encouragement was given to the League leaders exiled from Marseilles to recapture the city. Various exiles met in Algiers and Naples to plot the assassination of the king, and there was always a ready welcome for those who sought refuge from the French regime at Milan which was governed by the Spanish general Dom Pedro Henriques de Azevedo, Count of Fuentes, from 1600 to 1610.[22] But after the collapse of the Duke of Bouillon's rebellion in 1604, these attempts to destabilise France faded away.

France's responsibility for maintaining peace in Europe appears in the range of its diplomatic initiatives, for the wars of religion had not reduced royal diplomatic activity, although they had limited its success. An ambassador was despatched to Constantinople and the old alliance between the King of France and the sultan was revived.[23] A similar embassy was despatched to Sweden to engage a Scandinavian ally to the Bourbon cause in Europe.[24] The king even received overtures from the Spanish Moors in 1602 and sent an envoy to them, signing a secret agreement in 1603.[25] France's most substantial efforts were reserved for the smaller states of northern Italy, Switzerland and Germany, many of them traditional allies of the French crown during the sixteenth century. This was where Henri IV's government deployed its most able and experienced diplomats. Some of these were former Huguenot diplomats like Jacques Bongars (1554–1612), the king's German envoy, or Sully's younger brother, Philippe de Béthune (?–1619), who served in Venice from 1595 to 1601 and then in Rome until 1605.[26] Others were in the pattern of Méric de Vic (?–1621), Henri IV's ambassador to the Swiss Confederation, a Catholic servant of the monarchy of proven loyalty and experience.[27] Some of the king's advisors – especially among the Protestants and former servants of the king in his Protestant days – were more aggressive in proposing alliances abroad to exploit every Habsburg weakness, demanding a direct benefit from every subsidy or pension granted to a sovereign power. Others – particularly the king's foreign minister, Nicholas de Neufville, seigneur de Villeroy (1549–1617) – were more cautious. They did not wish to encourage France's allies to entertain greater hopes from her support than were realistic. They were anxious to reach a more lasting *détente* with Spain and to avoid committing the king to actions which might eventually leave him isolated and vulnerable against Habsburg power in Europe. They were prodigal with French subsidies abroad, regarding them as an investment in France's ability to influence future events without binding commitments.

The situation in northern Italy indicates how finely matched and intricately interrelated France's alliances became. France's diplomats found it difficult to make any headway against Spanish influence in northern Italy after the peace of Lyons. The French ambassador remarked in 1602: 'Italy is bound from head to foot to Madrid. Once upon a time, the House of Ferrara, the Duke of Urbino, the Prince of La Miranda and many smaller princes were either French in their affections or neutral. . . . Now all that has been lost to Spain.'[28] France's diplomats gradually cultivated new friends – none more assiduously that Philippe de Béthune in Rome, to whom Pope Clement VIII once remarked that he wanted to see more French prelates in the Holy City to balance those from Spain.[29] As gestures to the Holy See, the Jesuits were accepted back throughout France in 1603 and the French government offered to mediate between James I, the new king in England, and Philip III in Spain. The French cardinals and French pensions in Rome made their influence felt in the elections for a new Pope in 1605.[30] Relationships also improved in Venice, mainly as a result of the logic of events. The Venetian Republic's vulnerability to Adriatic pirates (encouraged by Naples) and its need for diplomatic assistance to maintain its sphere of influence in the central Alps made it turn, rather reluctantly, towards a French alliance. When, in May 1606, Pope Paul V placed Venice under an interdict for having extended state control over the ecclesiastical and moral life of its inhabitants beyond an acceptable degree, France supported the Venetian council and the interdict was removed in April 1607.[31] It was a small sign of France's new ability to play a difficult diplomatic hand well and protect an important ally in delicate circumstances.

Venice was important to France because, through it, lay a means of influencing the central Alps. Thanks to the diplomatic finesse of Méric de Vic, France's ambassador to the Swiss Confederation, the traditional alliance between most of the thirteen Protestant cantons and France was successfully renewed at Soleure in October 1601 (and confirmed in Paris the following year.[32] The Austrian and Spanish Habsburgs had an alliance with the six Catholic cantons of the Swiss Confederation. The object of French policy in the region was to try to close the Spanish routes through the Swiss passes to their Austrian relatives or to the Rhine while opening those passes which led through the Protestant Swiss Confederation towards Venice. Apart from the Simplon pass, a long and difficult route through the Valais to the canton of Fribourg, the most important passes lay through the Engadine valley and the Valtelline, both in the territory of the confederation of the *Grisons*, or the Grey Leagues. These were an association of three cantons of local landowners who were predominantly Protestant.[33] The *Grisons* were bounded by Milan, Venice, the Tyrol and the Swiss Confederation. The Valtelline was administered by the *Grisons* but it was inhabited by villagers who were largely Catholic. The valley was leased out by treaty to the highest bidder for its exclusive military use. Given the vital strategic importance of the valley, no effort was spared by either Habsburg or Bourbon in order to secure exclusive rights to the use of the Valtelline. France was successful in December 1601 in securing exclusive rights to the valley's use. Then, in 1603, the Venetians also managed to cajole the *Grisons* into granting them a right of passage through the valley. The Spanish governor of Lombardy, Count Fuentes, was so irritated by this strategic victory that he redoubled his efforts to win over the *Grisons* and sent Catholic agents to arouse religious antipathies in the Valtelline. In October 1603, he also began the construction of a formidable fort (Fort Fuentes) at the entrance to the valley so that he could demonstrate Spain's military might and intimidate the *Grisons*. These moves had their effect when, in 1607, the Venetians attempted to move some troops through the Valtelline and provoked an uprising among its inhabitants. Eventually the Protestant landowners regained control, restored order and executed some of the ringleaders in the Valtelline so that French and Venetian influence was once more restored to the valley and Spanish were, for the moment, excluded. Once again, French diplomacy had proved successful in sustaining its alliances in a sensitive region, but a price had been exacted in terms of the destabilising of the central Alps and these instabilities would re-emerge at the beginning of the Thirty Years War a decade later.

The most important alliance in northern Europe became the French treaty obligations, arrived at in 1603, to give the Dutch (in conjunction with England) financial assistance disguised as France's repayment of its war debts.[34] Up to 1603, the Dutch had been highly suspicious of French passivity after the peace of 1598. Their envoy in Paris, d'Aerssen, was afraid that the French were merely concerned to maintain the war in the Netherlands so that 'inwardly calm, there would be just enough [warlike] exercise to remove the transitory distempers [from France] and keep the Spanish occupied'.[35] France's annual subsidies to the Dutch became considerable – over 2 million *livres* in some years after 1603 – but France did not intervene militarily to assist the Dutch. The siege of Ostende, begun in July 1601, ended in Dutch defeat in 1604 and Spanish efforts against Prince Maurice of Nassau succeeded to the extent of bringing the Dutch to consider a cessation of hostilities. French mediation was vital in the period from 1607 until 1609 when the twelve year truce was concluded at Antwerp. The French ambassador ensured that the truce was for as brief a time as possible and that it held no hidden obligations beyond those of a simple truce for the Dutch. The treaty of Antwerp was, in many ways, the most humiliating of all the pacifications accepted by Spain after 1598 and a fitting climax to the period of peace after 1601 which France had, to a great extent, managed to mould to its own advantage.

The remaining area in which French diplomacy was particularly active lay among the German princes of the Holy Roman Empire. Henri IV had relied on many of them for loans during the war of the league; but he remained unimpressed by their overall ability to coordinate themselves into an effective alliance. The German Protestant princes had failed to act together in 1591, 1594, 1596 and 1599, and Henri IV remarked sceptically on their 'long-winded Diets which never achieve anything'.[36] Their internal conflicts and divisions made them of little use in any larger diplomatic setting. As a result, Henri IV concentrated on winning the support of neighbouring princes and cities on the Rhine, showing particular regard for Strasbourg and the duchy of Lorraine.[37] Of course, France could not ignore what went on in the lower Rhineland; the least stable state was the small, composite territory on the eastern border of the Netherlands, the dukedom of John William the Simple, Duke (since 1592) of Clèves, Berg and Jülich, Count of Ravensburg and Mark. The lands were in a quadrant of the Rhine, Ruhr and Meuse, of great strategic importance for supplies to Spanish Flanders or for any potential invasion of the Netherlands. John William, already senile and childless, proved incapable of resisting an invasion of his territories in September 1598 by a contingent of the Flanders army under Francisco de Mendoza.[38] The Dutch mobilised forces and, along with some German princes of the Westphalian defensive League, rallied to remove these Spanish troops in April 1599. Henri IV did not immediately react to the invasion, despite the strategic importance of the area[39]:

> For I do not wish to draw on myself the fire which consumes them for this is probably what they would like to happen. I have too often put on my knapsack only to find that I have received no support from them or from anyone else. I am above all concerned to establish my authority and restore my realm. This is my sole objective for the immediate future . . . .

Once the Spanish had withdrawn, Henri IV offered to guarantee the security of the principality with a contingent of troops provided to the Elector Palatine. By this date (June 1599), the king was confident that his move would not be misinterpreted in Madrid, that he could call on clause 24 of the pacification of Vervins (which guaranteed the territorial integrity of the German princes) and that he could maintain the stability of the region against further invasions by either side.[40]

But the problem of Jülich – Clèves reappeared when Duke John William died in March 1609. Legally, the position of the inheritance was very complicated since there were at least eight claimants (two of whom were members of the French aristocracy) and no agreement among them as to how to proceed to settle their dispute. In the event, the Emperor Rudolf II proclaimed his right to mediate between the contending parties and appointed an interim administrator to the duchy. The two main claimants, the Dukes of Brandenburg and Neuburg forestalled him and agreed among themselves on a joint administration of the duchy. This openly ignored imperial authority and, in June 1609, the emperor proclaimed the sequestration of the duchy and, a month later, Spanish troops moved to invade the citadel of Jülich. The French government's initial reactions were cautious. The truce of Antwerp was only signed on 9 April 1609 and France was anxious not to see its ratification postponed or disturbed. Secondly, Henri IV was not convinced that he enjoyed the material support of the German Protestant powers. Although his agent Jacques Bongars had worked tirelessly to secure their loyalty, some of the princes had supported Bouillon against the king in 1606.[41] When the Protestant princes eventually signed their famous 'Evangelical Union' at Ahausen in 1608, they explicitly rejected France being associated with it.[42]

When it was obvious that France could expect the support of many important German Protestant princes, its position became clearer. In October 1609, Henri IV issued an ultimatum to the emperor to remove his administrator and the Spanish troops from the duchy and, in January 1610, the princes of the 'Evangelical Union' began to mobilise. Henri IV also called his troops to muster in Champagne, ready to conduct an invasion of the lower Rhineland. By May 1610, an army of 50,000 – roughly the same size as had been used in the successful Savoyard campaign in 1600 – was prepared to invade the duchy, and the Dutch and English had agreed to contribute some troops. In addition, France concluded an offensive and defensive alliance with Savoy in which the Duke of Savoy was to attack the duchy of Milan with French assistance at some date later in 1610.[43] At this moment of great international tension, Henri IV was assassinated on 14 May 1610, as he prepared to leave Paris to join his army. We shall never know whether, had he lived, the sequence of events would have produced a climax to the *Pax Gallicana* and further asserted French influence in Germany, or whether it would merely have been the prelude to a major European armed confrontation.

THE GRAND DESIGN

The events of 1609–10 have led historians to question the motives and purpose of French foreign policy from 1598 until 1610. Some historians have suggested that its purpose was unequivocally to remove all Spanish authority from Europe outside the Spanish peninsula by any means possible. The suggestion is based on a passage from Sully's *Economies Royales* in which he spoke of a 'Grand Design'.[44] But the passage cannot be accepted even as authentic evidence for Sully's point of view during the king's own lifetime. It appeared in the published version of the memoirs in 1662 and was neither in the various manuscripts nor in the printed edition of 1638. It seems as though Sully added it at a late stage in order to prove that he had foreseen France's diplomatic position in 1659. It was undoubtedly the case that some royal advisors pressed the king to be more adventurous in his foreign policy commitments. Sully was widely believed to have advocated on several occasions a French offensive against the Spanish in Flanders.[45] But there is no sign that such advice formed the basis of French foreign policy. Nineteenth-century historians suggested that the 'Grand Design' lay in diplomatic initiatives to formulate strategic alliances of nations rightly struggling to be free – a united Italy, a confederated Switzerland, a concerted Germany – through which France would eventually defeat the Habsburgs.[46] All the evidence suggests that French diplomats and advisors were sceptical of the likely success of overall confederations and as aware of the underlying religious and political issues which divided their allies as of the common causes which might, at any one moment, temporarily unite them.

If there was no 'Grand Design', it is clear that France's foreign policy was operating in a coordinated and effective fashion which suggests a coherent attitude sustaining it. Recent historians have stressed as the important theme France's desire to maintain European peace while articulating France's strength within it. They have shown how prudent and cautious French foreign policy was in the months before the king's assassination.[47] Henri IV kept contacts with Madrid, and the ambassador, Don Inigo de Cardenas, remained in Paris throughout the period of mobilisation. Henri IV had not offered the Moors any assistance when they were expelled from Spain in 1609. As late as the beginning of May 1610, the Tuscan ambassador in Paris was encouraged to act as marriage broker in a proposed alliance between the Dauphin Louis and an Infanta. Evidence from the first gentleman of the chamber and from Cardinal Richelieu suggests that the king was anxious to restrict his dispute to the Austrian branch of the Habsburgs. There was already some evidence that Rudolf's resolve was weakening, especially as the imperial administrator fled from Jülich in the face of the impending military invasion. Was not Henri IV concerned to maintain the status quo in Germany, demonstrate France's authority to German princes and come to a lasting *détente* with Spain?

If this *was* the case, it is clear that the maintenance of peace in 1610 would have depended on an international diplomacy of great skill and some brinkmanship. It is impossible to judge whether Henri IV had calculated correctly or not the diplomatic and military strength required to achieve his objective. Villeroy certainly believed he had, and wrote on 3 June 1610: 'If our good master were not dead, he would not have had to bother to cross the Seine. The keys of Jülich would have been brought to him.'[48] Whether this assessment would have proved to be a correct one would also have depended on whether France could restrain more unstable allies like Savoy. It would also have depended on whether the king could successfully have dissipated the war fever which he had aroused in a country where martial glory and nobility were intimately related and where there were powerful social pressures for external aggression. It is possible to imagine that the show of force which Henri IV clearly intended to mount in May 1610 would have made France's position internationally clear, and that this clarity would have prevented major hostilities breaking out. The uncertainty over France's position in 1620 was an important factor in persuading the Habsburgs in Vienna and Madrid to adopt a robust attitude towards the Palatinate and the expiring Dutch truce and thus became a material cause for the outbreak of the Thirty Years War.

REFERENCES AND NOTES

1. G. Parker, 1972, pp. 50–82.
2. D. Lamar Jensen, 1964, pp. 197, 208–9, 216.
3. F. Braudel, 1973, Vol. II, pp. 1209–16.
4. There is no effective study of Spanish intervention in France during the wars of the League beyond that of J. de Croze, 1866.
5. I. Raulich, 1896–1902, Vol. I, pp. 314–45. The background to the loss of Saluzzo is given in A. Pascal, 1960.
6. J-H. Mariéjol, 1947, chs iii–iv. On Spain and Lyons, see J. Saignieux, 'Philippe II et les ligueurs lyonnais', *l'Humanisme lyonnais au XVIe siècle*, Presses universitaires de Grenoble, 1974, pp. 221–30.
7. G. Cabourdin, 1977, p. 53.
8. LN, No. 1984. M. Yardeni, 1971, pp. 297–330.
9. D. J. Buisseret, 1968. p. 177.
10. C. Dufayard, 1892, ch. X.
11. R. Ritter, **1955**, pp. 127–8.
12. On Spanish and papal motives, see F. Braudel, 1973, pp. 1219–22. Bellièvre believed 'it was the most advantageous peace France had secured for five hundred years'.
13. H. de Péréfixe, *Histoire du roi Henry le Grand*, 1749, pp. 558–9.
14. J. Nouaillac, **1908**, p. 87 (15 Sept. 1600).
15. E. Rott, 1882, pp. 95–7. On the negotiations, see Cayet, Vol. XIII, pp. 133–8.
16. A. Dufour, 1965, pp. 429–31.
17. E. Rott, 1882, p. 97. J. Nouaillac, **1908**, pp. 97–8.
18. D. J. Buisseret, 1964b; 1968, pp. 122–8.
19. *Ibid*.
20. V. Chomel, 1976, pp. 122–4.
21. E. Rott, 1882, pp. 438 *et seq*.
22. R. E. Mousnier, 1973, pp. 44–6.
23. D. Lamar Jensen, 1974, pp. 22–46. Saint Priest, 1877, pp. 64–8; 398–438.
24. *Revue Henri IV*, Vol. II, pp. 25–33.
25. J. de Caumont, duc de La Force, *Mémoires*, 4 vols, 1824, Vol. I, pp. 217–20, 389–45.
26. L. Anquez, 1887, pp. xiii – lxix. E. Rott, 1882, pp. 104–5; R. Couzard, 1900.
27. E. Rott, 1882, p. 181.
28. Quoted in *Ibid*, p. 115.
29. *Ibid*, p. 122.
30. *Revue Henri IV*, Vol. I, pp. 133–41. Cf. R. Couzard, 1900.
31. W. Bouwsma, *Venice and the Defense of Republican Liberty*, University of California Press, Berkeley, 1968, chs vii and viii.
32. E. Rott, 1882, pp. 194–8.
33. *Ibid.*, ch. i and pp. 170–94.
34. M. Lee, 1970, 21–7. J. Dumont, **1728**, Vol. V, p. ii, pp. 30–1.
35. J. Nouaillac, **1908**, p. 148.
36. L. Anquez, 1887, p. 76.

37. *Ibid.*, pp. 88–95.
38. *Ibid.*, pp. 70–4.
39. *Ibid.*, p. 74.
40. J. Dumont, **1728**, Vol. v, pp. 563–4.
41. L. Anquez, 1887, pp. 98–115.
42. *Ibid.*, p. 128.
43. E. Rott, 1882, p. 435.
44. Sully, **1881**, Vol. xvii, pp. 421, etc.
45 J. Nouaillac, **1908**, pp. 95, 105.
46. This appears in the works of L. Anquez, E. Rott and others.
47. Principally J. M. Hayden, 1973.
48. Cited in *Ibid.*, p. 11.

CONCLUSION

THE ASSASSINATION

Henri IV was assassinated in his coach while it was stuck in conges-
tion in the rue de la Ferronerie in Paris on 14 May 1610. His assassin,
a strong, red-haired man called Ravaillac, stabbed him three times
with a short knife before being arrested by the king's travelling
companion, the Duke of Epernon.[1] Ravaillac was interrogated by the
parlement of Paris but, despite being tortured, he protested that he
had acted as a completely free agent and that neither Jesuit nor aris-
tocrat, Spanish pension or former League fanatic had encouraged
him to undertake the regicide. On the scaffold, he was scalded with
burning sulphur, red-hot pincers, molten lead, boiling oil and resin
before his arms and legs were attached to horses which then pulled
in different directions. After an hour and a half, Ravaillac died. The
crowd tried to prevent his receiving the usual last prayers and urged
the horses to pull harder. After his death 'the entire populace, no
matter what their rank, hurled themselves on the body with their
swords, knives, sticks or anything else to hand and began beating,
hacking and tearing at it. They snatched the limbs from the execu-
tioner, savagely chopping them up and dragged the pieces through
the streets.' According to Nicholas Pasquier, one woman ate some
of the bits.

The assassination was the work of one individual who found it
impossible to forget the recent past. For no king had survived more
attempts on his life by 1610 than Henri IV. There were at least
twenty-three other known plots to eliminate him, clustering mainly
about the times of greatest uncertainty in the reign – 1593–94,
1597–98, 1602 and 1604. The most serious of these occurred on 27
December 1594 when a young law student from a family of Parisian
drapers who had studied classics and philosophy at a Jesuit college
was apparently inspired to kill the king after reading a devotional

treatise. His dagger narrowly missed the king's throat and hit his cheek, breaking one of his teeth. Chastel was tortured, hanged, drawn and quartered and his family's house was razed to the ground and a sombre pillar erected in its place bearing the edict as an inscription against such regicide. The Jesuits were implicated and expelled by the *parlement* of Paris. Chastel's failure did not deter others, but plots grew less common after the turn of the century. The last concrete piece of evidence for any concerted attempt on the king's life before 1610 comes from the testimony of a former gendarme of the Duke of Guise and the Duke of Biron. He related the story of a gathering of malcontents in Naples in the wake of the unsuccessful revolt of the Duke of Biron. The participants included a former secretary to Biron, a renegade League leader from Marseilles, a Jesuit, and a captain called Roux whose attempted disaffection in Provence was known to the French authorities as early as 1597. Ravaillac may also have been present. The plot never materialised and the successful assassination by Ravaillac was a cruel *momento mori* to these earlier efforts.

Despite his apparent immunity, popular fear that the king would die a sudden death and that France would be immediately plunged into renewed civil war remained strong. Astrologers regularly predicted that he would die a violent death and some even cited 1610 as the likely year. The first president of the *parlement* of Toulouse received reports of the king's death from various quarters of his province and had to issue denials. Investigations conducted after the king's assassination in 1610 revealed that spontaneous, false rumours of the king's death were current on the days *before* 14 May in places as far apart as Douai, Lille, Antwerp, Maastricht and Cologne. These fears put the Jesuits in a difficult position. They had not been the only Catholics to support the notion of tyrannicide during the League, but they fell victim to the disparate guilts raised by such a proposition later in the reign and became the scapegoats for them. These collective fears revealed a deep psychological unease, it has been argued, a suspicion that the peace of Henri IV's reign was only skin-deep.

THE LEGEND

The king had sedulously cultivated his image by careful propaganda during his reign which had stressed his indispensability. The manner of his death transfigured the king into an active legend.[2] The preachers who had done so much to popularise the League now rivalled one another in putting their oratorical talents behind the construction of the main elements of this legend in their funeral elegies. They praised his success in war and peace, calling on classical and Christian mythology (as well as French history) to ornament his heroic stature. Justice, pacifism, prudence, frugality, charity, the chorus of praise – based on the perceived benefits of his reign – was unanimous. They stressed his contribution to political stability. He had, like Castor and Pollux (they said) pacified the seas and cleansed the realm of 'polluted waters'. He had made the 'waters of royal finance flow again' and constructed 'reservoirs to store them in'. He 'had extinguished the brazier of discontent in France'. His death was a martyrdom 'for he has died innocently for the purpose of bringing peace to the kingdom'.

Other groups added to the legend. The Jesuits, afraid that they would be blamed for the assassination, hastened to praise the king and acquired his heart to bury in their chapel at La Flèche. The Protestants, aware of the prosperity which had come their way in the security of his reign, spoke of him as the best king Providence had granted them. The judges of the *parlements* chose to ignore their dislike at his occasional interference in their jurisdiction, wept at the news of his death and, fearful of renewed sedition, granted full regent powers to his wife. Henri IV proved, in his legend as in his life, a man for all seasons and his stature grew in the generation after 1610. The political changes associated with the government of Richelieu and Mazarin turned Henri IV's reign into something of a golden age. The Protestants looked back during the civil wars of the 1620s to the security and protection of the first decade of the century. The judges of the epoch of the Fronde regarded benevolently the tranquil period from 1598 to 1610 in comparison with the political turbulence of the years after 1630. Peasants, faced with unprecedented rises in the *taille* to pay for the Thirty Years War, declared open revolt in many provinces and were joined by some nobles and towns on behalf of an old order which Henri IV appeared to cement and which Richelieu and Mazarin seemed intent on destroying. Churchmen and preachers, faced with the task of writing elegies on the deaths of Richelieu and Mazarin, found the contradictions between traditional Catholic moral values and the imperative demands of 'reason of state' much more overt than they had been under Henri IV. One of these bishops, Hardouin de Péréfixe, was well placed to express the legend of Henri IV. He was tutor to the young Louis XIV and he wrote a *History of Henry the Great* for use in the king's education. The account is as much moral philosophy as accurate history, with a considerable emphasis on the prudence of the king. The collection of royal aphorisms at the end of the book are a homely French counterpart to the popular maxims associated with the name of Guicciardini. Written in the aftermath of the worst years of the century for the French peasantry (1648–52), it was the first account to mention Henri IV as the king who had wanted to see a chicken in every pot for the French peasant. This aphorism evoked a king who had the welfare of his subjects at heart, but contemporaries would have seen the wider allusion. It was customary to represent anarchy in engravings and prints of the period in terms of reversed images (for instance, the donkey in the cart with a man between the halters). It was also habitual to represent the world as a pot or *marmite*. Therefore, when Henri IV was alleged to have wanted to see a chicken in the pot, the allusion was not just to a king who had put meat into the peasants' diet, but also to one who had set the world to rights and refounded the stability of the old order.

MYTH AND REALITY

Reality could never have matched the legend. Henri IV could not eliminate the forces of instability in France. What he could do was establish a political consensus. Religious fanatics, factious princes, dissident lawyers, Spanish infiltrators, corrupt treasurers, violent provincial nobles, peasants in revolt – still existed but the climate was much less kind towards them, and they were much less close to the meniscus of political life by 1610. The established institutions – universities, lawcourts, treasury, mints and Catholic Church – all felt a new confidence in their ability to contain instability. More importantly, the hierarchical society, on which the *ancien régime* depended, had been strengthened. Although based on rank and privilege, the society of Henri IV's France did not prove completely closed to wealth, ideas and change when it was blessed by royal favour. It was, of course, the case that contentious issues which divided social groups in France were avoided – issues such as the relationship between church and state and the extent to which the state should pursue Catholic aims at home or abroad. There was an air of relativism about these matters in the first decade of the century. Louis le Caron reminded the king – he scarcely needed to be told – that the 'public good' often 'changes according to circumstances and events'. With this in mind, Henri IV was Gallican and ultramontane as the occasion suited, and pro-Catholic or pro-Protestant when the circumstances required it. But the relativism was justified, not as cynical Machiavellism, but as the necessary prudence for the existence of public peace and the justification was widely accepted.

It could be argued that it was impossible for France to forget its recent past. Although Henri IV ordered the destruction of all official documents and published memoirs of the troubles, a morbid interest in the events of the wars of religion remained strong in the earlier years of the new century. Stability remained an ideal which was never completely attainable in practice. But it would be wrong to suggest that what was achieved rested on a mere fortunate coincidence of the exhaustion of France after the civil wars and the exhaustion of Spain from its long struggle against heresy in northern Europe. This would be to fail to recognise that, until 1600, Henri IV's regime was on trial, based on a series of negotiated agreements in which success was not a foregone conclusion. Nor would it recognise the extraordinary achievements of Sully in finance, which produced a unique strengthening of the financial position of a major government in western Europe in the early seventeenth century. Finally, it would ignore the important fact that Spain was brought to the negotiating table not by its own exhaustion alone, but by the vigorous French military efforts, especially in 1597 and 1598.

When France passed into the hands of an eight-year-old king in 1610, renewed civil war was widely predicted. Contemporaries looked backed to a previous minority of Charles IX in 1560 which had seen the beginning of the civil wars, and were struck by the ominous comparisons. In 1560, as in 1610, France was in the hands of a sickly boy-king. In 1560, as in 1610, the regent came from the Médicis family (and the reputation of the one cast doubts on the prospects for the other). In 1610, as in 1560, there were attempts to envelop the regent in an exclusive Catholic wing at court (that after 1560 was called the triumvirate; after 1610 it was the *dévots*). In 1560, a Prince of Condé was ready to lead the opposition to the regent as the prince of the blood. In 1610, his grandson was in exile in Milan and apparently preparing to do likewise. But the expected explosion did not occur and, in the end, it is the differences, rather than the similarities, which strike the historian. Firstly, Marie de Médicis, while not of the same stature as Catherine, had a series of able and experienced ministers to rely on. She maintained nearly all Henri IV's team, save Sully (they became known collectively as the *dotards* because they were all over seventy years of age). Secondly, she never became the prisoner of the dévot faction at court in the same way as Catherine became beholden to the triumvirate. The edict of Nantes was reissued in its entirety eight days after Henri IV's assassination and confirmed in 1612, 1614 and twice in 1615. She did not press for the acceptance of the decrees of the Council of Trent at the estates general in 1614–15. Although contemporaries saw the marriage of Louis XIII to the Infanta in October 1615 as similiar to the marriage of Charles IX to a Spanish princess in 1565 at Bayonne, and presumed it would have the same consequences, in fact, Marie de Médicis' government assured France's Protestant allies at home and abroad that the marriage indicated no abrupt change in policy. Thirdly, Marie de Médicis was not faced with impending bankruptcy. The reserve treasury established by Sully was not exhausted until

1614 and the revenue from the *taille* continued to rise until 1616, while the receipts from the *gabelles* remained strong until the economic crisis of 1619–21. It is true that Marie de Médicis spent more and was charged with extravagance at the estates general in 1614. But the spending did not seriously damage the equilibrium of the budget before 1614 and ministers justified the increase in pensions as necessary to consolidate the loyalties of princes during a minority.

Finally, the Prince of Condé faced greater difficulties in raising revolt in France than his grandfather had done in 1562. Condé left court in January 1614 and initially attracted the support of other princes who felt badly treated by Henri IV. From the fortress of Mézières in Champagne, he attempted to rally troops and secure the loyalties of various provincial governments. But the military forces that were raised were not substantial enough and only the Duke of Bouillon had real stomach for a fight and he turned into a mediator when faced with a confident royal government which pre-empted the position of the princes by assembling a royal army, negotiating with the princes, calling an estates general and declaring the king's minority at an end. In the months before the opening of the estates general, there was a flood of pamphlets on political affairs, but the princes of blood gained little popular support for their cause, being accused of breaking the peace. The regent government exploited the popular sentiment and influenced the election of delegates to the estates to ensure that the princes of the blood had few supporters at the assembly. In comparison with the estates general of 1560, those of 1614 were attended by a larger number of royal office holders among the third estate and this ensured a fundamental royalism. Among the demands of their *cahier* was a request that it be declared to be a fundamental law of France that the king held his crown from God alone. Other demands, it is true, presented a case for reform in the state which included the reduction of taxes, reform of the church, the abolition of venality and the retrenchment of expenditure. Unlike the estates of 1560, the delegates of 1614 found no panacea such as the secularisation of church property behind which they could unite, so that their various demands remained a curious mixture of the realistic and the idealistic. Henri IV's stability had not involved any fundamental reforms, and herein lay a substantial hostage to fortune in the period from 1610 to 1630, as would appear in the assembly of notables of 1617 and 1626–27. After the minority of Louis XIII, it is true that there was renewed civil dissension in France. Stability, consciously realised, was also reversible, particularly when government fell into the hands of favourites. But the campaigns against the princes in 1619 and 1620 and with the Huguenots in 1621–22 and 1627–28 were ones which the king did not lose. With the pressures from the Thirty Years War in the 1630s, they produced the political changes of the government of Cardinal Richelieu and Mazarin which are associated with the first generation of French absolutism.

REFERENCES AND NOTES

1. These, and the following details on the assassination, are taken from R. E. Mousnier, 1973.
2. The legend of Henri IV is explored through the funeral sermons in J. Hennequin, 1977, *Henri IV dans ses Oraisons funèbres ou la naissance d'une légende*. A longer perspective of the legned is to be found in the valuable study by M. Reinhard, *La légende de Henri IV* (1936).

BIBLIOGRAPHY

ABBREVIATIONS

The following abbreviations have been used:

Annales	*Annales, Economies, Sociétés, Civilisations*
Bib Ec Ch	*Bibliothèque de l'Ecole des Chartes*
Bib H R	*Bibliothèque d'Humanisme et de la Renaissance*
BSHPF	*Bulletin de la Société d'Histoire du Protestantisme Français*
EHR	*English Historical Review*
FHS	*French Historical Studies*
PHSL	*Proceedings of the Huguenot Society of London*
16C J	*Sixteenth Century Journal*

Works in French are published in Paris, and works in English in London, unless otherwise indicated. Publishers are not indicated for works before 1945.

1. PRIMARY SOURCES

Barnavi, E. (1976–77) 'Le Cahier de Doléances de la ville de Paris aux Etats Généraux de 1588', *Annuaire-bulletin de la société de l'Histoire de France*, pp. 81–154.

Bernard, A. (1842) *Procès-verbaux des états-généraux de 1593*.

Blouyn, M. (1976) *Les troubles à Gaillac*, (ed.) Negre, E. Editions du collège d'Occitanie, Toulouse.

Bodin, J. (1789) *Receuil de tout ce qui s'est négocié en la chambre du tiers estat 1577*.

Brantôme (1864–82) *Oeuvres complètes*, (ed.) Lalanne, L., 11 vols.

Brun-Durand, J. (1885) *Mémoires d'Eustache Piémond (1572–1608)*. Valence.

Brutus, Etienne Junius (1979) *Vindiciae contra Tyrannos*. Droz, Geneva.

Buisseret, D. J. (1963) 'Lettres inédites de Sully aux Trésoriers-généraux de France à Caen (1599–1610)'. *Annales de Normandie*. Vol. XIII, pp. 269–304.

Busbecq (1845) 'Les lettres d'Olivier Ghislain de Busbecq', *Archives curieuses de l'Histoire de France*, Vol. X.

Carew, Sir George (1749) 'A relation of the State of France . . .' in *An Historical View of the Negotiations Between the Courts of England, France and Brussels*, (ed.) Birch, T., pp. 417–528.

Catherine de Médicis, Lettres, (1880–1909), (ed.) La Ferrière, H. de, Vols I–V (1880–96); Puchesse, B. de, Vols VI–XI (1897–1909).

Champollion-Figeac, J. (1841–74) *Documents historiques inédite*. 4 vols.

Chéruel, A. (1860) *Journal d'Olivier Lefèvre d'Ormesson*.

Chevalier, J. (1885) *Mémoires des frères Gay pour servir à l'histoire des guerres de religion*. Montbéliard.

Cheverny (1881) *Mémoires de Philippe Hurault, comte de Cheverny*, (ed.) Michaud and Poujoulat. Vol. X, pp. 463–576.

Cromé (1977) *Dialogue d'entre le maheustre et le manant*, (ed.) Ascoli, P. Droz, Geneva.

Davila, H. (1647) *The Historie of the Civill Warres of France*.

Desjardins, A. (1859–86) *Négociations diplomatiques de la France avec la Toscane*, 6 vols.

Devic and Vaissète (1872–1904) *Histoire générale de Languedoc*, 16 vols. Toulouse.

Douais, C. (1890) 'Etat du diocèse de St Papoul et sénéchaussée du Lauragais en 1573', *Mémoires de l'Académie des sciences et arts de Toulouse*, 10th Series, pp. 473–89.

Dumont, J. (1728) *Corps universel diplomatique du Droit des gens*, 8 vols. Amsterdam.

Du Plessis-Mornay, Mémoires (1824–25) *Mémoires et correspondance de Du Plessis-Mornay*, (ed.) de la Fontenelle de Vaudoré, A. D. and Anguis, P. R., 12 vols.

Estoile (1875–96) *Mémoires-Journaux*, (ed.) Brunet, G. *et al.*, 12 vols.

Estoile (1943) *Journal de l'Estoile pour le règne de Henri III*, (ed.) Lefèvre, L-R. Gallimard.

Estoile (1948–1958) *Journal de l'Estoile pour le règne de Henri IV*, (ed.) Lefèvre, L-R., 2 vols. Gallimard.

Franklin, A. (1876) *Journal du siège de Paris en 1590*.

Gaches, J. (1879) *Mémoires*, (ed.) Pradel, C.

Gamon, A. (1881) *Mémoires d'Achille Gamon*, (ed.) Michaud and Poujoulat, Vol. VIII.

Gassot, J. (1934) *Sommaire Mémorial (1550–1623)*, (ed.) Champion, P.

Gérard, G. de (1887) *Les Chroniques de Jean Tarde*.

Granvelle (1841–52) *Papiers d'Etat du cardinal de Granvelle*, (ed.) Weiss, C., 9 vols.

Groulart, C. (1881) *Mémoires*, (ed.) Michaud and Poujoulat, Vol. XI.

Halphen, E. (1880) *Lettres inédites; Charles Faye et Jacques Faye*.

Haton, C. (1857) *Mémoires contenant le récit des événements accomplis de 1553 à 1582*, (ed.) Bourquelot, F., 2 vols.

Henri III, Lettres (ed.) François, M. Société de l'Histoire de France, 3 vols in progress.

Henri IV, Lettres (1843–76) (ed.) Xivrey, B. de and Guadet, J. 9 vols.

Hotman, F. (1972) *Francogallia*, (ed.) Giesey, R. and Salmon, J. H. M. Cambridge UP.

Jean de la Fosse (1866) *Journal d'un curé ligueur de Paris sous les trois derniers Valois*, (ed.) de Barthélemy, E.

Lalanne, L. (1858) *Mémoires de Marguerite de Valois*.

La Noue, F. de (1967) *Discours politique et militaire*, (ed.) Sutcliffe, F. E. Droz, Geneva.

La Roche Flavin, B. de (1617) *Treze livres des parlements de France*. Bordeaux.

Loutchizky, J. (1873–96) 'Collection des procès-verbaux des assemblées politiques des réformés de France', *BSHPF*, Vol. XXII (1873) pp. 546–58; Vol. XXIV (1875) pp. 314–22, 359–67, 402–9; Vol. XXVI (1877) pp. 351–7, 401–7; Vol. XLV (1896) pp. 418–41.

Loutchizky, J. (1875) *Documents inédits pour servir à l'histoire de la Réforme*. Kiev.

Lucinge, R. de (1954–55) 'Miroir des princes ou grands de France', *Annuaire-Bulletin de la société de l'histoire de France*, pp. 95–186.

Lucinge, R. de (1964) *René de Lucinge: lettres sur les débuts de la Ligue*, (ed.) Dufour, A. Droz, Geneva.

Lucinge, R. de (1966) *René de Lucinge: lettres sur la cour d'Henri III*, (ed.) Dufour, A. Droz, Geneva.

Loyseau, C. (1611) *Oeuvres*.

Mémoires de Nevers (1665) 2 vols.

Monluc, B. de (1964) *Commentaires*, (ed.) Courteault, J. de. Edition La Pléiade.

Montaigne, J. de (1962) *Essais*, (ed.) Rat, M., 2 vols. Gallimard.

Nouaillac, J. (1908) *Un envoyé hollandais à la cour de Henri IV; lettres inédites de François d'Aerssen à Jacques Valcke (1599–1603)*.

Pasquier, E. (1723) *Oeuvres*, 2 vols. Amsterdam.

Pasquier, E. (1966) *Etienne Pasquier: lettres historiques pour les années 1556–94*, (ed.) Thickett, D. Droz, Geneva.

Philippi, J. (1918) *Histoire des Troubles de Languedoc (1560–1600)*, (ed.) Guiraud, L. Mémoires de la société archéologique de Montpellier, Vol. VI.

Pigafetta, F. (1876) 'Relation du siège de Paris', *Mémoires de la société de l'histoire de Paris*, Vol. II, pp. 1–105.

Pradel, C. (1894) 'Mémoires de Batailler sur les guerres civiles à Castres et dans le Languedoc', *Archives historiques de l'Albigeois*, Vol. III, pp. 1–60.

Quick, J. (1692) *Synodicon in Gallia Reformata*, 2 vols.

Registres de Paris (1866–) *Registres de délibérations de la ville de Paris*, (ed.) Bonnardot, F. *et al.*, 9 vols.

Revue rétrospective (1834) 'Henri III et les prédicateurs de son temps', Vol. II, pp. 267–78.

Ibid. 'Documents historiques sur l'assassinat du duc et cardinal de Guise', Vol. III, pp. 432–55.

Richart, A. (1869) *Mémoires sur la Ligue dans le Laonnais*. Laon.

Ritter, R. (1955) *Lettres du Cardinal de Florence sur Henri IV 1596–8*. Edition B. Grasset.

Romier, L. (1910) *Lettres et chevauchées du bureau des finances de Caen sous Henri IV*.

Saulnier, E. (1913) *Journal de François, bourgeois de Paris, 23 décembre 1588–30 avril 1589.*
Saulx-Tavannes, G. de (1881) *Mémoires de Gaspard de Saulx-Tavannes,* (ed.) Michaud and Poujoulat, Vol. III.
Stegmann, A. (1979) *Edits des guerres de religion.* Librairie J. Vrin.
Sully (1881) *Economies Royales,* (ed.) Michaud and Poujoulat, Vol. XVI, XVII.
Sully (1970) *Les Economies Royales de Sully,* (ed.) Buisseret, D. and Barbiche, B., Vol. I. Klinsieck.
Taix, G. de (1625) *Mémoires des affaires du clergé de France.*
Tommaseo, N. (1838) *Relations des ambassadeurs vénitiens sur les affaires de France au XVIe siècle,* 2 vols.
Valois, C. (1914) *Histoire de la Ligue, oeuvre inédite d'un contemporain.*
Villeroy (1881) *Mémoires de Villeroy,* (ed.) Michaud and Poujoulat, Vol. XI.
Waquet, H. (1960) *Mémoires de chanoine Jean Moreau sur les guerres de la Ligue en Bretagne.* Quimper.

2. SECONDARY WORKS

Adams, S. L. (1975) 'The road to La Rochelle: English foreign policy and the Huguenots, 1610–1629', *PHSL,* Vol. XXII, pp. 414–29.
Airo-Farulla, J. (1975) 'Les Protestants et l'acquisition des offices à la fin du XVIe siècle', *BSHPF,* Vol. CXVI, pp. 503–12.
Anquez, L. (1859) *Histoire des assemblées politiques des réformés de France, 1573–1622.*
Anquez, L. (1887) *Henri IV et l'Allemagne d'après les mémoires et la correspondance de Jacques Bongars.*
Appollinaire, P. (1892) 'Conversion et dernières années du connétable Henri de Montmorency', *Annales du Midi.* pp. 101–9.
Ascoli, P. (1974) 'A radical pamphlet of late 16th century France; *le dialogue d'entre le maheustre et le manant*', *16C J,* Vol. V, pp. 3–22.
Ascoli, P. (1977) 'French provincial cities and the Catholic League', *Occasional Papers of the American Society for Reformation Research,* Vol. I, pp. 15–37.
Aubert, F. (1947) 'A propos de l'affaire de la rue St-Jacques (4–5 septembre 1557) . . .', *BSHPF,* Vol. XCIV, pp. 96–102.
Babelon, J. P. (1958) *Musée de l'histoire de France.* Imprimerie Nationale.
Babelon, J-P. (1965) *Les demeures parisiennes sous Henri IV et Louis XIII.* Le Temps.
Baccrabère, G. (1956) *Les Visites pastorales dans les paroisses rurales du diocèse de Toulouse aux XVI et XVIIe siècles.*
Baehrel, R. (1961) *Une Croissance; la basse Provence rurale.* SEVPEN.
Bailhache, J. (1929) 'Un atelier inconnu, Maringues, 1591–3', *Revue numismatique,* Vol. XXXII, pp. 128–36.
Bailhache, J. (1930) 'l'Atelier temporaire de Melun, 1592–4', *Revue numismatique,* Vol. XXXIII, pp. 71–6.

Bailhache, J. (1932) 'La monnaie de Montmorency pendant la ligue à Montpellier, Beaucaire, Béziers et Villeneuve d'Avignon', *Revue numismatique*, Vol. XXXV, pp. 37–91.

Barbiche, B. (1960) 'Les commissaires députés pour le régalement des tailles en 1598–9', *Bib Ec Ch*, Vol. CXVIII, pp. 58–96.

Barbiche, B. (1963) 'Une tentative de réforme monétaire à la fin du règne de Henri IV: l'édit d'août 1609', *Dix-septième siècle*, Vol. LXI, pp. 3–17.

Barbiche, B. (1978) *Sully*. Albin Michel.

Bardon, F. (1974) *Le portrait mythologique à la cour de France sous Henri IV et Louis XIII*. A. and J. Picard.

Barnavi, E. (1980) *Le Parti de Dieu* (Publications de la Sorbonne, Series NS Recherches, 34). Nauwelaerts, Louvain.

Batiffol, L. (1930) *Le Louvre sous Henri IV et Louis XIII*.

Baudry, J. (1920) *La Fontenelle le ligueur et le brigandage en Basse-Bretagne pendant la ligue, 1574–1602*. Nantes.

Baudson, E. (1947) *Charles de Gonzague, Duc de Nevers et de Rethel et de Mantoue*. Edition A. Perrin.

Baulant, M. (1953) *Lettres de négociants marseillais; les frères Hermite, 1570–1612*. A. Colin.

Baulant, M. and Meuvret, J. (1960) *Prix des céréales extraits de la mercuriale de Paris (1520–1698)*, Vol. I. SEVPEN.

Baumgartner, F. J. (1973) 'The case for Charles X', *16C J*, Vol. IV, pp. 87–98.

Baumgartner, F. J. (1976) *Radical Reactionaries; the political thought of the French catholic league*. Droz, Geneva.

Baumgartner, F. J. (1978) 'Renaud de Beaune, politique prelate', *16C J*, Vol. IX, pp. 99–114.

Baumgartner, F. J. (1979) 'Crisis in the French episcopacy; the bishops and the succession of Henri IV', *Archiv für Reformationsgeschichte*, Vol. XX, pp. 276–301.

Bautier, R. H. and Karcher-Vallée, A. (1959) *Les papiers de Sully aux archives nationales*. Imprimerie Nationale.

Bayard, F. (1971) 'Les Bonvisi, marchands-banquiers à Lyon, 1575–1629'. *Annales*, Vol. XXVI, pp. 1234–69.

Bayard, F. (1974a) 'Les chambres de justice de la première moitié du XVIIe siècle', *Cahiers d'histoire*, Vol. XIX, pp. 121–40.

Bayard, F. (1974b) 'Etude des comptants ès mains du roi sous Henri IV', *Bulletin du centre d'histoire économique et sociale de la région lyonnaise*, Vol. III, pp. 1–27.

Beame, E. (1966) 'The limits of toleration in sixteenth century France', *Studies in the Renaissance*, Vol. XIII, pp. 250–65.

Becquart, N. (1974) 'Les aliénations du temporel ecclésiastique au diocèse de Périgueux de 1563 à 1585', *Annales du Midi*, Vol. LXXXVI, pp. 325–41.

Bellaud-Dessalles, J. (1902) *Les évêques italiens de l'ancienne diocèse de Béziers (1547–1668)*.

Benedict, P. (1975) 'Catholics and Huguenots in sixteenth century Rouen; the demographic effects of the religious wars', *FHS*, Vol. IX, pp. 209–34.

Benedict, P. (1978) 'The St Bartholomew's massacres in the provinces', *Historical Journal*, Vol. XXI, pp. 201–25.

Benedict, P. (1981) *Rouen during the Wars of Religion*. Cambridge UP.

Bennassar, B. (1969) *Recherches sur les grandes épidémies dans le nord de l'Espagne à la fin du XVIe siècle*. SEVPEN.

Benoist, C. (1900) *La Condition juridique des Protestants sous le régime de l'édit de Nantes*.

Bercé, Y-M. (1974) *Histoire des Croquants. Etude des soulèvements populaires au XVIIe siècle dans le sud-ouest de la France*, 2 vols. Droz, Geneva.

Billioud, J. (1951) *Histoire du commerce de Marseille de 1515–1599*. Plon.

Bireben, J-N. (1975) *Les hommes et la peste en France et dans les pays européens et méditerranéens*, 2 vols. Mouton.

Bitton, D. (1969a) *The French Nobility in Crisis (1560–1640)*. California UP, Stanford.

Bitton, D. (1969b) 'History and politics; the controversy over the sale of offices in early seventeenth century France' in *Action and Conviction in Early Modern Europe*, (ed.) Rabb, T. K. *et al.* Princeton UP. pp. 390–403.

Black, J. B. (1914) *Elizabeth I and Henri IV*.

Blanchet, A.. (1930) 'Les pinatelles', *Revue numismatique*, Vol. XXXIII, pp. 235–7.

Bloch, M. (1973) *The Royal Touch*. Routledge and Kegan Paul.

Boase, A. (1977) *Vie de Jean de Sponde*. Droz, Geneva.

Boilisle, A. M. de (1873) *Histoire de la maison de Nicolay*. Nogent le Rotrou.

Bonney, R. J. (1976) 'The secret expenses of Richelieu and Mazarin', *EHR*, Vol. XCI, pp. 825–36.

Bonney, R. J. (1981) *The King's Debts*. Oxford UP.

Bontems, C. *et al.* (1965) *Le Prince dans la France des XVI et XVIIe siècles*. PUF.

Bosher, J. F. (1973) 'Chambres de justice in the French monarchy' in *French Government and Society, 1500–1850*. Athlone Press. pp. 19–40.

Bouillé, R. de (1849) *Histoire des ducs de Guise*, 4 vols.

Bourrachot, L. (1963) 'Le diocèse d'Agen entre 1592 et 1607 vu par son évêque' in *Moissac et sa région. 19e congrès de la fédération des sociétés* pp. 129–43.

Boutruche, R. (1966) *Bordeaux de 1450 à 1715*. Fédération Historique du Sud-Ouest, Bordeaux.

Boyer, P. (1921) *Le barrau toulousain*. Toulouse.

Braudel, F. (1973) *The Mediterranean and the Mediterranean World in the Age of Philip II*. Collins.

Buisseret, D. J. (1964a) 'The French Mediterranean fleet under Henri IV', *The Mariner's Mirror*, Vol. I, pp. 297–306.

Buisseret, D. J. (1964b) 'Les ingénieurs du roi Henri IV', *Bulletin de géographie*, Vol. LXXV, pp. 13–84.

Buisseret, D. J. (1965) 'The communications of France during the reconstruction of Henri IV', *Economic History Review*. Second Series, Vol. XVIII, pp. 43–53.

Buisseret, D. J. (1966) 'A stage in the development of the intendants; the reign of Henri IV', *Historical Journal*, Vol. IX, pp. 27–38.

Buisseret, D. J. (1968) *Sully*. Eyre and Spottiswoode.

Buisseret, D. J. (1972) *Huguenots and Papists*. Ginn.

Cabourdin, G. (1977) *Terre et hommes en Lorraine (1550–1635)*, 2 vols. Université de Nancy II.

Cameron, K. (1974) 'Henri III – the anti-christian king'. *Journal of European Studies*, Vol. IV, pp. 152–63.

Cameron, K. (1978) *Henri III. A Maligned or Malignant King?* University of Exeter.

Chadourne, J. P. (1969) 'Les bouchers parisiens au XVIe siècle . . .', *Positions de l'école des chartes*. pp. 17–24.

Chamberland, A. (1903) 'Recherches sur les réformes financières en Champagne à l'époque de Henri IV et de Sully', *Travaux de l'Académie de Reims*, Vol. CXI, pp. 243–71.

Chamberland, A. (1904) *Le conflit de 1597 entre Henri IV et le parlement de Paris*.

Champion, P. (1937) *Catherine de Médicis présente à Charles IX son royaume*.

Champion, P. (1939) 'La légende des mignons', *Bib H R*, Vol. VI, pp. 494–528.

Charbonnier, F. (1919) *La Poésie française et les guerres de religion*.

Charbonnier, F. (1923) *Pamphlets protestants contre Ronsard (1560–77)*.

Charleville, E. (1901) *Les Etats généraux de 1576*.

Charrière, E. (1848–61) *Négociations de la France dans le Levant*, 4 vols.

Chaunu, P. and Gascon, R. (1977) *Histoire économique et sociale de la France de 1450–1660*, Vol. I, i. PUF.

Chénon, E. (1892) *Les marches séparantes d'Anjou, Bretagne et Poitou*.

Chomel, V. (1976) *Histoire de Grenoble*. Privat, Toulouse.

Cloulas, I. (1958) 'Les aliénations du temporel ecclésiastique sous Charles IX et Henri III (1563–1587). Résultats généraux des ventes', *Revue d'Histoire de l'Eglise de France*, Vol. XLIV, pp. 5–56.

Cloulas, I. (1964) 'Les acquéreurs des biens ecclésiastiques vendus dans les diocèses de Limoges et de Bourges sous les règnes de Charles IX et Henri III', *Bulletin de la société archéologique et historique du Limousin*, Vol. XCI, pp. 87–140.

Cloulas, I. (1979) *Catherine de Médicis*. Fayard.

Coligny (Actes du Colloque, 1972) (1974) *l'Amiral de Coligny et son temps*. Société du Protestantisme français.

Constant, J-M. (1977) 'Quelques problèmes de mobilité sociale et de vie matérielle chez les gentilshommes de Beauce aux XVI et XVIIe siècles', *Acta Poloniae Historica*, Vol. XXXVI, pp. 83–94.

Coope, R. (1972) *Salomon de la Brosse and the development of the classical style*. Zwimmer.

Courteault, P. (1909) *Un cadet de Gascogne; Blaise de Monluc*.

Couzard, R. (1900) *Un ambassadeur à Rome sous Henri IV, d'après des documents inédits*.

Croix, A. (1974) *Nantes et le pays nantais au XVIe siècle, Etude démographique*. SEVPEN.

Croze, J. de (1866) *Les Guise, les Valois et Philippe II*, 2 vols.

Crump, L. (1926) *A Huguenot Family in the Sixteenth Century*.

Cummings, M. C. (1974) 'The long robe and the sceptre', PhD, Colorado University.

Dareste, R. (1850) *Essai sur François Hotman*.

Davies, J. M. (1979) 'Persecution and Protestantism: Toulouse, 1562–1575', *Historical Journal*, Vol. XXII, pp. 31–51.

Davillé, L. (1909) *Les Prétensions de Charles III, Duc de Lorraine, à la couronne de France*.

Davis, N. Z. (1975) *Society and Culture in Early Modern France*. Stanford UP.

Decrue de Stoutz, F. (1889) *Anne, duc de Montmorency, connétable et pair de France*.

Decrue de Stoutz, F. (1890) *Le parti des politiques*.

Delumeau, J. (1959) *La vie économique et sociale à Rome dans la seconde moitié du XVIe siècle*. Edition de Boccard.

Delumeau, J. (1968) *Naissance et affirmation de la réforme*. PUF.

Derblay, C. (1927) *Roger de Comminges, sieur de Sobole, gouverneur de Metz (1553–1615)*.

Descimon, R. (1982) 'La Ligue à Paris (1585–1594); une révision', *Annales*, Vol. XXXVII, pp. 72–111.

Desgraves, L. (1960) *Les Haultin (1571–1623)*. Droz, Geneva.

Desjardins, A. (1879) 'Les parlements du roi', *Séances et travaux de l'Académie des sciences morales et politiques*, Vol. XXXIX, pp. 478–505, 614–33.

Dewald, J. (1976) 'The 'perfect magistrate'; *parlementaires* and crime in Sixteenth Century Rouen', *Archiv für Reformationsgeschichte*, Vol. LXVII, pp. 284–300.

Dewald, J. (1980) *The Formation of a Provincial Nobility; the magistrates of the parlement of Rouen, 1499–1610*. Princeton UP.

Deyon, P. (1963) 'Variations de la production textile aux XVIe et XVIIe siècles; sources et premiers résultats', *Annales*, Vol. XVIII, pp. 948–9.

Dickerman, E. H. (1968) *Bellièvre and Villeroy*. Brown U. P.

Dickerman, E. H. (1972) 'The man and the myth; Sully and the *Economies Royales*, FHS, Vol. VII, pp. 307–31.

Divers Aspects de la Réforme au XVIe et XVIIe siècles (1975). Société de l'Histoire du Protestantisme français.

Dolan, C. (1981) *Entre Tours et Clochers; les gens d'église à Aix-en-Provence au XVIe siècle*. Publications du centre d'études de la Renaissance de l'université de Sherbrooke.

Doucet, R. (1948) *Les Institutions de la France au XVIe siècle*, 2 vols. A. and J. Picard.

Drouot, H. (1911) 'Vin, vignes et vignerons dè la côte dijonnaise pendant la Ligue', *Revue de Bourgogne*, Vol. I, pp. 343–61.

Drouot, H. (1937a) *Mayenne et la Bourgogne*, 2 vols. Dijon.

Drouot, H. (1937b) 'La première ligue en Bourgogne et les débuts de Mayenne (1974–79)', *Etudes bourguignonnes sur le XVIe siècle*, Vol. II.

Drouot, H. (1951) 'Les conseils provinciaux de la Sainte-Union (1589–95)', *Annales du Midi*, Vol. LXV, pp. 415–33.

Ducourtieux, P. (1925) *Histoire de Limoges*.

Dufayard, C. (1892) *Le Connétable Desdiguières*.

Dufour, A. (1965) 'La paix de Lyon et la conjuration de Biron', *Journal des Savants*, pp. 428–55.

Dumoouin, M. (1895) 'Jacques de la Fin', *Bulletin historique et philologique*. pp. 170–286.

Dussert, A. (1929) 'Le baron des Adretz et les états de Dauphiné, 1562–3', *Bulletin de l'Académie delphinale*, 5th Series, Vol. xx, pp. 110–18.

Dussert, A. (1931) 'Catherine de Médicis et les états de Dauphiné, préludes du procès des tailles et arbitrage de la reine mère en 1579', *Bulletin de l'Académie delphinale*, 6th Series, Vol. ii, pp. 123–89.

Ehrman, S. H. (1936) *The Letters and Documents of Armand de Gontaut, Baron de Biron*, 2 vols. New York.

Ehrman, J. (1972) 'Tableaux de massacres au XVIe siècle', *BSHPF*, Vol. cxviii pp. 445–55.

d'Estaintot, R. (1862) *La Ligue en Normandie (1588–1594)*.

Fagniez, G. (1897) *l'Economie sociale de la France sous Henri IV*.

Fauney, J. (1903) *Henri IV et l'édit de Nantes*.

Fayard, E. (1876) *Aperçu historique sur le parlement de Paris*, 3 vols.

Foisil, M. (1976) 'Harangue et rapport d'Antoine Séguier, commissaire pour le roi en Basse-Normandie, 1579–80', *Annales de Normandie*, Vol. xxvi, pp. 25–40.

Forneron, H. (1893) *Les ducs de Guise et leur époque*, 2 vols.

Frêche, G. and G. (1967) *Les prix des grains, des vins et des légumes à Toulouse*. Privat, Toulouse.

Galpern, A. N. (1976) *The Religions of the People in Sixteenth-Century Champagne*, Cambridge, Mass., Harvard U. P.

Gambier, P. (1957) *Le président Barnabé Brisson, ligueur (1531–91)*. Librairie Perrin.

Garrisson, F. (1950) *Essai sur les commissions d'application de l'édit de Nantes*. Montpellier.

Garrisson-Estèbe, J. (1968) *Tocsin pour un massacre: la saison des Saint-Barthélemy*. Editions Le Centurion.

Garrisson-Estèbe, J. (1980) *Protestants du Midi (1559–1598)*. Privat, Toulouse.

Gascon, R. (1971) *Grand commerce et vie urbaine au XVIe siècle*, 2 vols. SEVPEN.

Gilmont, J-F. (1981) *Jean Crespin: un éditeur réformé du XVIe siècle*. Droz, Geneva.

Girard, A. (1932) *Le commerce français à Seville et Cadiz au temps des Hapsburgs*.

Goubert, P. (1960) *Beauvais et le beausaisis au XVIIe siècle*. CNRS.

Goubert, P. (1961) 'Sur le front de l'histoire des prix au XVIe siècle', *Annales*, Vol. xvi, pp. 791–803.

Goubert, P. (1976) *Clio parmi les hommes*. Mouton.

Goy, J. and Le Roy Ladurie, E. (1972) *Les fluctuations du produit de la dîme; conjoncture décimale et domaniale de la fin du moyen âge au XVIIIe siècle*. Mouton, The Hague.

Graham, V. E. and Johnson, W. M. (1979) *The Royal Tour by Charles IX and Catherine de Medici*. University of Toronto.

Grant, A. J. (1951) *A History of Europe from 1494 to 1660*. Methuen (orig. edn 1927).

Green, V. H. H. (1969) *Renaissance and Reformation*. E. Arnold (orig. edn 1954).

Greengrass, M. (1979) 'War, politics and religion in Languedoc during the government of Henri de Montmorency-Damville (1574–1610)', D. Phil., University of Oxford.

Greengrass, M. (1981) 'Mathurin Charretier; the career of a *politique* during the wars of religion in France', *PHSL*, Vol. XXIII pp. 330–340.

Guilleminot, G. (1977) 'Religion et politique à la veille des guerres civiles; recherches sur les impressions françaises de l'année 1561', *Positions des thèses, école des Chartes.* pp. 77–83.

Gundersheimer, W. L. (1966) *The Life and Works of Louis Le Roy.* Droz, Geneva.

Gutton, J. P. (1970) *La société et les pauvres. L'example de la généralité de Lyon.* Société d'édition 'Les belles lettres'.

Hanotaux, G. A. A. (1886) *Origine des Intendants des Provinces.*

Harding, R. R. (1978) *Anatomy of a Power Elite.* Yale UP, New Haven.

Harding, R. R. (1980) 'The mobilisation of the Confraternities against the Reformation in France', *16 C J*, Vol. XI, pp. 85–107.

Hauchecorne, F. (1950) 'Le parlement de Bordeaux pendant la première guerre civile', *Annales du Midi*, Vol. LXII, pp. 329–40.

Hauchecorne, F. (1970) 'Orléans au temps de la Ligue', *Bulletin de la société archéologique et de l'histoire du Orléanais*, Vol. V, pp. 267–78.

Hauser, H. (1912–15) *Les sources de l'histoire de France*, 4 vols.

Hauser, H. (1932) *La vie chère au XVIe siècle; 'la response de Jean Bodin à M. de Malestroit, 1568'.*

Hayden, J. M. (1973) 'Continuity in the France of Henry IV and Louis XIII: French foreign policy, 1598–1615', *Journal of Modern History*, Vol. XLV, pp. 1–23.

Hayden, J. M. (1974) *France and the Estates General of 1614.* Cambridge UP.

Hayden, J. M. (1977) 'The social origins of the French episcopacy in 1614', *FHS*, Vol. X, pp. 27–40.

Henrard, P. (1870) *Henri IV et la princesse de Condé (1609–10).* Brussels.

Hickey, D. (1978) 'Procès des tailles et blocage sociale dans le Dauphiné du XVIe siècle', *Cahiers d'Histoire*, Vol. XIII, pp. 25–49.

Highfield, J. R. L. and Jeffs, R. (1981) *The Crown and Local Communities in England and France in The Fifteenth Century.* Alan Sutton, Gloucester.

Higounet, C. (1971) *Documents sur l'Histoire de Gascogne.* Privat, Toulouse.

Hilaire, J. (1952) 'Une vente de biens ecclésiastiques au diocèse de Béziers en 1563', *Congrès régional, fédèration des sociétés savantes du Languedoc*, pp. 146–58.

Hours, H. (1952) 'Le conseil d'état à Lyon pendant la Ligue; contribution à l'étude des gouverneurs de province', *Revue historique de droit français et étranger*, pp. 401–20.

Huppert, G. (1977) *Les Bourgeois Gentilshommes.* University of Chicago.

Jackson, R. A. (1972) 'Elective kingship and 'consensus populi' in sixteenth century France', *Journal of Modern History*, Vol. XLIV, pp. 155–71.

Jacquart, J. (1974) *La crise rurale en Ile de France (1550–1670).* SEVPEN.

Jensen, D. Lamar (1964) *Diplomacy and Dogmatism. Bernadino de Mendoza and the French Catholic League.* Harvard UP, Cambridge, Mass.

Jensen, D. Lamar (1968) 'Franco-Spanish diplomacy and the Armada' in *Essays in Honour of G. Mattingly*, (ed.) Carter, C. H. J. Cape. pp. 205–21.

Jensen, D. Lamar (1974) 'French diplomacy and the wars of religion', *16C J*, Vol. V, pp. 22–46.

Jouanna, A. (1976) *l'Idée de race en France au XVIe siècle (1494–1614)*, 3 vols. H. Champion.

Joutard, P. *et al.* (1976) *La Saint-Barthélemy ou les résonances d'un massacre*. Delachaux and Niestlé, Neuchâtel.

Jung, M-R. (1966) *Hercule dans la littérature française du XVIe siècle*. Droz, Geneva.

Kaiser, C. (1982) 'Les cours souveraines au XVIe siècle; morale et contre-réforme', *Annales*, Vol. XXXVII, pp. 15–32.

Karcher, A. (1956) 'l'Assemblée des notables de St Germain-en-Laye', *Bic Ec Ch*, Vol. CXIV, pp. 115–62.

Kelley, D. (1970) *Foundations of Modern Historical Scholarship*. Columbia UP, New York.

Kelley, D. (1973) *François Hotman: a revolutionary's ordeal*. Princeton UP.

Kelley, D. (1981) *The Beginning of Ideology*. Cambridge U.P.

Kierstead, R. F. (1968) *Pomponne de Bellièvre*. Northwestern UP, Evanston.

Kingdon, R. M. (1956) *Geneva and the Coming of the Wars of Religion in France (1555–1563)*. Droz, Geneva.

Kinser, S. (1966) *The Works of Jacques-Auguste de Thou*. M. Nijhoff, The Hague.

Kleinman, R. (1962) *Saint François de Sales and the Protestants*. Droz, Geneva.

Koch, P. (1940) 'Jérémie Ferrier, pasteur de Nîmes (1601–3)', *BSHPF*, Vol. XXXIX, pp. 9–21.

Kretzer, H. (1977) 'Remarques sur le droit de résistance des Calvinistes français au début du XVIIe siècle', *BSHPF*, Vol. CXXIII, pp. 54–75.

Labatut, J-P. (1972) *Ducs et pairs de France au XVIIe siècle*. PUF.

Labitte, C. (1849) *De la démocratie chez les prédicateurs de la ligue*.

Laborde, F. (1886) *François de Châtillon*.

Labouchère, G. (1923) 'Guillaume Ancel, envoyé résident en Allemagne d'après sa correspondance', *Revue d'Histoire Diplomatique*, Vol. XXXVII, pp. 160–88.

Lacoste, G. (1883–86) *Histoire générale de la province de Quercy*, 4 vols. Cahors.

Lamet, M. S. (1979) 'Reformation, war and society in lower Normandy, 1558–1610', Ph.D., Ann Arbor.

Lapeyre, H. (1955) *Une famille de marchands, les Ruiz: contribution à l'étude du commerce entre la France et l'Espagne au temps de Philippe II*. SEVPEN.

Laronze, C. (1890) *Essai sur le régime municipal en Bretagne pendant les guerres de religion*.

Lavisse, E. (1901–1911) (ed.) *Histoire de France*. 9 vols.

Lebègue, R. (1929) *La Tragédie religieuse en France: les débuts (1514–1573)*.

Lebigre, A. (1980) *La Révolution des curés; Paris, 1588–94*. Albin Michel.

Lebrun, F. (1965) 'Registres paroissiaux et démographie en Anjou au XVIe siècle', *Annales de démographie historique*, pp. 49–50.

Leclercq, P. (1979) *Garéoult: un village de Provence dans la deuxième moitié du XVIe siècle*. CNRS.

Lee, M. (1970) *James I and Henri IV*. University of Illinois Press, Urbana.

Lelong, J. (1909) *Charles Loyseau; une biographie*.

Léonard, R. (1961) *History of Protestantism*, 2 vols.

L'Epinois, H. de (1886) *La Ligue et les Papes*.

Lequenne, F. (1942) *La Vie d'Olivier de Serres*.

Le Roy Ladurie, E. (1966) *Les Paysans de Languedoc*, 2 vols. SEVPEN.

Le Roy Ladurie, E. (1971) *Times of Feast, Times of Famine*. Allen and Unwin.

Le Roy Ladurie, E. and Couperie, P. (1970) 'Le mouvement des loyers parisiens de la fin du moyen âge au XVIIIc siècle', *Annales*, Vol. XXV, pp. 1002–23.

Le Roy Ladurie and Morineau, M. (1977) *Histoire économique et sociale de la France de 1450–1660*, Vol. I (pt ii). PUF.

Le Roy Ladurie, E. (1979) *Le carnaval de Romans*. Gallimard.

Les Travaux et les jours dans l'Ancienne France (Exposition, catalogue de la Bibliothèque Nationale, 1969). Imprimerie Nationale.

Lettenhove, K. de (1891) 'Un mémoire de la reine Margot', *Revue d'Histoire Diplomatique*, Vol. IV, pp. 161–75.

Ligou, D. (1968) *Protestantisme en France de 1598 à 1715*. SEDES.

Lloyd, H. (1981) 'The political thought of Charles Loyseau (1564–1627)', *European Studies Review*, Vol. XI, pp. 53–82.

Lods, A. (1889) 'l'Edit de Nantes devant le parlement de Paris', *BSHPF*, pp. 124–138.

Lublinskaya, A. (1968) *French Absolutism: the crucial phase*. Cambridge UP.

Madden, S. H. (1982) 'l'Idéologie constitutionelle en France; le lit de justice', *Annales*, Vol. XXXVIII, pp. 32–63.

Malvezin, T. (1883) *Histoire du commerce à Bordeaux*. 4 vols. Bordeaux.

Mariéjol, J-H. (1928) *La vie de Marguerite de Valois, 1553–1615*.

Mariéjol, J-H. (1947) *Charles-Emmanuel, Duc de Nemours, Gouverneur du Lyonnais, Beaujolais et Forez (1567–1595)*. Librairie Hachette.

Mattingly, G. (1959) *The Defeat of the Spanish Armada*. J. Cape.

Maugis, E. (1914) *Histoire du parlement de Paris de l'avènement des rois Valois à la mort de Henri IV*.

Maupeou, J. de (1959) *Histoire des Maupeou*. Fontenay-le-Comte.

Ménard, L. (1750–68) *Histoire des antiquités . . . de Nîmes*. 5 vols. Nîmes.

Merle, L. (1958) *La métairie et l'évolution agraire de la Gâtine poitevine de la fin du Moyen Age à la Révolution*. SEVPEN.

Meyer, J. C. P. (1978) 'Reformation in La Rochelle: religious change, social stability and political crisis, 1500–1568', Ph.D. Thesis, University of Iowa.

Michaud, C. (1981) 'Les aliénations du temporel ecclésiastique dans la seconde moitié du XVIe siècle. Quelques problèmes de méthode', *Revue de l'Histoire de l'Eglise de France*, Vol. LXVIII, pp. 61–82.

Michaud, H. (1972) 'Ordonnancement des dépenses et le budget de la monarchie, 1587–9', *Annuaire-Bulletin de la société de l'Histoire de France*, pp. 87–120.

Miron de l'Espinay, A. (1885) *François Miron et l'administration municipale de Paris sous Henri IV de 1604 à 1606*.

Mirot, L. (1918–19) 'l'Hôtel et les collections du connétable de Montmorency', *Bib Ec Ch*, Vol. LXXIX, pp. 311–413; LXXIX, pp. 152–229.

Morice, Dom (1742–46) *Mémoires pour servir de preuves à l'histoire de*

Bretagne, 3 vols.

Mousnier, R. E. (1941) 'Sully et le conseil d'état et des finances; la lutte entre Bellièvre et Sully', *Revue Historique*, Vol. CII, pp. 68–86.

Mousnier, R. E. (1970) *La Plume, La Faucille et le Marteau*. PUF.

Mousnier, R. E. (1971) *La Vénalité des offices sous Henri IV et Louis XIII.* PUF.

Mousnier, R. E. (1973) *The Assassination of Henri IV. The tyrannicide problem and the consolidation of the French absolute monarchy in the early seventeenth century*. Faber.

Mousnier, R. E. (1979) *The Institutions of France under the Absolute Monarchy (1598–1789)*. Chicago UP.

Mouton, L. (1924) *Le duc et le roi*.

Neale, J. E. (1943) *The Age of Catherine de Medici*.

Nicholle, H. A. (1976) 'Anglo-French trade (1540–1640)', Ph.D., London School of Economics.

Nicholls, D. J. (1977) 'The origins of Protestantism in Normandy: a social study', Ph.D. Thesis, University of Birmingham.

Nouaillac, J. (1912) 'Henri IV et les Croquants du Limousin. La mission de l'intendant Boissise', *Bulletin historique et philologique*, pp. 312–50.

Orlea, M. (1980) *La noblesse aux Etats généraux de 1576 et de 1588*. PUF.

Palanque, J-R. (1975) *Le Diocèse d'Aix-en-Provence*. Beauchesne.

Pallasse, E. (1943) *La sénéchaussée et siège présidial de Lyon pendant les guerres de religion*. Lyons.

Pallier, D. (1975) *Recherches sur l'imprimerie à Paris pendant la Ligue*. Droz., Geneva.

Pannier, J. (1911) *l'Eglise réformée de Paris sous Henri IV*.

Parker, D. (1981) 'Law, society and the state in the thought of Jean Bodin', *History of Political Thought*, Vol. II, pp. 253–84.

Parker, G. (1972) *The Army of Flanders and the Spanish Road, 1567–1659*. Cambridge UP.

Pascal, A. (1960) *Il marchesato di Saluzzo e la Riforma protestante, durante il periodo della dominatione francese (1548–1588)*. Sansoni, Florence.

Patterson, W. B. (1972) 'The Huguenot appeal for a return to Poissy' in *Schism, Heresy and Religious Protest*, (ed.) Baker, D. CUP, pp. 247–57.

Patterson, W. B. (1975) 'Jean de Serres and the politics of religious pacification' in *Church, Society and Politics* ed. Baker, D. Oxford UP. pp. 223–44.

Paultre, C. (1906) *De la repression de la mendicité et du vagabondage en France sous l'ancien régime*.

Permezel, J. (1935) *La politique financière de Sully dans la généralité de Lyon*. Lyons.

Perrens, F-T. (1872) *l'Eglise et l'état en France sous le règne de Henri IV*, 2 vols.

Picot, E. (1901) *Italiens en France au XVIe siècle*.

Picot, G. (1874) 'Recherches sur les quarteniers cinquanteniers et dizainiers de la ville de Paris', *Mémoires de la société de la ville de Paris*, Vol. I, pp. 132–66.

Picot, G. (1888) *Histoire des Etats généraux*, 4 vols.

Pineaux, J. (1973) *La polémique protestante contre Ronsard*. Didier.

Poirson, A. (1862–67) *Histoire du règne de Henri IV*, 2nd edn, 4 vols.

Powiss, J. (1973) 'Officiers et gentilshommes; a *parlementaire* class in sixteenth century Bordeaux?', *Bordeaux et les Iles Brittaniques*. Université de Bordeaux. pp. 27–36.

Préclin, E. (1930) 'E. Richer, sa vie, son oeuvre, le richérisme', *Revue d'Histoire Moderne*, Vol. V, pp. 241–69.

Prentout, H. (1925) *Les Etats provinciaux de Normandie*. Caen.

Proudhon, J. (1959) 'La réception de l'édit de Nantes en Bourgogne (1599–1600)', *Annales de Bourgogne*, Vol. CXXIV, pp. 225–49.

Prouzet, J. (1975) *Les guerres de religion dans le pays d'Aude* (1560–96).

Pujol, E. (1876) *E. Richer. Etude historique et critique sur la rénovation du gallicanisme au commencement du XVIIe siècle*, 2 vols.

Raffin, L. (1926) *Saint-Julien de Balleure, historien bourguignon*.

Ranum, O. (1980) 'The French ritual of tyrannicide in the late sixteenth century', *16C J*, Vol. XI, pp. 63–82.

Raulich, I. (1896–1902) *Storia di Carlo Emanuele, duca di Savoia*, 2 vols. Milan.

Reure, C. (1897–98) 'La presse politique à Lyon pendant la Ligue', *Annales de la Charité*, Vol. XXVI, pp. 161–88; XXVII, pp. 5–35.

Revue Henri IV (1909) Republished Mégariotis, Geneva 1979.

Richard, P. (1901) *Pierre d'Epinac*.

Richet, D. (1965) 'Une société commerciale, Paris–Lyon dans la seconde moitié du XVIe siècle', *Bulletin de la société d'hist de Paris*, Vol. XCII, pp. 30–2.

Richet, D. (1976) 'La formation des grands serviteurs de l'état', *l'Arc*, Vol. LXV, pp. 54–61.

Richet, D. (1977) 'Aspects socio-culturelles des conflits religieux à Paris dans la seconde moitié du XVIe siècle', *Annales*, Vol. XXXII, pp. 764–89.

Robiquet, P. (1886) *Paris et la Ligue sous le règne de Henri III*.

Roelker, N. L. (1968) *Queen of Navarre – Jeanne d'Albert*. Harvard UP, Cambridge, Mass.

Rolle, F. (1865) *Collection des Inventaires-sommaires: Lyon*.

Romier, L. (1925) *Catholiques et Huguenots à la cour de Charles IX*.

Romier, L. (1960) *A History of France*. Methuen.

Rosenberg, D. L. (1978) '*Social experience and religious choice: a case study – the protestant weavers and woolcombers of Amiens in the Sixteenth Century*', Ph.D., Yale University.

Rott, E. (1882) *Henri IV, les Suisses et la Haute Italie – la lutte pour les Alpes (1598–1610)*.

Rousselet, M. (1957) *Histoire de la Magistrature Française*, 2 vols.

Russell Major, J. (1966) 'Henri IV and Guyenne; a study concerning the origins of royal absolutism' *FHS*, Vol. IV, pp. 363–83.

Russell Major, J. (1974) 'Bellièvre, Sully and the assembly of notables of 1596', *Transactions of the American Philosophical Society*, New Series, Vol. LXIV, pp. 3–34.

Russell Major, J. (1980) *Representative Government in Early Modern France*. Yale UP, New Haven.

Russell Major, J. (1981) 'Noble income and inflation and the wars of religion in France', *American Historical Review*, Vol. LXXXVI, pp. 21–48.

Saint-Jacob, P. de (1961) 'Mutations économiques et sociales dans les campagnes bourguignonnes à la fin du XVIe siècle', *Etudes rurales*, Vol. I, pp. 34–49.

Saint-Priest, le Comte de (1877) *Mémoires sur l'ambassade de France en Turquie.*

Salmon, J. H. M. (1975) *Society in Crisis: France in the Sixteenth Century.* E. Benn.

Salmon, J. H. M. (1979) 'Peasant Revolt in the Vivarais (1575–80)', FHS. pp. 25–40.

Sauval, H. (1724) *Histoire et recherches des antiquités de la ville de Paris*, 3 vols.

Sauzet, R. (1979) *Contre-réforme et réforme Catholique en Bas-Languedoc* (Publications de la Sorbonne, NS Recherches 30). Nauwelaerts, Louvain.

Schalk, E. (1976) 'The appearance and reality of nobility in France during the wars of religion: an example of how collective attitudes can change', *Journal of Modern History*, Vol. XLVIII, pp. 19–31.

Schnapper, B. (1957) *Les rentes au XVIe siècle. Histoire d'un instrument de crédit.* SEVPEN.

Serbat, L. (1906) *Les assemblées du clergé de France. Origines. organisation, développement (1561–1625).*

Skinner, Q. (1978) *The Foundations of Modern Political Thought*, 2 vols. Cambridge UP.

Snyders, G. (1965) *La pédagogie en France aux XVI et XVIIe siècles.*

Soman, A. (1973) 'The theatre, diplomacy and censorship in the age of Henri IV', *Bib H R*, Vol. XXXV, pp. 273–88.

Soman, A. (1974) *The Massacre of St Bartholomew: reappraisals and documents.* M. Nijhoff, The Hague.

Soman, A. (1978) 'The *parlement* of Paris and the great witch hunt (1565–1640)', *16C J*, Vol. IX, pp. 30–44.

Sommenvögel, C. and Bäcker (1892–1919) *Bibliothèque de la compagnie de Jésus.* 12 vols. Brussels and Paris.

Spooner, F. C. (1958) 'La Normandie à l'époque des guerres civiles; un problème de l'économie internationale', *Annales de Normandie*, Vol. VIII, pp. 199–213.

Spooner, F. C. (1972) *The International Economy and Monetary Movements in France, 1493–1725.* Harvard UP, Cambridge, Mass.

Spooner, F. C. (1973) 'Monetary disturbance and inflation, 1590–3; the case of Aix-en-Provence' in *Mélanges en l'honneur de Fernand Braudel; Histoire économique du monde méditerranéen, 1450–1650*, Privat, Toulouse. pp. 582–93.

Stocker, C. (1978) 'Public and private enterprises in the administration of Renaissance monarchy; the first sales of office in the *parlement* of Paris (1512–14)', *16C J*, Vol. IX, pp. 4–25.

Sutherland, N. M. (1973) *The Massacre of St Bartholomew and the European Conflict (1559–72).* Macmillan.

Sutherland, N. M. (1980) *The Huguenot Struggle for Recognition.* Yale UP, New Haven.

Sutto, C. (1977) 'Le contenu politique des pamphlets anti-Jésuites français à la fin du XVIe siècle', in *XVII Colloque International de Tours.* J. Vrin. pp. 233–46.

Sypher, G. W. (1963) 'La Popelinière's *Histoire de France*; a case of historical objectivity and religious censorship', *Journal of the History of Ideas*, Vol. XXIV, pp. 41–54.

Sypher, G. W. (1980) '"Faisant ce qu'il leur vient à plaisir": the image of Protestantism in French Catholic polemic on the eve of the religious wars', *16C J*, Vol. XI, pp. 59–84.

Taillandier, A. (1845–46) 'Election du député de la prévoté de Paris aux Etats-Généraux de 1588', *Bib Ec Ch*, 2nd Series, Vol. II, pp. 422–59.

Tait, R. G. (1977) 'The king's lieutenants in Guyenne, 1581–1610', D. Phil., University of Oxford.

Thickett, D. (1979) *Etienne Pasquier (1529–1615)*. Regency Press.

Thirsk, J. and Cooper, J. P. (1972) *Seventeenth Century Economic Documents*. Clarendon Press, Oxford.

Thomas, A. (1882) *Inventaire sommaire des archives communales de Limoges antérieur à 1790*. Limoges.

Thomas, A. (1910) *Le Concordat de 1516, ses origines, son histoire au XVIe siècle*, 3 vols.

Tilley, A. (1899) 'Some pamphlets of the French wars of religion', *EHR*, Vol. XIV, pp. 451–70.

Trocmé, E. and Delafosse, M. (1952) *Le commerce rochelais de la fin du XVe siècle au début du XVIIe siècle*. SEVPEN.

Trudel, M. (1973) *The Beginnings of New France*. McClelland and Stuart, Toronto.

Trullinger, R. S. (1972) 'The royal administration of Brittany under Henri IV', Ph.D., Nashville University.

Tuetey, A. (1882–83) *Les Allemands en France et l'invasion du comté de Montbéliard*.

Van der Essen, L. (1933) *Alexandre Farnèse, prince de Parme, gouverneur général des pays-bas,* 2 vols. Brussels.

Van Doren, L. Scott (1974) 'Revolt and reaction in the city of Romans, Dauphiné (1579–80), *16C J*, Vol. V, pp. 71–100.

Van Doren, L. Scott (1975) 'Civil war taxation and the foundation of French absolutism: the royal *taille* in Dauphiné, 1560–1610', *Proceedings of the Western Society for French History*, Vol. III, pp. 35–53.

Veyrassat-Herrem, B. and Le Roy Ladurie, E. (1968) 'La rente foncière autour de Paris au XVIIe siècle', *Annales*, Vol. XXIII, pp. 541–55.

Viguier, J. (1906) *Les contrats et la consolidation des décimes à la fin du XVIe siècle*.

Villages déserts et histoire économique, XVe–XVIIIe siècles (1965). SEVPEN.

Viñas, A. (1939) 'Felipe II y la Jornada de las Barricadas', in *Hommage à Ernst Martinenche*. pp. 514–33.

Vivanti, C. (1967) 'Henri IV, the Gallic Hercules', *Journal of the Courtauld and Warburg Institute*, Vol. XXX, pp. 167–97.

Vogler, B. (1965) 'Le Rôle des Electeurs palatins dans les guerres de religion (1559–1592)', *Cahiers d'Histoire*, Vol. I, pp. 51–85.

Warren, A. (1967) 'Les pamphlets de 1563 et l'assassinat du duc de Guise', *Bulletin philologique*. pp. xlii–xliii.

Welter, L. (1946) 'Les aliénations du bien ecclésiastique en Auvergne au XVIe siècle', *Bulletin historique et scientifique de l'Auvergne*, Vol. LXVI, pp. 114–51.

Wolfe, M. (1972) *The Fiscal System of Renaissance France.*

Yardeni, M. (1966) 'l'Ordre des avocats et la grève du barrau parisien en 1602', *Revue d'Histoire Economique*, Vol. XLIV, pp. 481–507.

Yardeni, M. (1971) *La conscience nationale en France.* Nauwelaerts, Louvain.

Yates, F. (1947) *The French Academies in the Sixteenth Century.* The Warburg Institute, London.

Yates, F. (1954) 'Dramatic religious processions in Paris in the late sixteenth century', *Annales musicologiques*, Vol. II, pp. 215–70.

Zeller, G. (1879) 'La conspiration du maréchal de Biron', *Compte rendu des séances et travaux de l'Académie des sciences morales et politiques*, Vol. CXI, pp. 130–59.

Zeller, B. (1964) *Aspects de la politique française sous l'ancien régime.* PUF.

FIGURES AND MAPS

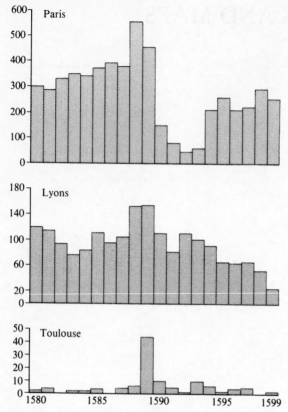

Fig. 1. Extant imprints from the presses at Paris, Lyons and Toulouse

NOTE
It must be remembered that extant imprints do not accurately reflect the total number of titles printed each year in any centre. Surviving books and pamphlets represent only a small fraction of the total material in print in any year in the sixteenth century. In addition, there are numerous dubious imprints which have been excluded from these calculations. Sources used:

1. H. L. Baudrier, *Bibliographie lyonnaise*, 13 vols. Lons, 1895–1921.
2. J. Mégret and L. Desgraves, *Répertoire bibliographique des livres imprimés en France au seizième siècle*, Bibliotheca Bibliographica Aureliana, lxiii, fasc. 151. Baden-Baden, 1975.
3. D. Pallier, 1976.

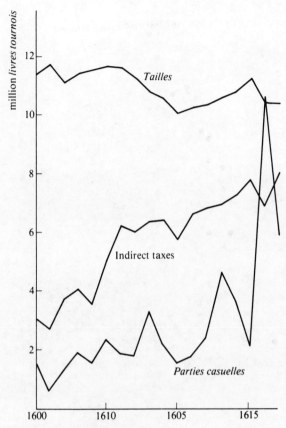

Fig. 2.   Royal income, 1600–17

NOTE
The basic source for income to the treasury in the reign of Henri IV is: J. R. Mallet, *Comptes rendus de l'administration des finances du royaume de France.* London and Paris, 1789.
The figures can be presented in several different ways; I have adopted the method used in J. M. Hayden, 1974.

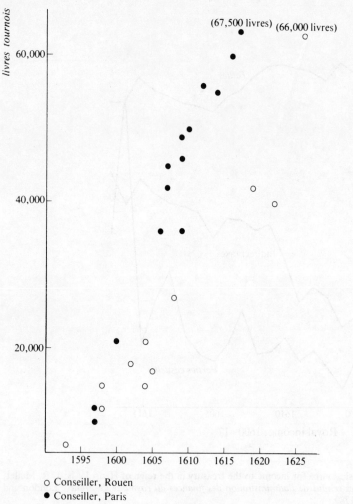

Fig. 3.   Office prices in the *parlements* of Paris and Rouen, 1590–1620

o Conseiller, Rouen
● Conseiller, Paris

NOTE
Office prices can only be calculated with difficulty, generally from notarial archives. Because the market was not completely public, prices could differ for similar offices, sometimes by wide margins. This table overestimates the rise in prices in the early seventeenth century because the market was obviously depressed during and immediately after the League. Sources used:
1. R. Mousnier, 1971.
2. R. J. Bonney, *Political Change in France under Richelieu and Mazarin.* Oxford, 1978.
3. R. Mousnier (ed.), *Lettres et mémoires adressés au Chancelier Séguier (1633–49)*, 2 vols. 1964.
4. J. Dewald, 1980.

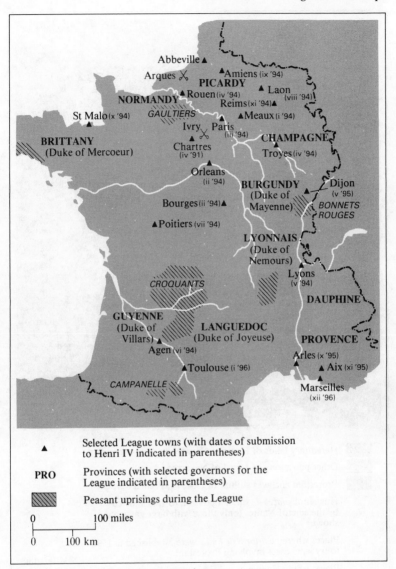

Map 1. France during the Catholic League

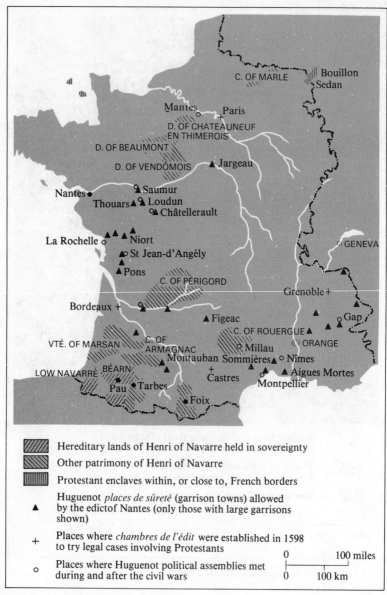

Map 2. Protestant France *c.* 1600

Hereditary lands of Henri of Navarre held in sovereignty

Other patrimony of Henri of Navarre

Protestant enclaves within, or close to, French borders

▲ Huguenot *places de sûreté* (garrison towns) allowed by the edict of Nantes (only those with large garrisons shown)

+ Places where *chambres de l'édit* were established in 1598 to try legal cases involving Protestants

o Places where Huguenot political assemblies met during and after the civil wars

0   100 miles

0   100 km

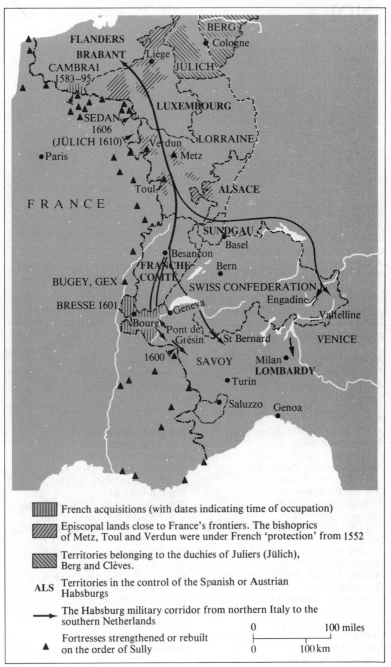

Map 3. France's frontiers, 1589–1610

INDEX

Ferrier, Arnaud du, 26, 69
Feuillants, 161
Flanders (Spanish Netherlands), 54, 192, 195
Florence, Cardinal of, (Alessandro de Médicis), 96, 189
Folembray, Treaty of, 59
Forget de Fresnes, Pierre, 93
Fort Barraux, 192
Fouquet, Guillaume, Marquis de La Varenne, 161
Francogallia, 12–13, 44
Frégoso, Janus, 160
Fuentes, Dom Pedro Henriques de Azevedo, Count of, 192, 194

gabelles, 88, 104–5, 206
Gaillac, 2
Gallican rights, 142–3, 162
Gap, 7
Gassot, Jacques, 21, 151
Gâtines cross, 6
Gaultiers, 126
Geneva, 1–2, 7, 12, 84, 182
gens d'armes, 174–8, 182–3
Gerson, Jean, 162
Gex, 191
Godin, Nicolas, 55
Goulart, Simon, 11
Gourgues, Ogier de, 127
grande guerre, 122
Granvelle, Cardinal, 9
Grenoble, 192
Grisons, 194
Guincestre, Jean, 40
Guise, House of, 8, 22–3, 39
    Charles, Duke of, 57, 103, 175
    François, Duke of, 8
    Henri, Duke of, 8–9, 29, 42, 46–9, 53, 172–5
    Cardinal de (Louis de), 37 n169
Guyenne, 69, 109, 126, 133

Harlay, Achille de, 153
Harlay de Sancy, Nicolas, 93
Henri II, King of France, 21
Henri III, King of France, 13–17, 20–7, 42–50
Henri IV, King of Navarre, and of France,
    abjuration of, 60, 73–5, 92, 154–5
    and alliances in Europe (1601–10), 192–97
    and assassination of, 201–2
    and buildings of, 133
    and coronation, 58

and *Croquants*, 128
and defence of the frontiers, 189–92
and ecclesiastical reform. 159–62
excommunication of, 41
and financial problems of (1589–96), 91–6
and Huguenot movement, 69–72
and Jülich-Clèves, 196–8
and the League, 58–62
legend of, viii–ix, 202–4
marriage of, 22, 69
and Moors, 192, 198
and nobility, 178, 182, 183–4
and pacification of France, 69–70
and *parlements*, 154, 156–7, 163
and representative assemblies, 108
and O. de Serres, 130
and Sully, 97–107
Hennequin, Aymar, 152
Holy Spirit, Order of the, 25
l' Hôpital, Michel de, 8, 10, 111
hospitals, reform of, 18, 133
Hotman, Charles, sieur de la Rocheblond, 40–1
Hotman, François, 8, 11–13, 27–8, 42, 164, 165
Hotman de Villiers, Jean, 87 n52
Huguenots, 2–5, 7, 9–11, 13, 17, 22, 42, 48–9, 68–85, 133, 203
    political assemblies of, 7, 13–14, 33 n98, 70, 74–6, 78, 84

James I, King of England, 84
Jeronimites, 25
Jesuits, 142, 161–2, 193, 201–2
John William the Simple, Duke of Clèves, 195
Joinville, 39
Joyeuse, House of, 176
    Anne, Duke of, 22
    François, Cardinal de, 26, 139 n112, 152, 160
    Henri de Bouchage de, frère Ange, 178
Jülich-Clèves, 196–8

Iberra, Don Diego de, 56
Ile de France, 117, 172, 174
Infanta, (Isabella Clara Eugenia), 57, 192
Italians, 19–20, 25, 102
Ivry, battle of (14 March 1590), 58–9

La Fère, 94
Laffemas, Barthélemy de, 132–3
La Fin, Jacques de, 181